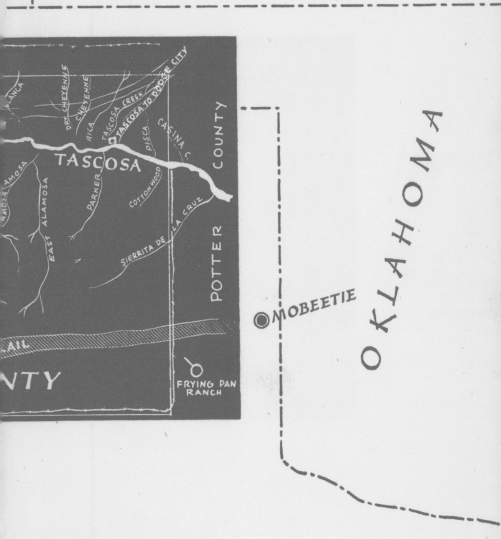

Maverick Town
THE STORY OF Old Tascosa

Maverick Town
THE STORY OF Old Tascosa

By JOHN L. McCARTY

with chapter decorations by
HAROLD D. BUGBEE

NORMAN
UNIVERSITY OF OKLAHOMA PRESS
1946

COPYRIGHT 1946 BY THE UNIVERSITY OF OKLAHOMA PRESS

PUBLISHING DIVISION OF THE UNIVERSITY

ALL RIGHTS RESERVED

COMPOSED AND PRINTED AT NORMAN, OKLAHOMA, U.S.A.

BY THE UNIVERSITY OF OKLAHOMA PRESS

FIRST EDITION

For the people, living and dead,
who saw Tascosa rise and fall

FOREWORD

As FREDERICK JACKSON TURNER has shown, the processes of settlement in western America were epochal, but it does not follow that they were orderly, or that they always resulted in permanence. The reality of cultural conquest is reflected in the institutions that fail, as well as in those that succeed. If we direct our attention to the failures, we cannot escape the ghost towns of the West—places that still live in the memories of men, though their physical remains, and even their exact locations, are sometimes conjectural.

Tascosa, Texas, is such a place. In a prairie world cut in half by a typical western river lies the site of one of the greatest towns of the open-range world two generations ago. Its story is of the life and death of a town. In large outline, it could be that of many another early-day community; but in many ways Tascosa was unique: so much of the history of the open range centered there and so many things came first to Tascosa that it telescoped into a few decades the history of a people and the development of an industry.

Yet Tascosa did not spring full grown from the southwestern prairie. As a matter of fact, it had antecedents which reflect at least three cultural phases in the development of the West:

It was first a camping place for Indians and explorers, then a Comanchero trading point, and after that part of a group of Mexican pastoral settlements. In the heydey of Tascosa's existence it became an open-range trading center and the legal capital of ten counties of a cattle empire. At this time it was the stamping ground of some of the most notorious "bad men" of the West, a focal point for cattle thieves and cowboys bent on pleasure and mischief, and the home of a group of great "little" men, both Mexican and Anglo-American. These men, welded together in common brotherhood by the bounty of grass and the solitude of distance, united against the warring forces of nature and the "big" men, who for the most part represented foreign investors seeking to control the country and fence it for their own use.

Tascosa played a vigorous role in a fabulous era of the Southwest, and its decline was as rapid as its meteor-like rise to importance. The railroad, boomed by the brilliant editor of *The Tascosa Pioneer* as Tascosa's greatest asset, actually started the town toward oblivion because it spawned many rivals and other shipping points. Barbed-wire fence was first tested on ranches in the vicinity, and the ranchmen literally "fenced Tascosa in," throwing the trail herds and business from its trade area elsewhere. Basically, however, from the time mavericking changed from employee initiative for the outfit to rugged individualism and cattle theft, Tascosa was doomed. In the open-range world, where everyone had equal claim and equal opportunity, Tascosa thrived; but when the cattle kingdoms fenced the country, the ranchmen organized, and the XIT began using business methods in ranching, Tascosa's days were numbered. In far less than a quarter of a century, a boom town had risen and fallen again to a mere settlement.

While the story of Tascosa is worth the telling for its own sake, in addition, it shows the manner of men who settled the West and discloses the effect of a succession of cultures on the land.

For guidance in the original research for and the writing of this book, I am deeply indebted to Dr. Ima C. Barlow of the History Department of West Texas State College. Dr. Hattie M. Anderson and Dr. L. F. Sheffy of the same department have aided in various ways, and the encouragement of Dr. H. Bailey Carroll of the University of Texas has been most worthwhile.

Foreword

Much of the research was made possible by a grant through the Texas State Historical Society from the Rockefeller Foundation for the study of the history of the Great Plains.

Deepest appreciation must also be expressed to Gene Howe of Amarillo, publisher of *The Globe-News*, for granting me the time to make the study and for his co-operation in allowing free access to newspaper files.

The task of thanking those individuals to whom I am indebted is overwhelming, for their number is legion. Most of them are listed in the bibliography, but many who have aided in supplying background material are not mentioned by name. To all of them, the named and the unnamed, I am grateful.

To Mel Armstrong, former Oldham County sheriff and son of Tascosa's first justice of the peace, must go a special word of thanks.

Earl Vandale, book collector and lay expert on all matters historical in the Southwest, Bishop Laurence J. Fitz-Simon, historian, and Harold Bugbee, the artist who more nearly depicts the Old West than anyone else since Remington and Russell, have lent important aid to a co-operative undertaking.

Then, I owe a debt of gratitude to my family—Susie, my wife, and Evelyn Jeanne, James Louis, and Wilbur Don, our children—whose patience, inspiration, and co-operation have made writing this book a pleasurable task.

JOHN L. McCARTY

Amarillo, Texas
March 25, 1946

THE CHAPTERS

ILLUSTRATIONS

1. A

THE GREAT BUFFALO PLAINS
made a rough, broken troug[h]
than the prairie lands north an[d]
the valley was a temperamen[t]
tributaries which covered a w[ide]
the last of the active volcanoes
States (Mt. Capulin) to far b[eyond]
looked like the breasts of a slee[ping]

Midway in the course of t[he]
there was an easy crossing. Seve[ral]
north side in gentle patterns of lo[w]
minated in broad *vegas* of spring[s]
the river to the south the grasslar[d]
to two-mile swath which extende[d]
four miles, the grass reaching to th[e]
mals that grazed it. At the west e[nd]
trails made by hordes of buffaloes
back hill and wound in a long cur[ve]
trees and mesquite into a world of

Bel[ow]
cult to tr[
The buf[
found th[
south pl[
plorers.
trails. T[
crossing
mouths[
covered
neers tr[
the wo[
mount[
village

T[
gion a[
hundre[
Ameri[
handle[
juts in[
in Ok[
The [
the S[
becan[
cosa,
strug[
rang[

men[
beau
Earl[
Indi[
west[
dev[
live[

3

w or above this point animals and man found it diffi-
averse the big valley with its obviously young river.
aloes and other wild animals, endowed by instinct,
his crossing the easiest way from the north to the
ins on the great *El Llano Estacado* of the Spanish ex-
Indians and early explorers wisely followed their
he animals bedded down in the rich valley before
the river, and men followed their example. Thus the
of these winding creeks and their shrub- and tree-
banks became camping places on the road the pio-
aveled east and west across the sea of grass between
oded sections of the young United States and the
ins of the West. It was a location ideally suited for a
or a town.

he few maps of four hundred years ago show the re-
"Gran Quivira." Some of the geographers of one
d years ago wrote across that blank space "Great
can Desert." Present-day maps show it as the Pan-
of Texas and adjacent territory. Some of the region
to eastern and northern New Mexico, No Man's Land
ahoma, southern Colorado, and southwestern Kansas.
iver, once called the Rio Colorado, now is known as
uth Canadian. The natural crossing and camping place
he in the seventies and eighties the range capital, Tas-
famed for its conflicts between cultural groups and the
gle between the nesters and the cattle kings of the prairie
land empire of Texas.

The valley seems always to have attracted the "little"
Those who sought food, shelter, and happiness in a
iful country lived there during its spectacular history.
est of these were the Pre-pueblo or Panhandle Culture
ans. They are believed to have migrated to the South-
from Central America and were a sedentary people who
ted most of their time to hunting and farming. They
in large communal houses of fairly-well-developed ar-

Maverick Town
THE STORY OF *Old Tascosa*

chitecture, some of the dwellings even having more than one story.

The later nomadic tribes of Indians had a great affection for the plains country and for the places in it where water, shelter, and camping ground afforded them haven and protection. Millions of buffaloes roamed the plains, and these animals furnished the roving Indians with food, with hides for shelter, clothing, and harness, and with bones for tools. The road of the pioneers was a road to and from the hunting grounds of the Indians, one of the camping spots being the Canadian River Valley with its easy crossing. It was for years one of a few places where the Indians and the Mexican traders, familiarly known as *Comancheros*, met to exchange contrabrand goods, cattle, horses, and women and children captured from the white settlements. At some seasons of the year surface lakes and buffalo wallows provided excellent water on the plains, but more often the only water to be found flowed in small creeks or in the river. Therefore, explorers and hunters attempted to follow the river or to move from one watercourse to another. The occasional severe winter and spring storms gave added attraction to the Canadian River Valley because of its sheltered canyons and the broad *vegas* of tall grass. Travelers, during dry weather, made excellent speed across the flat plains when they knew the road that led them to water, the camping places, and the location of the oases in this teeming desert—a desert that never existed except on a map and was more accurately described by those who traversed it as a "prairie sea of grass."

The courtly Coronado and his conquistadors blazed the trail of explorers in 1541 to become the first Europeans on the Staked Plains and in the Canadian River Valley. Coronado used bones and buffalo chips piled into mounds to mark his trail, for the plains were as trackless as the sea except to those occasional men born not to get lost. The Indians tricked Coronado into the plains country to search for the Seven

Cities of Cíbola, whose houses were lined with gold and turquoise. The guide intended that the expedition be lost in the wild country, but Coronado was able to extricate his party from the trap into which they had marched, the streams which break the plains being a big factor in his success. The guide lost his neck. Later Father Juan de Padilla of the Coronado party returned to the plains from New Mexico to become the first Christian martyr in America when he was killed by those he sought to convert.

After Coronado, Juan de Oñate in 1599 came into the Southwest and sent Zaldivar to the buffalo plains to capture some "cows." He built a corral near the Canadian River, where the buffaloes killed three of his horses and wounded several more. Nevertheless, Zaldivar became the first European buffalo hunter.

The French made good use of the route to cause trouble between the Indians and the early Spanish settlers of New Mexico. The Spaniards, jealous of their colonial rivals who were settling along the Mississippi River, suspected the French of using the Indians as confederates in an attempt to gain possession of the province of New Mexico. Therefore, they sent several missions against the French, one being that of Villasur in 1720, which went out to gain information. One member of this party was Captain Jean l'Archevêque, a Frenchman who had been taken as a prisoner to Mexico and who, after obtaining his freedom, had become a trader in Santa Fé. Somewhere in the Southwest—many historians believe on the Canadian—the Indians killed most of the party. Among the dead was Captain l'Archevêque, whose name was, however, to be carried forward by a grandson who affected the region in more violent ways than his grandsire.

The Louisiana Purchase in 1803 carried the boundary of the United States, fixed for years at the Mississippi, across the Great Plains into an uncharted domain. President Jefferson, desirous of having this new territory explored and of developing the fur trade of the Missouri River country, sent out an expedition from St. Louis in 1803 led by Lewis and Clark. Its route was across the northern part of the Great Plains, over the mountains, and to the Pacific Ocean. The party's return in 1806 brought the nation its first real information about the country west of the Mississippi. Travel and trade followed.

In July, 1806, Lieutenant Zebulon M. Pike left St. Louis to explore the southwestern part of the Louisiana Purchase. He crossed the plains, discovered the great peak in Colorado which has since carried his name, and was captured by the Spaniards and taken to Chihuahua. Upon his release he brought back the story of the high price of cloth in Santa Fé, news resulting in a thriving business between United States and Santa Fé merchants and in the opening of the Santa Fé Trail, with its main route one to two hundred miles north of the Canadian River route.

General Thomas James—the famous Illinois militia leader, Indian fighter, and trader—secured permission from President John Adams to trade with the Indians and brought his stores by boat to Fort Smith, Arkansas. From there he packed into the Comanche Indian territory along the Canadian River, where he traded until 1824. Thus the ancient road became important as a trade route for the commerce of the prairies.

The Canadian crossing became a regular rendezvous and an important stop on the trail of the Indians from the Midwest and the Mississippi coast regions to Chihuahua and Mexico City via El Paso del Norte. Mexican traders also used the route and the camping place when carrying tanned buffalo hides and other products to the plazas and fairs in the prosperous towns of Mexico. Indians who traveled from the prairie midwest of the Arkansas and Oklahoma regions across the plains to trade centers in Mexico also favored the route. It was a logical way for persons crossing from St.

7

Louis or Fort Smith to Spanish settlements in New Mexico. When the gold rush to California began in 1849, the road offered from one to two months more of winter-free weather than the Santa Fé or Oregon trails. Here in the period of the forty-niners, when Captain Randolph B. Marcy of the United States Army led several expeditions over the route, twin boys were born in camp. The caravan, which had made up at Fort Smith, rested awhile as the first Anglo-Americans born in the Texas Panhandle became accustomed to life. They were true American pioneers.

On this old road, at the easy crossing of the Canadian, people of many cultures and many purposes rested after braving the Llano Estacado and its grass, sun, solitude, and ever dominating world of sky. Here they found food, water, and shelter. Then they moved on, seeking the gold or grass or other treasure that far horizons offered. Some time in the eighteen sixties, however, a number of Mexican families settled on the south bank of the river below what came to be known as Parker Creek. They attempted irrigation of small farms and gardens but found that the water from the creek and the soil did not mix—the water caked the soil, causing it to bake like cement about the plants. When the first Anglo-Americans settled in the country, they found an irrigation ditch and a few graves remaining. As in so many forgotten places in the enchanted West, there were no markers on the graves. The red clay of the adobe shacks had crumbled into earth again; and the grass, as Senator Ingalls so eloquently described it, was "growing its comforting cover over the mounds."

The Comanchero trade probably had its beginning in the annual trek of Mexicans and Indians to the buffalo plains for their big hunts. These hunts were great sport as well as a prime means of obtaining food, clothing, and primitive tools. The buffalo was highly important to the Indian and, in a slightly less measure, to the Mexican. The hunts also

8

brought to the language of the Southwest a colorful term describing a daring character and its first sportsman—the *Cibolero*, or buffalo hunter. The Mexican, who used the lance and rode a fast, carefully trained horse was the Cibolero. Stripped to the waist except for a colored turban-like head-piece which flowed in the wind like a banner carried by a fast battle charger, the Mexican hunter crowded his horse closer and closer to the fleeing buffalo. With split-second precision he brought his long lance with flint- or steel-tipped point from over his shoulder down his side and literally rode the point of it into the heart or lungs of the buffalo. Some-times a shaft broke; and a well-trained horse, pressing home for the kill, unknowingly jabbed the jagged, broken end through the stomach or side of his rider. Sometimes buffalo, horse, and man went down in a spill together, an exceedingly dangerous accident in a herd of stampeding buffaloes. The Indians used the same technique as the Mexicans in hunting buffaloes but often substituted short-bow and arrow for the lance, although sometimes both were employed. The Cibo-lero, dashing, colorful horseback hunter of the West, brought home dried or jerked buffalo meat, hides, and horns. He also brought beads, stone and shell ornaments, and occasionally a horse or a cow from his contact with the Indians, whom he met at the easy crossing of the Canadian and at other wa-tering and camping places in the plains country.

Indian and Mexican hunters got along together very well. One of the reasons for the friendly intercourse between the two, and a big factor in the development of the Coman-chero trade, was the significant treaty made with the Co-manche Indians in 1786 by Don Juan Bautista de Anza, pa-triot governor of New Mexico. By this treaty the Comanches were practically vassals of the Spanish throne as far as their relations with the province of New Mexico were concerned. Pledged in friendship to New Mexico alone, they preyed on unsettled Spanish claims in Texas and by provisions of the treaty kept off all interlopers, especially Frenchmen and Anglo-Americans. The treaty, however, did not keep the Comanches from raiding the provinces of Chihuahua and Durango in Mexico until they were almost depopulated of both cattle and men. Nor did it affect the conscience of Mexican traders from the towns of New Mexico in exchanging goods with the Indians.

It was easy for the Cibolero to mix his hunting with trading or to quit the sport of lancing buffaloes for profitable commerce with the Indians he had met on the hunt. When the Cibolero started trading, he became known as a Comanchero, and his business was called the Comanchero trade. He was typically a greasy, poverty-stricken New Mexican, who, with a few carts, some burros, a small stock of trinkets, and an utter lack of conscience or principle, joined a caravan of his countrymen and struck a deep-cut trail for the Llano Estacado and rendezvous with the Comanche Indians. That he dealt in *"contrabando"*—earthly goods of struggling Texans stolen by the Comanches during bloody forays—did not deter him. Where the goods came from did not matter to him nor, as a rule, to the rich merchant who financed him. The trade was an extremely shady transaction in stolen goods, cattle, women, and children. The Mexicans swapped trinkets, cloth, liquor, guns, and ammunition. The Indians had the scalps as well as the horses and cattle of settlers who dared live on the outer fringe of Anglo-American civilization in early-day Texas. The Comancheros, and some outlaw Americans as well, fared prosperously on the trading trips and generally took time for buffalo hunts while they were on the Great Plains. Some of their goods were hauled in great, wooden-wheeled carts or *carretas*, but most of it was carried in packs on the backs of patient burros. The Comancheros met the Indians at Las Tecovas, Las Linguas, and other springs where camps had been made over the Panhandle region. A great volume was carried, to the profit of

traders at Santa Fé and Las Vegas. In some instances, United
States Army officers conspired with traders at the New
Mexico border forts to profit at the expense of the government. Several notable trials were held in connection with
business in which army officers were involved, but generally
there was no court to which anyone had recourse.

From Central Texas Colonel Samuel Cooper, assistant
adjutant general, reported to Washington in 1858 that he had
seen the great broad trail used by the Comanches to drive
their stolen stock to be disposed of by traders. That trail led
far to the northwest of the Central Texas settlements to the
ominous caprock of the Llano Estacado, a favorite haunt of
the Comanches. From these vast uplands the embittered Indians looked down upon a relentless tide—the ragged, restless, approaching edge of white settlement. Between the
western fringe of the Cross Timbers and the Staked Plains
lay a buffer region bordering the Pease River, a never-never
country of wild, red, broken hills, where game was scarce,
water alkaline, and life almost impossible. Indians crossed it
at rapid gaits, white men not at all unless pressed. Across it
crawled the bitter trail which led to the "Valley of Tears"
on the Quitaque, the last stop on the way to oblivion for
grieving mothers and children who were captives of the Comanches; for it was here that the children were taken from
their mothers and all relatives separated, so that there would
be less chance for escape and that child captives might sooner
be absorbed by the tribe.

El Llano Estacado in the eighteen fifties was home to
the wildest bands of Indians the North American continent
ever knew—the Comanches. With the rising of the sap in
the spring, the blood of the warriors surged, sending them
on ambitious forays. Young, adventurous braves and grizzled,
crafty, old warriors, who had raided with Bajo del Sol in
Mexico, all gathered on the plains to meet the Comancheros.
At snug oases, sheltered from the wild winds that beat the

plains and near living waters, their wilderness trading posts nestled far from government authorities or the avenging guns of the Texans. There the Comancheros waited for them. If by chance the Comancheros arrived at a slack time when the Indians had no stock to trade, the Mexicans settled themselves in camp and lent the Indians their guns—which had been secured from forts and Anglo-American traders—so that the Comanches might go on forays in the Cross Timbers. While they were gone, the Mexicans made merry, anticipating the arrival of *"mucho contrabando."*

During the Civil War raiding became easier and more profitable in Texas. The men had gone off to fight, and the price of cattle was increasing. The establishment of Fort Bascom on the north bank of the Canadian River at the edge of New Mexico on August 15, 1863, actually stimulated the unlawful trade and set the stage for practices which later had much influence on the Canadian River Valley and on the life of Billy the Kid and his gang of killers and cattle and horse thieves. In the vicinity of Fort Bascom were Indian reserves, and cattle for beef became a necessity to both soldiers and Indians. To satisfy the demand, daring cowmen began the big cattle drives into the country. These drives started the Indians on a new and easier thievery, with the cattle virtually delivered to them. Charles Goodnight and Oliver Loving put the first herd through from Texas to New Mexico in 1866; and with the trail blazed, much of it following an ancient Indian route, thousands of head of cattle were soon started on the long journey from Texas to the forts and reservations. As the drives became numerous, the Indians went into camp around Horsehead Crossing on the Pecos and stole a part or all of every herd that started through. Charles Goodnight said: "I personally know that the Indians captured five herds and sold them to the New Mexico traders, accounting for some eight to ten thousand head. I proved before U. S. Court by Mexicans who bought the cattle from the Indians, who put the total of cattle at 300,000 head. The loot in horses was estimated at 100,000 head."[1]

Some of the army officers at Fort Bascom worked with the Comancheros and outfitted caravans to be sent on the plains for trade with the Indians. Other unprincipled Anglo-Americans worked with or financed the Comancheros.

A. B. Norton, superintendent of Indian affairs in New Mexico in 1867, reported: "Last year on my arrival here, I found that an unrestrained commerce was being carried on between the Comanches and the Mexicans, and that thousands of cattle stolen by the Comanches from the people of Texas were being traded for by the Mexicans having trade permits from General Carelton and from my predecessor; in fact, the territory was filled with Texas cattle.

"What a disgrace that our government should permit this plundering of the people of the frontiers of Texas by the Comanches to be encouraged by her own citizens giving the Indians a market for their booty."[2]

Late in the eighteen sixties, after years of fruitful piracy, the sun began to sink on the prosperous day of the Comancheros. Although no one then realized the import of the scattered groups of white buffalo hunters, who defied the Medicine Lodge Treaty to hunt on the plains, this army of killers was the force which finally drove the Comanches back on the reserve in Oklahoma to accept the dictates of the government. The buffaloes, constituting food, clothing, and shelter for the Indians, were practically exterminated by 1875; and the Comancheros' trade was destined to be history when the buffaloes were gone.

The easy crossing of the Canadian was on the western edge of the buffalo plains, the most wonderful hunting ground in the Southwest. The American hide-hunters, with their

[1] Edna Kahlbau, "The Comancheros of the Panhandle," *The Amarillo Sunday Globe–News*, November 2, 1941.
[2] *Ibid.*

deadly rifles, their excellent equipment, and their large forces, were not long in almost wiping out the animals. Champion of the hunters was J. Wright Mooar, who, with his brother and a few other hunters, obtained the army's tacit consent to cross the Red River and hunt in the Panhandle of Texas. This action definitely broke the Medicine Lodge Treaty. In 1874 a horde of hunters poured across the Red River in quest of hides; and out of their encroachment grew the battles of Adobe Walls, McClellan Creek (where Lieutenant Baldwin charged the Indians with his infantry loaded in wagons), and many other lesser Indian battles of the Panhandle. The Miles and Mackenzie campaigns and the complete subjugation of the Indians resulted from this broken treaty.

Colonel Mackenzie in his clean-up campaign against the Indians, which was concluded in 1875, found the plains white with bleaching buffalo bones. In crossing the plains, he found José Tafolla in full caravan, cruising about in search of trade with the Comanches. Tafolla, backed by army officers at Fort Bascom, operated on a big scale and used many carts and wagons heavily loaded with goods. After he was strung up to the tongue of a wagon, he disclosed the refuge of several hundred Indians in the Palo Duro, Tule, and Blanco canyons. A rope can be a good persuader.

The Comancheros also found a natural enemy in the buffalo hunters. A crew of hunters routed a considerable camp of Comancheros on one occasion. Again, after a fight on the Yellowhouse, where the Indians worsted a group of hunters, the Indians, to get revenge, raided the south plains territory down as far as Fort Griffin. They stole every horse they could lay hands on, leaving almost one hundred hunters on foot. A group of about thirty of the latter, under the leadership of Jim Greathouse and including Wild Bill Kress and "Sol" Reese, started on borrowed horses to retake their animals and punish the Indians. While searching for them, they met twelve Mexican Comancheros on the Las Linguas, waiting for rendezvous with the Indians, and in the ensuing battle killed the Comancheros to a man.

The destruction of the buffaloes, forcing the Indians to the reservations, killed the Comanchero trade, but the Canadian River Valley and its Mexican-Indian camping places lost traffic for only a short while. At that time the good land about Las Vegas, Mora, and Taos in New Mexico was crowded. When news reached these places that the Indians were on the reservation at Fort Sill, eager opportunists took advantage. The Comancheros and the Ciboleros had told many stories of the fine grazing lands of the public domain along the Canadian River. Many of the Comancheros themselves, cut off from their contraband trade, fell back on their original pursuit of sheep raising. Thus, Mexican sheepherders and settlers drove their flocks to the Canadian Valley, down the Tierra Blanca and Frio draws to the meadowland headquarters of the Palo Duro. Grazing with or just behind them came the great outfits with thousands of sheep and many herders or *pastores*. Most of the grass was short mesquite or rich buffalo grass, and stock fared better on it than on taller grasses. Indeed, the plains offered a treasure-land of grass, which had nothing on it of consequence now that the buffaloes were gone.

Many of the Comancheros, now turned sheepmen, grazed their great flocks into the Texas Panhandle but continued to use sharp practices as they had done in their trade with the Indians. In Texas, property was assessed as of January 1. In New Mexico, it was assessed as of March 1. The herds of these men were never in Texas in large numbers on the first of the year but had left New Mexico well ahead of March 1. Thus taxes were lost to both states somewhere between January 1 and March 1.

Among the families who came into the country, however, were some who built plazas and became good citizens. During this period the Placita de la Borregos was established on the south bank of the Canadian River, less than a mile from the site, on the north bank, which had been a favorite stopping place over the years and which was to become famous as Tascosa. Justo and Ventural Borregos led a group of Mexican families and *pastores* from Taos in this venture. They erected a single line of rock and adobe houses and a hundred yards away built sheep corrals around two small buttes near the riverbank. Later Juan Dominguez and his family built a group of adobes facing the Borregos home, their settlement becoming known as the Juan Dominguez Plaza. During the next few years, as the number of sheepmen owning small flocks increased, many plazas were erected up and down the river from the Borregos site. Some of these were Salinas, Trujillo, Valdez, Ortega, Chávez, Tecolote, Agapito Sandoval, Las Tecovas Springs, Casimero Romero, and Atascosa plazas.

At Borregos and the other plazas life was simple. The residents handled sheep, goats, and horses. Almost anything they wanted to eat could be had from the land. They spent much time hunting and fishing. Occasional trips to Anton Chico, Springer, Las Vegas, Salinas, and other trading points were made but were not absolutely necessary. Diet and clothing alike were simple.

The Mexicans loved a good time, and their parties were lively affairs. Mexican *bailes,* or dances, were well attended, entire families usually coming together. Dances lasted all night, and no one was in a hurry to go home. Cowboys and hunters often came, too, and many romances growing out of acquaintances made at *bailes* resulted in Anglo-Mexican unions. The Mexican girls were a real attraction to the cowboys. At these dances music was usually made by guitar and fiddle; and the dancers stepped to the Mexican quadrille, the American quadrille, and picturesque waltzes. In the Mexican dances, the figures were executed by the music, while the Americans promenaded and swung to calls.

Henry Kimball and Theodore Briggs, among a group of soldiers at Fort Union who went on a big hunt along the Canadian in 1874, later told interesting stories of their experience. They followed the old Mexican and Indian trails down the valley. The Borregos adobes sparkled like a little city of diamonds and rubies in the morning sun as Kimball and Briggs rode into the plaza and alighted at the greeting of the Borregos clan. The dogs were chased to the rear of the houses and made to stop barking, and little children bashfully peered out from behind doors and the big, sweeping skirts of their mothers. The soldiers enjoyed a pleasant visit before going about their hunt. Then they crossed the river and camped under the trees which had been used by Marcy, Carson, the emigrant trains, the Comancheros, and the Indians. They found the valley a paradise abloom. The river was fringed with willows and bushes. Beavers had built dams across the river and across Tascosa Creek. Bird life was plentiful. Wild game included several members of the cat family, gray prairie wolves, giant lobos, coyotes, antelopes, bears, and elk. Wild turkeys thrived. Kimball observed the great expanse of meadowland, the trees in some of the valleys, and the abundance of wild fruit; and he vowed that when his term of enlistment was up, he would return to this spot to live.

However, he found the valley on the verge of one of its feuds. The plaza sheepmen even then were concerned for their ranges. Each of the plazas was located at a spot with favorable grass and water and protection from storms. Large bands of sheep—some owned by rich, powerful, and often ruthless New Mexican politicians and merchants—were drifted into the country, overrunning the grazing grounds of the smaller sheepmen. Some of the Mexicans built stone fences adjacent to their plaza homes, taking advantage of bluffs and hills to fence in water and meadow grass. These fences, however, were meager protection from the outside. Simply shooting the invaders appealed to some, but even this method could not check the relentlessly oncoming flocks wanting free grass.

In the winter of 1875, Charles Goodnight, Texas Ranger, trail blazer, and rancher, drove a large herd of cattle from Colorado into New Mexico, just above the Canadian River Valley plazas. He had fallen in love with this country, which he had explored while working as a ranger. However, his presence there, on the borderland of the range he hoped to pre-empt, was promptly challenged by important owners of the large bands of sheep. The small sheepmen looked on as the two larger forces clashed. Jack Potter, a well-known trail driver, reported that the country was in a continual disturbance over water and grass in 1875 and 1876. The Mexican *pastores* and owners of small flocks of sheep about the plazas heard of the coming of cattle and cowboys with excited concern. A threat to their existence other than the big sheep owners of their own nationality was now a stern reality. Men on both sides oiled their shooting irons, and a number of bad men felt their trigger fingers itching. Among these was Sostenes l'Archevêque, no champion of the little sheepmen but a dangerous member of their group with a bitter hatred for any gringo and a developing lust for gold.

2. Sostenes and "Those Californians"

ONE MAN'S GREED and his hatred for the gringos instigated
the earliest decisive war against the little sheepmen, but it
was fought neither by the cattlemen nor by the holders of
the large flocks. His actions took out of the hands of the big
sheepmen and the cattlemen, both ambitious for the free grass
in the public domain, the decision impending in the Canadian
River Valley and changed the conflict from a cultural struggle to a personal issue involving robbery, murder, and revenge.

Sostenes l'Archevêque, whose career was as violent as
the times, was one of the earliest of many bad men in the
Southwest. This lithe, six-foot, four-inch, panther-like man
was born in Santa Fé, the son of a French father and a Mexican-Indian mother. He was the grandson of Jean l'Archevêque, the Frenchman who had been killed by the Indians in
1720. He had blue eyes and blonde hair, and the *señoritas*
called him handsome. He lived as a Mexican in New Mexico
and the Canadian River Valley.

Another of the early bad men in the same region was

William Bonney, familiarly known as "Billy the Kid," who was born in Brooklyn and reared in the turbulent New Mexico of the sixties and seventies. He was probably the most publicized outlaw of the Wild West; however, those old enough to remember will tell you that Billy the Kid when compared to Sostenes was a weakling. Perhaps they reach this shocking conclusion not from a comparison of the notches in the two men's guns but from the difference in the attitudes of the two killers.

William Bonney, the Brooklyn-born boy, carved twenty-one notches on his six-shooter. He started a career of wholesale slaughter to avenge the murder of the only man who had ever treated him decently. Once he became embroiled in the feuds of the raw West, there was no turning back. He was mired in intrigue and outlawry, but he lived by the strict gun code of the West. He was a hero to many of his acquaintances. Some who knew him only by reputation and legend shared this admiration. The feud in which he was a principal actor still lives up and down the piñon hills and the sage-covered draws of eastern New Mexico and over the wind-swept plains of the Texas Panhandle. There is plenty of "Kid money" in the Southwest today.

The feeling for Sostenes l'Archevêque is exactly the opposite of that for Billy the Kid. In his brief career he is said to have killed twenty-three white men, and he became so disagreeable to his own people that Colas Martínez, the Mexican guide and sheepman and his brother-in-law, said to Colonel Charles Goodnight, the early-day cowman and the most powerful influence for order and law in the Panhandle: "Don't worry about Sostenes. I will kill him myself if he makes any more trouble."[1]

Sostenes' father had been slain by an American at the little town of Sapello in eastern New Mexico, and the hatred

[1] Clarence R. Wharton, *L'Archevêque,* 17–19.

of the lad, Sostenes, for Americans soon knew no bounds. "When I grow up, I will kill every white man I meet," he vowed, and he came near to keeping his word.[2]

Many of the persons who helped in reconstructing the story of Sostenes do not believe that he could have killed as many men as legend credits him. The Mexican likes his outlaws mean and does not mind carving a few verbal notches on his legendary gun. Sostenes' reputation may have been enhanced by Mexican storytellers, but even if one or two incidents, which can be partially vouched for by persons yet living, are true, his deeds do not need embellishment. Perhaps it is the incident involving "those Californians," the mere mention of which sends shudders up and down the spines of many Mexicans in the Southwest today, that validates the case of Sostenes versus Billy the Kid.

As has been related earlier, the Canadian River region had been invaded by the *pastores* with their big bands of sheep long before the arrival of the cattlemen. No one knows when the earliest sheep grazed the valley of the Canadian or its many tributaries, but it is certain that the Mexicans had built their little mud and rock houses in parts of the Panhandle long before the Mooar brothers broke the Red River buffalo-hunting treaty with the Indians in the early seventies, for Frank Collinson, buffalo hunter and trail driver, found old houses on the Canadian and at Las Linguas in 1873, and Henry Kimball and his soldier companions found the valley of the Canadian fairly well populated with Mexicans when they entered it on the hunting expedition from Fort Union in 1874.

Thus, in the sixties and seventies the Panhandle belonged to the Mexican *pastores*, before the great cattle kings, Charles Goodnight and T. S. Bugbee, brought their first herds to the free-grass empire in 1876. It was the domain of Sostenes and the little sheepmen when the Californians came into it.

2 Wharton, *L'Archevêque*, 6.

In the summer of 1876 Miguel García and perhaps Baca were holding some 3,000 head of sheep near the confluence of Wildorado Creek and the Sierrata de la Cruz. One day as Miguel's herder let his flock graze slowly back toward the camp, he walked to a knoll and looked about the saucer-like world below, broken here and there by canyon bluffs and small buttes. As he looked off into the far distance, expecting to see Miguel at any minute, he was surprised to spy a large herd of sheep, for he knew of no other flock in this part of the country. He relayed the news to Miguel upon his arrival, and subsequent investigation revealed that the sheep belonged to two brothers by the name of Casner, soon to be known as "those Californians." With a Navajo Indian boy they were trailing a flock of several hundred fine sheep, hunting for a suitable open range. They had heard of the free grass of the famous Llano Estacado and the Palo Duro country, which that same year was attracting Goodnight.

Miguel told the Casners about the not-fully-occupied Palo Duro country and stressed the fact that the Canadian River region on into New Mexico was crowded. He also gave them specific directions to a good camping place at the head of Palo Duro Canyon. In acting thus, he was trying to protect his own interests and those of his friends, who did not want two gringos from California on their range.

In all, there were four members of the Casner family group, the father and three sons. They had been successful in a California gold mine and had minted twenty thousand dollars in twenty-dollar gold pieces at an Arizona mint. The two sons Miguel met had decided to invest in sheep, keeping as much money with them as possible, and find open country, for they were experienced frontiersmen. Although Miguel did not know the story of their wealth, he got the impression that they were rich and well equipped.

The next day, as the Californians continued their slow trek to the Palo Duro, Miguel rode to Borregos Plaza, near the south bank of the Canadian at the easy crossing of the river. There Colas Martínez, big sheepman, Comanchero, store operator, and boss of the Canadian River country, had his home. Many other Mexicans, including Sostenes l'Archevêque, the outlaw brother-in-law of Colas, also lived there.

In the interested group who heard of the Californians' invasion of the pastoral paradise was Sostenes. He immediately formulated a daring plan. Since he would need help to carry it out successfully, he would discuss it with his friend, Sacramento Baca. Perhaps he would assist him with the sheep and the loot, and also with old Colas, for Colas was usually against lawless expeditions.

Sostenes' enthusiasm was spurred by contact with Goodanuf, the notorious horse thief, whose men had also seen the Californians and evidence of their wealth. Sostenes made arrangements with Sacramento, who, although he refused to have a part in the actual deed, agreed to help in handling the loot and getting the community to acquiesce in the affair. Then one day Sostenes persuaded Ysabel Gurules, a Mexican boy, to accompany him on what was ostensibly a hunting trip. Ysabel rode a nag, and Sostenes rode one of the fastest horses at the plaza.

Sostenes led the way directly to the Casners' camp, where they found only one of the brothers. Sostenes talked with him long enough to hear that the other brother and the Indian boy were away with the sheep; then he shot the man at the first opportunity. Shocked, Ysabel wept and pleaded with Sostenes, but the outlaw slapped him and forced him to hide while he waited patiently for the second brother, whom he shot as he rode up to the tent.

Sostenes then ordered Ysabel to find and kill the Indian. When the Mexican boy protested, he was answered by another blow. Shaking with fear and horror, the boy mounted the fast horse and rode off. Once out of gunshot he put spurs to the horse and rode off at top speed for Borregos Plaza. He was a mile away before Sostenes realized that he was heading for home instead of following instructions, but the old nag left for Sostenes could not begin to catch up with the fleeter horse.

Sostenes cursed and then stopped to consider ways and means. He reasoned that perhaps it was best that Ysabel had not killed the Indian boy. He had found only a few coins in the pockets of the two men, although he had expected to find much gold. Perhaps the Indian could tell where the bulk of the gold was hidden. He had wanted Ysabel away from the camp while he looked for the gold, and he had thought it would be well also for his own safety if the little crybaby killed a man. Now he must work fast and attend to the matter himself after he discovered where the gold was hidden.

The Indian, with the help of his big sheep dogs, was moving the flock toward the camp when Sostenes rode out to meet him. Sostenes asked him many questions, but the herder, suspicious and fearful, failed to give satisfactory answers. One of the dogs snarled; and Sostenes, exasperated, shoved his gun into the Indian's stomach and demanded that he tell him where the Casner gold was hidden.

Just then he was hit from an unsuspected quarter. A sheep dog hurled himself at the intruder in a vicious attack that threw him off balance. He shot the dog, knocking him temporarily senseless, and flashed his gun back into the Indian's stomach, making a final demand for the gold. The Indian, paralyzed with fear, told him where a part of the treasure was hidden. He said that there was other gold, too, but he did not know where it was; the Californians had placed their gold in several hiding spots. Sostenes felt sure that the Indian was telling the truth. He also knew that the dead do not speak. Therefore, he clubbed the boy's head to a pulp with his gun. While he was attending to this grisly business, the second dog attacked, and he shot and killed it. Leaving the bloody scene, he hurried to the camp. Near the small

24

spring he found a heavy leather bag filled with coins. He fingered a handful of the money and felt the heft of the sack again and again.

No one has yet been able to explain the motive behind his next action. He tied his rope about the neck of one of the brothers, mounted his nag, and dragged the body to the rock cliff, where he kicked it off and watched it roll down the incline to the canyon and settle among some bushes. Then he fastened one of the Casner six-shooters at his hip, placed the gold in his shirt, and rode toward the plaza.

J. Evetts Haley has this to say of the loot that Sostenes found: "According to report, Sostenes failed to find the gold. Perhaps he got the money the Casners had received for their wool; the twenty-dollar gold pieces have never been found."[3]

Perhaps Haley is right, and it was only the wool-clip money about which the Navajo Indian boy knew, and his information about it was probably obtained accidentally. Sostenes, however, did carry away a large sum of money. The gold he failed to find or take with him has attracted several searching parties to the Palo Duro and the Canadian River. It is even predicted that someone will eventually stumble on one or more caches of twenty-dollar gold pieces in the Llano Estacado. It will be the gold which eluded Sostenes at the Casner brothers' camp or the money which Sostenes found there but could not carry with him.

Many of the occurrences of the next few days are shrouded in mystery, but there are living eye-witnesses to some of the events and other persons who have heard the stories at first hand.

It appears that Sostenes, that afternoon or later, was met halfway between the plaza and the sheep camp by Sacramento Baca. Baca reported that Ysabel had come into the plaza, with Sostenes' fine horse foaming from the hard ride,

---

[3] J. Evetts Haley, "Pastores del Palo Duro," (reprint from *Southwest Review*, Vol. XIX, No. 3 [April, 1934]), 11.

and had immediately told his father what had happened. The news spread fast in the small plaza; and Sacramento, who had every reason for protecting his own interests, rode out to meet the outlaw. Sostenes carefully inquired about the reaction to Ysabel's story. He was especially concerned with the attitude of his sister and her husband, Colas Martínez. Sacramento reported that they were very angry over the affair. Sostenes cursed Ysabel. Then he confided to Sacramento that perhaps they might find more gold about the camp, but Sacramento was afraid to have further part in the bloody business and suggested that they divide what money had been found. Sostenes, by now weary and somewhat apprehensive, divided the money with Sacramento; then he told him to go to camp and tell Colas that the two had fought, so that no one would suspect that Sacramento was an accessory to the murders. Sostenes himself would hide out for a while.

Colas Martínez had given his promise to Colonel Goodnight that he would take care of his brother-in-law if he became too unruly, and he intended to keep his word. Sostenes was leading all the Mexicans into trouble. In addition, there was no telling whom he might kill next. Therefore, Martínez called a council of the men of the community, who agreed that it would be better if Sostenes were dead. As a result of this conference a trap was set for him when he went to the home of Felix Gurules that night, having been lured there by the prospects of getting food. He entered an adobe room about twelve by fourteen feet in size. Across the doorway was a buffalo robe. In the center of the room was a table. Behind the table was another door leading into a small lean-to where the family cooked. As Sostenes crept through the front door, Miguel García and Felix Gurules, who were waiting inside, grabbed his arms and stabbed him in the back with a long knife. There were yells and the scuffling of feet. Colas stepped through the front door, cursing Sostenes for the misery he had caused, and fired twice point-blank into his body. Not even the gunshots stopped the struggle, but finally he was pinned to the floor, two men holding his hands and another with a knee in his stomach.

"You pull that knife out of my back, and I'll kill every one of you," screamed Sostenes.[4]

A blow on the head from a pistol knocked him unconscious for a moment only. Then he lunged, pulled, and tugged, trying to get up. He screamed and cursed, calling down all manner of evil spirits and curses on his enemies. One of the men tried to choke him. He was hit on the head again and again with the pistol and was only dazed by the blows. It was then that one of the battlers discovered a cross which Sostenes always wore on a small gold chain about his neck. The Mexican jerked it from his neck; and once the cross was gone, Sostenes lapsed into unconsciousness, dying early the next morning.

Besides the three participants mentioned above, other men witnessed the fight—Sacramento Baca, Francisco Nolan, Agapito Gurules, and Florentine.

Thus the bloody career of Sostenes was ended with his dying in the dark, killed by a group of his own people because they had found his actions unbearable. His end was not unlike that of Billy the Kid. Although at the beginning of his career as a killer, he had been motivated by revenge, he had no friends or principles to avenge. He could not even claim to be defending the interests of the plaza sheepmen and had degenerated into a killer for pure gain. No air of romance, no Robin Hood legends concerning him have sprung from the country where he ranged as they have about Billy the Kid. His grave on the south bank of the Canadian is unmarked. But one of his two daughters wrote historian Clarence R. Wharton: "My father was a very brave man.

[4] Colonel Jack Potter in an interview with the author.

Everybody feared him because he was not afraid of anything. He was the best shooter at that time and because he was such a good shooter the Texans had him killed. They were jealous of him."[5]

About a week after the fight, when Dyer and Hughes, employees of Colonel Charles Goodnight, were exploring the upper part of Palo Duro Canyon, they saw the Casner sheep and found the littered camp, the wounded dog, and the body of one of the brothers. Although near starvation, the dog was still faithfully and painfully herding the sheep. The cowboys drifted the sheep down the canyon and put Dave McCormick, hearty and lusty sheep-hating Irish cowboy, in charge of them. He was, however, very fond of pets and soon had a fast and intelligent friend and helper in the dog, whose eye had been shot out when Sostenes fired at him.[6]

The winter passed uneventfully, but Goodnight in his Pueblo, Colorado, home grew uneasy and decided to visit his Palo Duro ranch and the men he had left there. He came by way of Fort Dodge, Camp Supply, and Fort Elliott. After having made a surprising trade with Dutch Henry and his band of highwaymen that if they would not depredate in his country, he would not invade their domain, he reached the home ranch.

Finding his own property and men in good condition, Goodnight investigated the sheep and got all the information he could gather about their owners. He visited with his old friend, Colas Martínez, and found much to his satisfaction that Colas had effectively kept his word to rid the country of Sostenes.

When Goodnight returned to his home in Pueblo, he gave the story of the killing to the local paper, along with

---

[5] Wharton, *L'Archevêque*, 21.

[6] Haley, "Pastores del Palo Duro," 13. The remainder of the story of Sostenes has been reconstructed from *ibid.*, 14–16, and oral accounts of old-timers in the Panhandle.

a description of the property left by the victims, requesting that other papers in the West copy the article.

John Casner, the father, and his other son, Lew, who were prospecting near Silver City, New Mexico, and had in their party two Texans, Berry and Bell, read of the possible fate of their kinsmen and their sheep. The four men decided to go to the Panhandle and investigate. On a cold, blustery spring day in 1877 they arrived at the Goodnight home ranch in the Palo Duro Canyon, where they had no trouble in satisfying Dyer that the sheep were their property. They paid him for their keep and moved the flock to McClelland Creek.

When Goodnight returned to the ranch in the early summer, he met the Casners and got the impression that they were bad men, but, according to Haley, Dave McCormick disagreed with him. Retaliation for the killing of the two Californians and the Indian herder was rumored. Many Mexican *pastores* were running their bands of sheep from Francisco Baca's place a few miles above the head of the Palo Duro up the Tierra Blanca Creek and the Frio Draw into New Mexico. Some were good Mexicans and some were as rough as the country in which they lived. The Casners planned to rid that part of the Llano Estacado of Mexicans. Then they would drive them out of the whole Canadian Valley.

Goodnight heard rumors of their plans and warned that he would not permit such an outrage as they proposed; but the Casners swore that they were going ahead with their plans. Goodnight promptly pointed to his well-armed cowboys, with the promise of making war on the Casners if they carried out their threats. The Californians apparently accepted Goodnight's ultimatum, but their plans for revenge were not forgotten. Since they could not retaliate in wholesale fashion, they would go about it more methodically. They would wipe out Borregos Plaza and kill everyone who had had any part in the murder and robbery of the brothers.

29

John and Lew Casner had found some gold in an old shoe, but they knew that this was only a small part of what the brothers had brought with them. They believed that if they could find any of the rest of the money in circulation, they would have a positive clue to the murderers. They resorted to stratagem. Enlisting the aid of several Texans, they took a fast horse and made a visit to the Mexicans at the plaza. There they challenged Colas Martínez to a horse race, wagering five hundred dollars on the outcome. Both sides put up the money in the presence of witnesses, and among the Martínez money were some of the telltale gold pieces, which the Casners knew could have come only from their kinsmen. Although Martínez did not know it, the curse of Sostenes was reaching out to him in a strange way. The Texans and Californians lost the race and their money. Then they hired Colas Martínez and Felix Gurules to guide them to the canyon for a hunt and a look at the country.

They were some twelve miles down the river when the group started talking about the murder. The conversation was literally pulled out of the Mexicans, but the Californians and the Texans could speak the language like natives and they "savvied" the Mexican mind. Finally tiring of the game they were playing, one of the Casners let out an oath and shot Colas Martínez in his hand. Gurules spurred his horse into a small draw and raced for his life. Martínez grabbed his gun with his uninjured hand and fired, hitting one of the Texans in the stomach. The Texan returned the fire almost simultaneously, shooting the Mexican in the head. Martínez was riding his race horse, Huerfano, and that spirited animal bolted, dragging the Mexican a hundred yards before his lifeless body became disentangled from the stirrups. Felix Gurules, speeding for his life, used the cover of the draw and the trees and his knowledge of the country to get away, heading for his camp on the edge of the prairie. The Casners and their friends gave up the chase and gathered around the fallen Texan, who was suffering much agony from the wound given him by Martínez. In a short time the man died, and they buried him in a shallow grave.

In a brief caucus following this episode, the Casners determined to ride toward the place where the slain brothers had camped and there intercept the Mexican who had escaped them. The party of horsemen had been traveling for perhaps two hours when they saw a rider in the distance busily trying to round up a small herd of horses. They spurred their own animals into a gallop.

Felix Gurules, on racing away from them the day before, had ridden a roundabout route to his camp, kept by his nephew Ysabel. Pausing for only a short rest, he ordered Ysabel to be quick in loading their possessions and camp utensils. Then Felix rounded up the few horses in his charge. As a precaution he took his pistol out of his blanket saddle roll and put it in his pocket. There was no time for the gun, however, when the horsemen galloped to him. Bewildered, Felix reined his horse about and nervously awaited some word from them. That word never came, for every gun spoke at once. The riddled body of Felix Gurules crumpled in the saddle and tumbled to the ground. The horse bolted.

The Casners stopped but a moment and then went rapidly to the small wagon which could be seen a mile away. The boy, Ysabel, who was in the wagon, stopped when commanded. What happened then and there was retold by him on only a few occasions and then only to close friends. The men, as bloodthirsty as they were for revenge, hesitated to shoot a boy. They had been told that he had refused to have a part in the murder of the Casner brothers' Navajo herder and that he had reported Sostenes' crime. One of the Casners, however, wanted to kill every Mexican in the valley. The other was just as determined to turn the boy loose. For a time the argument, in which all took part, seemed on the verge of resulting in a fight to the death among themselves.

Ysabel begged and cried, pleading for his life. Finally one of the Casners shamed the others for wanting to kill a mere boy and won the decision. Ysabel Gurules was spared.

The Casners and their friends rode away in the direction of the sheep camps and the plaza, more determined than ever to rid the valley of Mexicans and to kill all of those who had had a part in the death of the brothers. Two of their victims, Agapito Nolan and Florentine, both participants in the punishment of Sostenes, were caught the next day, taken to a convenient chinaberry tree, and hanged with a small stay chain looped about their necks. Their bodies remained there for some days as ghastly evidence of the Californians' revenge.

When they returned to the plaza where everyone was in mortal terror, the Californians and their party interviewed Mrs. Colas Martínez, the sister of Sostenes. They goaded and taunted her about subjects of which she knew nothing and forced her to give them the money her husband had won in the horse race. This no doubt included money that Colas had taken from Sostenes after he had helped kill him.

Mexican messengers, riding day and night, spread the news of the trouble. Families deserted many plazas and camps to escape the plague that was called "those Californians."

"Those Californians," in the meantime, moved across the creek to Howard's Fort, operated as a base of supplies by G. J. Howard. Howard had come into possession of one of the Casner twenty-dollar gold pieces, and the Californians demanded to know from whom he had received it. He told them that Casimero Romero had paid for supplies with it and that Romero had said that it had been given to him by Colas Martínez. Then Howard gave up the money rather than have trouble. The party next headed for the home and stockade of Casimero Romero. When Romero would not come out to see them, they camped about his place for three days. While waiting, they reviewed their information. In some way they had learned of the encouragement Goodanuf and his gang had given Sostenes to kill and rob the brothers. They also heard that the Robbers' Roost band and Goodanuf had hoped to steal the sheep. Therefore, they decided to leave Romero and seek out Goodanuf and his hated and feared band.

The bandit learned that they were on his trail and went directly to Fort Elliott, where he surrendered to the military court. He was imprisoned in the post guardhouse for his own safety until county authorities could take him into custody. When the Casners arrived at the fort, they made a strong demand for his release to them, but the officers refused.

The great Panhandle country was at that time under the court jurisdiction of Clay County. Recourse to legal procedure made necessary a trip of two hundred miles to Henrietta. Bell and Berry, who it will be recalled were members of the Casner party, were sent after the sheriff, while the rest waited like hungry cats for a mouse. The sheriff, who wanted none of the affair, refused to come to Fort Elliott; but as a substitute deputized Berry to receive the prisoner and deliver him to Henrietta. Doubtless the sheriff felt sure that under the circumstances he would never receive a prisoner.

The federal authorities were helpful to Berry. When he presented his papers, they gave him the prisoner, a government ambulance, and five soldiers as guards. This was more help than Berry wanted. The Casners, however, were equal to the occasion. At midnight the first night out from the fort five Negro buffalo hunters, unheard-of previously in that country, charged the camp on Sweetwater Creek, their big Sharps buffalo guns covering the party. They demanded the prisoner, saying that they wanted to talk to him alone. A corporal, knees shaking and mouth dry, started to protest but was immediately hushed by a gun shoved into his stomach.

Haley, in describing the events that took place the next morning, wrote, tongue in cheek: "The innocent Berry and the excited soldiers found him [Goodanuf] tied to a cottonwood tree. But, as Dave McCormick concluded with a mighty pleased look on his face, 'they tied him so high his feet wouldn't reach the ground!'"

The Casners now had good reasons for leaving that part of the country. Taking their sheep, they left in as much of a hurry as the herders who fled into New Mexico.

During the next few years when Mexicans around Las Vegas, Mora, Taos, and other towns in New Mexico were asked why they had left the Panhandle, they would assume a pained expression and utter these words in tones of fear: "Ah! Those Californians."

3. The Coming of the Ranches

As THE THUNDERING of the great buffalo herds died out in the seventies, the lonesome, angry bawls of the longhorns coming up the trails from lower Texas announced the opening of a vast open-range world. Tough cattle, able to hold their own and gain ground against all the forces of nature in Mexico and South Texas, were herded by rugged individuals on hardened Spanish and mustang horses. It was as natural for these first cowboys to trail their herds by the route of the easy crossing on the Canadian as for all other men and animals to follow it. At the crossing they found a small, untamed plaza called by the natives Atascosa, a word meaning "boggy," which they used in describing the short, spring-fed creek meandering through the plaza. The cowboys pronounced the name more easily as "Tascosa" or slurred it, saying "Tascosy." To Tascosa came herds of maverick cattle and many human mavericks astray in a prairie world of crazy mirages. Here the cattle were cut into different herds. Here, too, the human mavericks lined up either with the "little" men or with the big outfits. The story of these mavericks, these little men, moving against tremendous odds in a maverick open-range world is one of the poignant sagas of the

West. In that world the bloody exploits of Billy the Kid and Sostenes l'Archevêque were the exceptions to the general rule, but many men lived near the border line of lawlessness.

The quiet of the sheepmen on the Canadian was rudely broken, as it had been once before, when the cowmen owning small herds came in and boldly claimed part of the open range. These cattlemen were as quick to realize the possibilities of profit from free land minus burdensome taxes as the owners of large flocks. Charles Goodnight's and Casimero Romero's agreement in the middle seventies, dividing the country between themselves, naturally bound no one else. The nester cattlemen were extremely practical and individualistic in their antagonism to sheep and to those who ran them. Some of the bitterest wars of the West were waged between the sheepmen and the cattlemen; and the small ranches were an important factor in the many conflicts arising in the Canadian River Valley between large and small interests, both Mexican and Anglo-American.

Some of the outfits ran both sheep and cattle or changed from sheep to cattle. The Trujillos, who came into the region about 1874, had a big ranch two miles above the mouth of Parker Creek, west of Borregos Plaza, and owned both sheep and cattle. John Hollicott, later manager of the LX Ranch, told friends that his horses all had mange that year and he believed that they had been infected while he was stopping at the Trujillo Ranch. It was no hard matter for the Trujillos, who were a large family, to change from sheep to cattle and include a little "mustanging" in their program.

Another outfit that ran both sheep and cattle, but began with sheep, was that of Scotchman James Campbell. In the course of his ranching he sold out twice and had two partners, Ledger and E. Godwin-Austen, both Englishmen. Campbell had his first headquarters on the Rita Blanca Creek northwest of Tascosa, where he ran several thousand head of sheep and some 3,500 head of cattle. Jim and Kid Dobbs

went to work for him late in 1878, when the first task given
them was dipping sheep. Kid Dobbs cut some 3,000 picket
staves for Campbell and then contracted to furnish Campbell's outfit with wild game. He got one dollar a head for
killing deer and antelope, as Campbell believed that paying
for the slaughter of game was much cheaper than killing his
own sheep or cattle to feed his men. Later Campbell and
Ledger sold their outfit and ranch location to the LE's.
Campbell then settled on a section of school land on the Rita
Blanca and with E. Godwin-Austen as a partner accumulated
a large property, which was finally sold to the LS Ranch.

In 1876, but perhaps earlier by weeks or months, Thomas
S. Bugbee moved from Kansas with a herd of cattle. He lo-
cated on Bugbee Canyon on the north side of the Canadian
River about seventy-five miles below Tascosa.

Charles Goodnight, who had been ranching in Colorado,
started for the Panhandle country in 1875 with 1,600 head
of cattle. As he pointed his herd into the Canadian Valley in
New Mexico west of Tascosa, he heard of the Adobe Walls
Indian fight and of the Indians still at large and "on the peck."
He decided to winter in New Mexico out of their range and
avoid trouble.[1]

This stay gave him time to hunt out the country more
thoroughly for a permanent location. In his explorations he
had the services of his Mexican friends, particularly Colas
Martínez. He found his range and his country in the Palo
Duro Canyon. After this he had a long and understanding
visit with the Mexican *pastores* and major-domos. He and
Casimero Romero, who represented a few sheepmen, agreed
to divide the country, the sheepmen staying in the Canadian
River Valley and west, Goodnight taking his cattle to the
Palo Duro Canyon and the range eastward. In late 1876,

[1] Roy Riddle, "Casimero Romero Reigned as Benevolent Don in
Brief Pastoral Era," *The Amarillo Sunday Globe-News*, Golden Anniversary Edition, August 14, 1938.

therefore, he moved his herd to the Palo Duro Canyon, but stopped en route to visit with Casimero Romero at his new hacienda.

Romero, accompanied by Agapito Sandoval and his family, had moved into the country in November, 1876, and had located his plaza behind some hills near a strong spring about one-half mile from Atascosa Creek. Romero had come in the grand manner. He was a *"mucho grande"* operator, a cultured and wealthy Castilian. It is interesting to contrast a description of his *entrada* with the coming of Briggs, Armstrong, and others representing the Anglo-American populace, who traveled on horseback or in one wagon with their meager possessions.

What a sight the Romero caravan must have been as it streamed slowly down the valley of the Canadian! Casimero moved on a scale befitting a grandee of Mexico. The train was composed of fourteen great lumbering schooners, peaked like a boat in front and back, which Romero had purchased from the United States Army. Their beds were painted blue, the color applied to all army property in those days, and each wagon was pulled by four yoke of oxen. The coach in which the family rode was a magnificent conveyance not unlike the stagecoaches plying the mail routes. The site of their embarkation was Mora County, New Mexico, where Casimero had ranched for a good many years before his son José was born in 1871.

From Chávez Plaza in New Mexico there was a clearly defined road leading eastward, probably the route followed by Captain Marcy in 1847, but as the Romero train neared Tascosa, the terrain close to the Canadian became so cut up by arroyos and canyons leading to the river that the Romero and Sandoval party was forced to take to the high hills, although they camped and watered at the stream at night. José Romero's description of the Canadian River then is important, as it reveals what rapid and widespread changes can take place in the topsoil and general topography of a country in a relatively few years:

"It was a beautiful stream, no sand bars at all. It was hardly more than 20 feet wide and had deep clear living water. Its banks were fringed along practically the entire distance we traveled with many bushes. Wild choke berries, plums—great big plums, too—wild gooseberries and grapes. There were many cottonwood nottes scattered along its banks. The cattle, when they came, destroyed the bushes. The trappers caught the beaver, their dams deteriorated, turning the water loose, and this altered the nature of the stream."[2]

The immigrants wintered just south of Tascosa. The great wagons were drawn into a circle well inside a grove of trees, and a tent was stretched. Then Casimero and Agapito and members of their party fell to cutting limbs from the cottonwoods for windbreaks. Altogether, their arrangement provided a very comfortable compound.

Casimero and Agapito explored the surrounding country in search of sites for their permanent plazas. Casimero favored the banks of the Canadian near a number of large springs, where a spacious *vega* flanked by high, protecting hills added to the value of the place. Hundreds of buffaloes came to this spring for water. Agapito found a homesite to his liking on Corsino Creek. The two clans worked together, putting up the Romero home first and then building one for the Sandovals.

The news of the beautiful streams and the rich grazing lands was not long in reaching Mora County and other sections of New Mexico, and the following year, 1877, the García, Valdez, and Sierna families came in, settling near where Punta de Agua and Rita Blanca creeks unite. They were joined by the Tafolla family soon afterwards. These

---

[2] Haley, *Charles Goodnight, Cowman and Plainsman*, 276–94.

families formed the Spanish nucleus of the frontier town of Tascosa. Most of them, like the Romero clan, were Castilians and substantial, peaceful folk bent only on colonization.

Henry Kimball brought only a blacksmith outfit—forge, anvil, horseshoes, hammers, tongs, and other small equipment—when he arrived. Kimball, it will be recalled, was the soldier who had been on a hunting party in this region in the fall of 1874 and who had vowed to return. His enlistment in the army had expired before that of his friend, Briggs, who was to accompany him on the venture; but since they had already agreed upon tentative sites for homes, Kimball came ahead. He went through the formality of moving on the site on the southern edge of Tascosa Valley where a big spring gushed from the side of the hill. There he erected early in 1876 a one-room house, the first built for an Anglo-American in the upper Panhandle, set up shop in his adobe hut beside the spring, and planted some small cottonwood switches he had gathered on the Canadian River. These switches grew into the giant trees which now shade the old LIT headquarters, so completely overshadowing the hillside and the spring that one has difficulty in believing that the hillside was ever barren of trees.

Briggs followed soon afterward. He settled on Rica Creek, about one and one-half miles up the river. He had plenty of water, fine grass, and big red bluffs for protection against the strong north winds.

Then in November, 1876, Casimero Romero moved in, and the little inland valley began to take on the aspects of a boom. Briggs, Kimball, and Romero were on the north side of the river; across the river from Romero and Kimball was the old Borregos Plaza; and next to it was the Juan Dominguez Plaza. These had grown to be large plazas modeled after the fashion of the day and very similar to some Indian and Mexican villages of the Southwest today.

Ellsworth Torrey, who according to some reports had

been a captain in the British Navy, had dreams of a cattle fortune, and with the backing of a Boston bank, also moved into the country about 1876. He settled on the south bank of the Canadian near Skunk Arroyo and had in his range some excellent springs and the peaks which now bear his name. The Torrey Peaks have long been famous landmarks—many exciting stories have been told of their use as hide-outs by Indians, Mexicans, and outlaws, and men have left their signs and marks on the rock walls.

Torrey and his wife had two sons, Charley and Bill, and two daughters. Charley was a fairly apt pupil in the cow business, and the family acquired approximately 25,000 head of cattle, which they sold to the LS Company when they left the region.

Torrey's experience with the outlaw, Billy the Kid, is said by some to have been the reason for his selling out and leaving the plains. Torrey had remarked that Billy and his band were ordinary horse thieves not fit to associate with decent people or to break bread with them. When this was reported to the outlaw, with four of his men he went to Torrey's headquarters and asked for feed for his horses and a meal for his men. The horses were fed and dinner was prepared. Torrey tried to serve Billy and his men before his family ate, but Billy insisted that the family eat with them. Then, after the meal was over, the young outlaw took Mr. Torrey outdoors and gave him a tongue lashing, threatening to shoot him if he spoke slightingly of his men again.

Billy the Kid had recently embarked on his lawless career, following the bloody wars in Lincoln County, New Mexico, in which he had been in the pay of John Chisum. Following the conclusion of the strife there, the Chisums had sent three herds of cattle to the Panhandle, where they built a dugout and some corrals at the foot of the breaks near the Canadian and below the mouth of Trujillo Creek, in the general vicinity of Torrey's ranch, about thirty miles above Tascosa. Charley Neebow, or Neilbold, was Chisum's wagon boss in the Panhandle, and some of the men with him were Johnny Newell, Bill Hutch, and Tom Pickett. Sally Chisum, daughter of one of the Chisums, came out to the camp headquarters for a stay in the winter of 1878. Then, in 1879, the Chisums moved their herds out of the Canadian River Valley range.

Billy the Kid, with the wages which he had drawn as gunman in the Lincoln County War cut off, gathered some of the other men in the same position about him and followed the Chisums to the Panhandle. There some of the men shuffled allegiance, some remaining with the Chisums, some throwing their lot with Billy the Kid, and others entering different fields or scattering to far places.

Other men also found refuge in the Canadian Valley. Padre Green had a ranch above the mouth of the Rita Blanca between the Trujillo and Campbell outfits in the late seventies. Green had allegedly been at one time a priest, hence the appellation "padre." There are several legendary stories of his activities in the Canadian region, including some not complimentary to his reputation. It was asserted that he collected tithes from the Mexicans, but it was not claimed that he administered any sacraments. He was in the valley in 1878 when Kid Dobbs came to the country. Tall and intelligent, he was in his fifties when he sold out to Dan Taylor and left the country. Taylor bought 800 head of cattle from Green that carried a Spanish brand.

Another small nester ranch was that of Mitchell and Falby, both of whom had Mexican wives. Its headquarters were at the head of the small canyon that today carries Mitchell's name. Mitchell, who was sometimes called Dr. Mitchell by the cowpunchers, ran a few cattle while Falby freighted. Their ranch improvements were later sold to the LIT, and the houses were used for a line camp.

Major George W. Littlefield of Texas sent a group of

his trusted trail drivers with a large herd of cattle gathered in Central and East Texas to Dodge City by way of the famous old Chisholm Trail, over which millions of head of cattle tramped their way to the railway market centers. When they reached Dodge City in the late summer of 1877, the drovers found the market glutted and the buyers not in a mood to deal with anyone except at prices that were sheer ruin. The trail boss, Phelps White, who had received reliable reports of the open-range paradise in the Panhandle of Texas, drifted the herd south into the Panhandle to winter along the Canadian. Thus some 3,500 cattle reached the mouth of the Pescado Creek in the fall of 1877. That winter cattle grazed on excellent grass that had plenty of substance to it. They had the protection of the bluffs, canyons, and trees. The cattle were in excellent flesh in the spring, but the market was still not favorable. Therefore, the owners decided to establish a ranch on the free acres of the Canadian.

The big squatter ranch had set up temporary headquarters about three miles west of Tascosa across Cheyenne (now Magenta) Creek, but a more suitable location was needed east of Tascosa. The site pre-empted by the blacksmith, Henry Kimball, where the water gushed out of the hillside in great volume and where there was open country far to the east and north except for settlers at Pescado and Sandoval plazas, was ideal. A trade was made whereby the Littlefield agents purchased Kimball's rights. One informant said the consideration was a good cow pony from a Mexican, one Francisco Romero, a brother-in-law of Kimball. C. S. (Bill) McCarty, one of Littlefield's trusted men, took charge of the ranch.

Thus came the LIT, the first brand burned in the immediate vicinity of Tascosa and the symbol of one of its largest squatter ranches. It remained the LIT brand and ranch through many ownerships. Major Littlefield, described as a "gentleman through and through,"[3] instructed McCarty to buy the small herds and improvements of the neighboring ranchers, but Littlefield never claimed any but squatter's right to all of the great stretch of acres grazed by his cattle. The ranch prospered under McCarty's management and gradually absorbed many little herds that found range in the neighborhood. One was that belonging to Goodrich and Beeman, who had brought several thousand head of cattle from New Mexico down the Canadian in 1877 in search of grazing ground.

Having heard of the great cattle fortunes possible in the Western Hemisphere, some Dundee, Scotland, men had formed the Prairie Cattle Company and had begun the organization of large ranch properties. They had bought the Cross L's from W. H. Hall of Crincero, New Mexico, on the Cimarron. Then they had bought cattle and had started a ranch on the Arkansas River in Colorado, branding JJ. Their first purchase was known as the New Mexico Division, their second as the Arkansas Division. Then they moved to the Panhandle to buy out the LIT's in 1881, and also purchased other Panhandle ranches and an Indian Territory brand. In 1883 they sold all of these to the Hansford Land and Cattle Company except the LIT, which the Prairie Company kept, adopting the brand and using the range. No land is mentioned in the instrument of sale because, as has been explained, the LIT's did not own any land but had merely preempted what they needed, as was the case with many ranches in those days. The sale involved all equipment and 17,247 head of cattle. Littlefield received notes for more than $125,-000, and the ranch became the Canadian Division of the Prairie Cattle Company's holdings. P. G. Head, sent from Scotland as general manager of the Prairie Company, had

[3] Laura V. Hamner, "Life Began in the Seventies" (manuscript). Much of the material that follows is taken from these manuscript volumes.

offices at Higgins, Colorado, and Bob Robinson was named manager of the Canadian Division.

The LIT's under the Prairie ownership continued running the scale from good to bad fortune and good to bad management with the years. The company was eventually sold to Lee Bivins, the ranch becoming a part of the Bivins estate; then it was owned by his son, Julian Bivins, and is now a part of Julian's estate following his death in an airplane crash in 1940. The old headquarters, however, are not as extensively used as once. The range suffered greatly during the drought years of the nineteen thirties. A caretaker stays at the headquarters, and for a brief period annually several cowboys are located there.

As the reports of the excellent open-range conditions in the Panhandle had intrigued the LIT's, so did they attract the founders of the LX Ranch, the first ranch in Potter County. W. H. (Deacon) Bates and David T. Beals, Bostonians, had established a ranch on the Arkansas River near Granada, Colorado, in 1870. H. C. Rosencrans, a Mr. Brown, and Erskine Clements, ranch bookkeeper, were associates. Bates and Beals had made a fortune in the early days of the Colorado country and had had excellent success on the Arkansas, but in 1876 they found the range there becoming crowded. Therefore, they sent John Ray, an old plainsman and a trusted employee, to survey the Canadian country before they moved their cattle. He came on horseback with a pack horse in the summer of 1876 to Tascosa and then rode down the river about twenty miles until he chanced upon a buffalo hunter's supply camp kept by a man named Pitcher, whose dugout store was on the north bank of the Canadian River a few steps northwest of the present United States Highway 87 bridge.

John Ray made a favorable report, and early in the summer of 1877 the first LX herd was driven to the Canadian. The LX Ranch headquarters were established on a creek

soon known as Ranch Creek, about two miles east of Pitcher's camp. The first improvements, consisting of a large
bunkhouse, an office, a kitchen, and a large warehouse for
ranch provisions and feed, were built of native stone chinked
with mud. Corn for the horses was freighted from Dodge
City, the nearest point of supply, 225 miles away. Later a
large stable, corral, blacksmith shop, and wagon sheds were
built of adobe. After establishing the headquarters, the ranchers went to Dodge City and bought several herds of young
steers. By the winter of 1877 thousands of cattle were fat-
tening on the luxuriant grass that covered the range, and
during 1878 four herds were brought from South Texas to
add to their number.

Charley Siringo, famous cowboy detective and writer,
has described the LX range and his experiences there in several of his books. He joined Bates and Beals in Dodge City
about July 4, 1877, and came with Bates, Bill Allen, Owl
Head Johnson, and others to the Panhandle with one of the
LX herds. En route they hunted buffaloes, mustangs, and
had many exciting adventures typical of the pioneer West.
Siringo reported a half-dozen Mexican families and a store
owned by Howard and Rinehart at Tascosa. He names as
neighbors on the range Goodrich, Tom Bugbee, Hank Cres-
well, Charles Goodnight, the LIT's, Lee and Reynolds, and
Nick Chaffin on the Lower Blue. According to his report,
Jim Kennedy, son of the famous South Texas cattle king of
the firm of Kennedy and King, brought in a herd of steers
and turned them loose above Tascosa.

Siringo related an experience which indicates that Pitcher—supplier to buffalo hunters and likely the first Anglo-
American resident of Potter County—encountered trouble
with the Mexicans in the region. Siringo wrote:

"About Christmas, 1878, we had an exciting chase after
thieves. Eight Mexicans came to Pitcher's post and loaded
all of his goods into large freight wagons and started south-

west with them. Pitcher went to the LX ranch and reported his loss. By the time the LX cowboys could collect enough men to form a posse the Mexicans had a good start on them, but after hard riding they were overtaken near the New Mexico line. For a time the Mexicans stood the posse off with their long range buffalo guns. Finally Jack Rigan, who could talk their language, was allowed to go to their wagons. On the promise that no harm would come to them, the Mexicans agreed to haul the goods back to Pitcher's camp. This bargain was carried out and what might have been a serious situation was settled without further ado. Shortly afterwards Pitcher left the country, following the buffalo hunters to the South."[4]

John Ray, who had explored the ranch location, was stationed at a line camp eight miles west of the headquarters on a nameless creek. Soon this creek and a butte preserved for posterity the name and memory of the lone rider who had scouted the LX Ranch. The LX grew and prospered. Many of its men had important roles in the life of Tascosa, and the ranch trade was for years a factor in Tascosa's growth. The original LX brand and a number of associated brands are still operated today, though not quite on their once-grand scale. Some of the early ranches were tremendous organizations involving huge amounts of money. These open-range empires, while hard to establish and precarious to operate, were typical of the years and of the country. They were essentially "big business" operations and dangerous gambles. The first two big outfits in the Canadian River Valley, the LIT's and the LX's, were established by moneyed men from other parts of the nation. These men had the means to hire able and daring subordinates and the power to take and hold the country once they found an open range worth taking.

W. M. D. Lee and the Reynolds brothers had been gov-

[4] Charles A. Siringo, *A Lone Star Cowboy*, 83–85.

ernment contractors and suppliers before Lee came to the Tascosa country to establish the LE brand in this period. A short time later he was bought out by the Reynolds brothers on a give-or-take trade, characteristic of the West. Lee then associated himself with Lucien B. Scott, a New York banker, made a deal with the Reynolds brothers to divide the range, bought out Godwin-Austen and Campbell on the former Duran range, and started the LS brand and ranch from the partnership known as the Lee-Scott Company.[5]

With its headquarters some fifteen miles southeast of Tascosa, the LS took kindly to the little plaza town and bought its supplies and stored them there. Thus was added a factor which was to make Tascosa grow as a trade, trail, and cattle center. The LS cattle found range north and south of the town for more than two hundred miles. It was a big world that the LS controlled and one entirely open south of the Canadian River. Cattle caught in the blinding, swirling snowstorms of the Panhandle could drift to the Pecos and on to the Rio Grande. This drifting, however, presented the LS range with a vexing problem, because to the south and to the west operated the cattle rustlers of New Mexico and the renegades led by men such as Billy the Kid. The cattle which drifted into the territory of these bad men were a welcome bonanza.

The foundation of the greatest ranch of them all—variously known as the Capitol Freehold Ranch, the Capitol Syndicate Ranch, or the XIT—was also laid in 1879. Destined to play an important role in the life of Tascosa and of Texas, the XIT, which was the ranch brand, was to be formed out of three million acres of the public domain. The state of Texas, having lost its capitol buildings in a fire, contracted with a syndicate, composed largely of Chicago capitalists, to build a new capitol, taking the land in exchange. The contract was

[5] Laura V. Hamner, *Short Grass and Longhorns,* 160–72.

let and work begun in 1879, but the XIT as a brand was not due to come on the scene actively until 1885.[6]

This ranch brought with it the beginning of great changes in ranching, for the XIT was the first ranch to apply business methods, rules, and regulations to the range. Heretofore, ranching had been largely an enterprise handled by one owner or a partnership. Often it had been carried on without too much regard for systematic accounting and straight-laced business formulas. The XIT organization, covering one of the greatest areas of grazing land in the world, had to operate by system and under definite business procedure. The XIT was ruled by strong men, whose efforts to dominate a country already occupied by nester ranchers, with others seeking entrance, must inevitably cause much conflict.

In 1881 the Frying Pan Ranch was established by two wealthy men, Glidden and Sanborn. Its brand was a small circle with a long bar in it that cowboys said resembled a frying pan. It was also known as the Skillet brand and as the Pan Handle. Headquarters of the ranch, which covered about 300,000 acres, were at Las Tecovas Springs, old Comanchero and Indian camping spot some twenty miles southeast of Tascosa.[7]

Dr. Henry C. Hoyt, who eventually became surgeon general of the United States Army in the Philippine campaign, was just out of medical school when King John Chisum of the Jinglebobs told him that Tascosa needed a doctor badly because of an epidemic of smallpox. He rode to Tascosa in 1877, accompanied by Hugh B. McCune. Chisum gave them a quarter of beef and water for their wagon, as an eighty-mile stretch, barren of water, lay between the Jinglebobs and Tascosa. Hoyt found the Panhandle sparsely popu-

[6] J. Evetts Haley, *The XIT Ranch of Texas and the Early Days of the Llano Estacado*, 54.

[7] Hamner, *Short Grass and Longhorns*, 207–15.

lated, and the smallpox epidemic soon faded. He had a fine
time hunting and living in the new country but was soon
without funds. Then he took a job on the LX Ranch, of
which W. C. (Bill) Moore was manager. Moore had learned
his cowpunching in California and had introduced California
methods and equipment to the Panhandle. Hoyt served him
as a range rider and camped at a line camp on Bonita Creek
with Latigo Jim, who chose to keep all other names to himself. Charley Siringo taught Hoyt to throw a lariat, and he
became an expert. Hoyt also learned to ride the wildest
horses. He made the acquaintance of Jack Ryan, junior foreman and top cowhand on the LX, and helped in gathering
strays that drifted with the storms. At one time he held down
one camp for thirty days with little food. Hoyt returned to
Tascosa, helped with the mail line, met Billy the Kid and his
gang, and formed a fast friendship with the outlaw. He rode
away from Tascosa on a fine horse given to him by the Kid.[8]

As Hoyt left the country, many settlers and nester cowboys had already begun to drift into the Panhandle. Two
of these were Jim and Kid Dobbs, who, after financial failure at buffalo hunting on the south plains in the spring and
summer of 1878, joined Jack Ryan, LX wagon boss, and
helped him locate some stray bunches of LX cattle. Ryan
brought the two Dobbs brothers to the LX headquarters in
August, and Moore put them to work. When winter forced
a reduction in the number of cowboys on the ranch, the two
with another LX cowboy rode to Tascosa with Billy the Kid.

At Tascosa the cowpunchers and the outlaws found
other cowboys, farmer boys, and ranchmen with small herds
seeking grazing lands. With the roundup of 1878 Tascosa
was clearly on its way to becoming the cattle-trading center
of the area. It gave every promise of growing with the development of the industry.

[8] Dr. Henry F. Hoyt, *A Frontier Doctor.*

4. Tascosa and Oldham County

IT WAS PERFECTLY NATURAL that Tascosa should have been an informal little community all of its life, but ownership of land called for maps, surveys, official names, and the other formalities that are necessary in an organized society. Thus it came about that in 1873 and 1874 Frank Maddox attempted the first survey of the Tascosa country in locating certificates for the Houston and Texas Central Railroad. Some persons claimed that most of his work was done at Sherman behind a desk and on a drafting board in his office. His own testimony before the Texas Supreme Court is enough to establish this rumor as a fairly accurate fact. The maps and the testimony also show that even this early the cards were being stacked in favor of the owners of large tracts of land against the best interests of the state and its later settlers.

The history of the West could in great part be written around the struggles for land with water on it or for the control of water in the areas of the public domain, for the rancher who controlled the water controlled the land. It must be remembered that this was before the day of windmills and the building of dams and the creating of artificial lakes. The surveyors and the big land companies laid the foundation, in the survey of the Canadian River country, for their immediate profit but for ill feeling and trouble later.

In the autumn of 1879 John Summerfield, surveyor for the firm of Gunter and Munson (later Gunter, Munson, and Summerfield), came from Grayson County, Texas, to the Panhandle to survey lands for the state and for his firm. He took care of the interests of his company, and with the aid of the inefficient work of Frank Maddox, his survey did not show a single school section bordering the south side of the Canadian River. The maps today show this discrepancy. With Summerfield came W. H. Ingerton, a lad of sixteen, as a flagman. He went back to Grayson County in 1880, when the survey was completed, but returned to the Panhandle as a cowboy with the first herd of GMS or T-Anchor cattle.

In 1882 W. S. Mabry was assigned to survey the Oldham County land district, which comprised a part of the three million acres the state of Texas had traded for its capitol building, the great land empire which formed the nucleus of the XIT Ranch. Many events of significance were to occur, however, before the XIT came into actual being and before much could be done in terms of varas, boundary lines, and legal rulings.

While the ranchers were moving into the outlying lands, other settlers were coming to the vicinity of Tascosa and establishing trades and businesses. There was an excellent reason for quickening activity in the Canadian River Valley. The day of the open range for the cattlemen was beginning in the Panhandle of Texas. Great herds were being trailed through the country to Kansas markets. Cowmen were moving to pre-empt the wide acres available to those who could get them and hold them as their own. All this activity was bringing new life and a new era to El Llano Estacado. It was spawning new trail trading centers and bringing with it all the trouble and excitement that boom conditions foster in a new country. The Canadian River Valley was soon to be the very heart of this new cattle world, the seat of business for many cattle kingdoms.

Shortly after Kimball arrived in the Tascosa Valley and just as Casimero Romero was getting his hacienda underway, G. J. Howard, a prominent man from Elizabethtown, New Mexico, when it was the capital of an inland mining empire, and his partner, Ira Rinehart, a German Jew and former sheriff at Elizabethtown, came from New Mexico to establish a general store at Tascosa. There they built a two-room adobe house with a flat roof. Included in their stock were whiskey, drugs, patent medicines, rifle and pistol shells, and staple foods. They were partners for a short time, and then in a mutually agreeable trade Howard sold his interest to his partner. He afterward established a store of his own.

In the spring of 1877, less than a year later, James E. McMasters, searching for a trading-post location, drove his wagon loaded with merchandise from Taos to the Canadian Valley. He pulled up on a grassy hilltop overlooking the new town. To his right was the site which was later to become Boothill Cemetery, its first occupant destined to be sent there by the man who was to become McMaster's partner.

McMasters jumped out of the covered wagon and drank in the scene before his eyes. The country was incomparably beautiful, from the rich waxy green of the sprouting cottonwoods to the cerulean blue haze that rose sharply above the red, yellow, and mauve hilltops in the breaks down the river. The stream with its border of willows and reeds added a touch of dependability to the location. James McMasters contemplated the view again as he sipped black coffee by his campfire. He noticed a beaver dam, and he saw a small, white-tailed deer frisk off to the river. A rabbit hopped down to the creek for a drink but paid no attention to him, even though the accustomed path to water lay only a few feet from the wagon. McMasters determined that he would remain here.

After supper, he looked speculatively at the two-room adobe house that stood about two hundred yards across the creek. It seemed inviting. He walked over and spoke to the man standing in the door, who was Howard. A short time later they formed a partnership.

In this manner came the second store to Tascosa, that of Howard and McMasters, and a name was added to the group of illustrious men, hardened on the frontier, who knew all of its evils and hardships and yet stood for the advancement of law and civilization. Kimball, Rinehart, Howard, McMasters—and later Armstrong, Brown, Willingham, and East —stood together in Tascosa's business and official affairs and breathed life into the little Western town.

On November 27, 1880, Howard and McMasters bought from Gunter and Munson of Sherman, who owned the section on which Tascosa was located, twenty-four acres of land on the north side of Main Street. They paid one hundred dollars for the land, which comprised most of the townsite of Tascosa. Then they built a large adobe storeroom and stocked it with everything that could be found in a general store or was needed in a new country. This merchandise was freighted by ox and mule teams at high rates from Dodge City, Kansas, or Springer, New Mexico.

W. H. Bush tells that once in the early history of this store a customer complained bitterly about paying twenty-five cents for a package of pins that sold for five cents almost anywhere else in the world. "Think of the freight," one of the proprietors laughed, ignoring the protest.

Ira Rinehart took an option on forty-one acres of the Tascosa townsite south of Main Street from Gunter and Munson in 1876 for $61.50, but the deed was not given until October 1, 1879.

On February 21, 1881, H. A. Russell paid Howard and McMasters one hundred dollars for a corner lot 70 by 140 feet at Spring and Main streets, on which he erected the Exchange Hotel. John Arnot, venerable Scottish pioneer, says that this proved the existence of a boom in Tascosa real estate.[1]

When Henry Kimball sold his claim at the springs south of Tascosa to the LIT's in 1880, he remained at the ranch for some time, plying his trade of blacksmithing. Soon, however, he found his business growing to such proportions that he needed a more centrally located shop. Therefore, he moved to the Main Street of the new town and erected a larger adobe, setting up an extensive blacksmithing trade.

Also in 1880 Jack Ryan, who had been a cowpuncher for the LX's in Potter County and who had stayed away from town long enough to save $160, heard of the boom in Tascosa and came to open a saloon in a building on the south side of Main Street. His business prospered, and in February, 1881, he bought a lot west of and adjoining the Exchange Hotel, erected an adobe, and moved into it. His sign read, "The Equity Bar."

As the cattlemen moved into the Canadian River country, they brought prospects which attracted John Cone, a wealthy businessman who wanted to establish a large general store at the new frontier village. His quest for business lots met a cold reception from both Howard and McMasters, owners of part of the townsite, and from Rinehart, who owned the rest of the land desirable as business property, in what appeared to be a mutual pact for keeping down competition. Cone, not to be thwarted by the lack of co-operation from the storekeepers, bought from Casimero Romero a small block of land a few hundred yards east of the business center which was being established by Rinehart and Howard and McMasters. He built a large store at this Lower or East

[1] John Arnot, "My Recollections of Tascosa Before and After the Coming of the Law," *The Panhandle–Plains Historical Review*, Vol. VI (1933), 58–79.

Tascosa site, which shortly was to be christened with a much more pungent title—Hogtown.

The necessity of naming the new townsite on the Canadian and securing its designation as a post office was called to the attention of Romero and his friends, and an application was submitted to the Post Office Department in Washington for the establishment of a post office at Atascosa. However, the department replied that the name of Atascosa could not be used by the new town as there was another post office and county by that name in Texas. The enterprising businessmen's committee of the new trading center merely dropped the "A," calling the new town Tascosa. This name was accepted by the federal authorities, and a post office was established—mistakenly recorded as being in Potter County —according to departmental records in Washington, on June 24, 1878, with Julius Howard as the first postmaster. Howard served until March 10, 1884, when his partner, James E. McMasters, succeeded him. In the meantime the records of the Post Office Department had been corrected and Tascosa properly assigned to Oldham County.

Thus a new town in the West was officially born. The name "Tascosa" came to mean many things to many people. The town was actually far from being a baby when it was given the official recognition of a name and a post office in 1878. In time it came to present more nearly than any other town a complete cross section of the rangeland West.

Within its limited area representatives of three races and three different types of civilization met with the inevitable human reactions and conflict. These were the Indians, the Mexicans, and the Anglo-Americans. The Anglos were a conglomerate group, including nesters, boys from the cotton patches of Texas, cowboys, bad men, English, Scottish, and Irish commoners and noblemen, Yankee and Confederate soldiers, Midwestern businessmen, gamblers, and prostitutes. The good and the bad of all three races merged in this small, inland, open-range area, far from railroads and established government.

Winding their way slowly up the caprock of the Llano Estacado in the wake of the trail herds and the stampedes of the gaunt longhorn cattle to claim a share of the public domain of good grass and opportunity came wave after wave of covered wagons. These wagons brought families, chickens, dogs, favorite field and garden seeds, occasionally some flower seeds, and a plow tucked out of sight. These were adventurous souls, and there are many who still assert that the family in the covered wagon represented the acme in pioneer daring and hardihood. Horace Greeley advised young men to go West, but a nation took his counsel to heart. Year after year the tide of immigration moved into the cattle country, sometimes flowing in great waves, sometimes ebbing in failure. Settlers sought a claim in the West. Some wanted to get away from the curse of malaria and cotton. Some, displaced by the Civil War, sought fortune in a new country. Others immigrated because they had grown too tough for their home communities. The great ships, the prairie schooners, sailed out across the sea of grass that led to Tascosa. The immigration of the Russells is typical of a family's trek to the cattle country.

Mrs. H. A. Russell marked a heavy ring around St. Valentine's Day, 1879. The day was a memorable one for the Russell family—father, mother, Charley, nineteen years old, Molly, sixteen, Claude, almost four, and little Clyde, barely three—and their old friend and companion, Charles Terry. They had reached a stopping place—Tascosa—in their long journey from Groesbeck in Limestone County, Texas, to La Junta, New Mexico, a small way station near Springer.

With two wagons—one pulled by four horses, the other by two—it had been a long, hard trip from Groesbeck to Waco, then across the Texas blackland belt into the hill and cross-timber country to Brownwood, and on across a virtual wilderness to Fort Griffin at the Double Mountain Fork of the Brazos River. They had rested there before striking out across the formidable and almost uncharted Staked Plains to the Goodnight ranch in the Palo Duro Canyon. After they had left Fort Griffin, they had passed several parties of buffalo hunters with loads of hides. When a terrific snowstorm had struck as they made their way slowly across the plains, the family had saved themselves from freezing to death only by burning their horses' feed boxes and all loose lumber on and in the wagons. After the storm had subsided, they had made their way to the Goodnight ranch headquarters in the Palo Duro Canyon, where they received a hearty welcome. Mrs. Goodnight especially seemed pleased to have women visitors, for few people came by the ranch, and in 1879 the visit of a woman was an occasion.

Molly Russell, now Mrs. J. E. May, of Vega, was old enough to be considered among the womenfolk. She enjoyed the stay at the Goodnight's and the drive up the Canadian to Tascosa and recalls vividly the scene that noonday of February 14, 1879, as the group drove to Borregos Plaza on the south side of the Canadian River. The plaza consisted of two long adobe houses which faced each other across a road leading down to the river and the rock and log corrals constructed around two small buttes. Although the buildings were old, the place offered human beings shelter, and the Mexicans rushed out of their homes to greet the visitors enthusiastically.

The Russells did not understand Spanish, but some of the Mexican boys who could speak English invited them to come in for dinner. The Mexicans and the Anglo-Americans exchanged pleasantries, and the Russells asked many questions about Tascosa. After the meal they started to cross the river, but as the stream was low and the ground marshy and boggy, the wagons bogged down. Mr. Russell carried the women and the two small boys across the river. Then, with his son Charley and Terry, he dug the wagons out of the mire, and the cavalcade proceeded to Tascosa.

In small, isolated Tascosa they found few residents. Charley Cummings and another fellow were operating a small restaurant, which had a kitchen and a tiny dining room. Henry Kimball's blacksmith shop was housed in a two-room adobe. He worked in one room and lived alone in the other. Ira Rinehart's store was doing business, and Mr. Rinehart had two rooms for living quarters for his family in the rear of the store. A short distance from Rinehart's was a two-room adobe house in which Mr. and Mrs. Jamerison and their two small daughters lived. Mr. Jamerison was running sheep on the plains, and his wife was alone with her children most of the time. All of these flat-roofed houses were on the south side of the road or street, while Howard and McMasters had their store building on the north side, with a room for each attached to the store. McMasters lived alone in one, while Howard had a housekeeper, a Mexican woman, Martina Romero, in the other. The Russells swelled Tascosa's population, for Mr. Russell promptly made a trade with Charley Cummings and his partner, buying their provisions and equipment at the restaurant.

In early spring of 1879 John Cone came to Tascosa and erected his combination store, saloon, and hotel in East Tascosa. Cone's store was a reality in May, 1879. Upper Tascosa immediately countered the Cone threat with a large hotel that boasted three bedrooms, built by Mr. Russell and completed in the summer of that same year.

Christmas, 1879, was a grand affair, and the village, which had grown during the year, observed its progress with a community tree set up in the Rinehart's living room and decorated with popcorn strings and balls, cranberry strings, and apples. Songs, music, and readings appropriate to the season gladdened the occasion. Guests present at the party were: Uncle Billy Ewing, a lovable old codger; Jack Wilson, a man about thirty-five years of age who stayed with Rinehart and Rinehart's fifteen-year-old son, Irvin; Howard and his Mexican housekeeper; McMasters; a clerk by the name of Bogman; the Jamerisons; Charley Cummings; Henry Kimball; Dr. Cummings, his wife, and their small daughter; John Cone's new partner, Edwards, his beautiful wife, and their six-year-old daughter, Idalene; the Cape Willinghams and the Marion Armstrongs and their five children; Lizzie Rinehart, Ira's daughter; and the Prevails. The town had indeed grown rapidly since the coming of the Russells early in the year.

The Exchange Hotel, which had a cow's head over its sign, well executed by an itinerant sign painter, charged fifty cents for a bed and fifty cents for a meal. A fifty-pound sack of flour cost the Russells six dollars, eggs were fifty cents a dozen, and butter fifty cents a pound. Beef was cheap, a fat yearling costing about six dollars.

When the Russells had vacated the two-room adobe house and restaurant they had bought at first, the Marion Armstrongs moved in to use it as a home. Then, shortly after Christmas, 1879, the Russells leased their hotel and made a temporary move to Las Vegas. But the New Mexico city did not appeal to them, and they returned to Tascosa and their hotel there within six months. They found that business had continued to improve at Tascosa and that more people were settling there.

At the time the Russells returned in 1880, there was already talk of organizing Oldham County. The leaders in the community had agreed that an organized county was desirable, and with that end in view had conferred with officials at Mobeetie, county seat of Wheeler County, to which Oldham was then attached for judicial purposes. Wheeler County itself was only a babe, having been organized on April 12, 1879; however, it had an area attached to it that was larger than most states. There was little opposition to the organization of Oldham County. Some of the heavy taxpayers of Wheeler County wanted to retain its property valuations on the rolls, but they recognized the futility of the opposition, and an election was ordered for December 8, 1880, to select officials for the new county and a county seat.

The officials had been virtually agreed upon in previous caucuses, but there were two rivals for the county seat. Upper Tascosa was pushed by Howard, Rinehart, McMasters, Russell, Armstrong, and McCarty of the LIT. Cone and Edwards championed the establishment of the county seat at Lower Tascosa and had the support of Romero and many other Mexican voters. There were two voting boxes in the county, Trujillo and Tascosa.

Mr. Russell missed the election and the big party the Russells, McCarty, and McMasters gave during the day. He had gone to Springer for a load of freight, and just about the time he got his wagons loaded for the return journey, his horses were stolen. His absence, however, did not stop the election or the big dinner at the hotel, which fed about one hundred persons, including all the Mexicans who came. McCarty, who was chief host, invited the Mexicans to dinner but would not eat with them. By agreement no whiskey was sold until after the votes were counted. Then there was a rush to the bar. Marion Armstrong went home, as he was practically a teetotaler and feared the effects of liquor on the actions of the crowd. The voters really celebrated that night and included in their revels the well-known practice of "shooting up the town."

Tascosa's big election party did not close without tragedy. The celebration which began with the count of the votes lasted until late at night; consequently it was very late when William Dudley Pannell, LIT cowboy, and a friend galloped toward the LIT headquarters on Cheyenne Creek, still in festive mood. Dud, as the cowboy was called, was riding a near-outlaw horse, which objected strongly to celebrating

the birth of Oldham County and the election of its officers.
Both Dud and his companion emptied their six-shooters into
the air as they left town, and Dud reloaded his gun with
difficulty. Nearing the creek across from their headquarters
home and bunkhouse, the two boys spurred the horses and
jerked out their six-shooters, twirling them over their heads
and shooting into the air. Dud's horse wheeled and danced
and bucked and snorted, becoming completely unmanage-
able. In the excitement either Dud's own gun or that of his
companion was discharged in such a manner that the bullet
struck the unfortunate cowpuncher in the back of the head.
He tumbled from the saddle to the ground. His friend,
shocked and dazed, tried to make him comfortable, but he
died within a few minutes, and the other cowboy stayed by
his side until morning.

Dud was buried near the site of his accident, his grave
marking the opening of the Cheyenne Cemetery, whose lone-
ly graves may be seen today as shallow depressions near
Magenta, with the markings almost obliterated by the ravages
of time and weather. A sandstone headstone properly carved
was erected at Dud's grave, and there it has remained to the
present time.

Upper Tascosa won the county-seat location. Cape B.
Willingham was elected first sheriff of the county, by far the
most important office. James E. McMasters, Pennsylvania
born and of Quaker parentage, was elected county judge;
C. B. Vivian, one-armed, brilliant, and with a fine sense of
humor, was elected county clerk; and Marion Armstrong
was named constable.

In his official capacity Armstrong called the first County Commissioners' Court to assemble on February 14, 1881,
and the officers began their duties. The commissioners elected or appointed were C. S. McCarty, George Strohm, Pablo
Herara, and Juan E. Chávez. W. H. Woodman filled in temporarily for C. B. Vivian. The court appointed Woodman

legal adviser and allowed a sum of $1,500 for his services for one year. Henry Kimball was employed as interpreter.

By virtue of its organization and position, Oldham County had attached to it for legal purposes the unorganized counties of Potter, Randall, Swisher, Deaf Smith, Dallam, Castro, Hartley, Moore, and Sherman. Thus Tascosa grew in importance as a court center as the county was settled. Later, as one after another of the counties grew strong enough to organize its own government, Tascosa lost the prestige it enjoyed at this time.

The actual organization of Oldham County was only the beginning of the struggle for formal government and that degree of civilization which makes for reasonable security. In fact, the establishment of order in Tascosa and in many other pioneer Western communities came much earlier than the orderly processes of law. Order was sometimes brought about by vigilante committees and sometimes by courageous and hardy individuals capable of commanding attention. Formal law soon followed, but almost always after conflict and struggle punctuated by the deafening blasts of Colt's forty-fives held by quick and determined hands.

5. The Mail Comes to Tascosa

THE MAIL came to the Panhandle in 1878 and 1879. Prior to its coming, old Dad Barnes had made an occasional ride to Dodge City delivering and receiving mail at the rate of fifty cents a letter. The story of the mail from this humble beginning has been a dramatic one, and the earliest attempts to establish mail delivery were hazardous ventures that seem almost fantastic in the retelling. E. W. Parker, surveyor and agent for the contractor of the route, scared the wits out of a number of cowpunchers as he went about his work; they thought he was a detective on the trail of murderers and robbers. Since Bill Moore of the LX Ranch had hired every renegade cowpuncher and outlaw that came along for the first roundup in 1878, he lost a number of them a short time later to one of the first visible evidences of progress, a surveyor for a mail line.

As Parker surveyed the line, he took advantage of the acquaintances he made to secure employees for the route. Many of the men he hired were cowboys or nesters newly arrived in the country. Cape Willingham and Marion Armstrong, both of whom were later to be leaders in bringing law and order to Tascosa, were two secured from the LX Ranch. The Willingham and Armstrong families were living together on Bonita Creek, where Armstrong had put in a garden for the LX in 1879. Willingham, fearless and commanding, was given the superintendency of the mail route from Tascosa to Dodge City. Armstrong helped build a stage and mail stand on Red Deer Creek and secured the job of carrying the mail from Mobeetie to Tascosa.

The story of Armstrong's trip to the Panhandle and his connection with the stage line illustrates the manner of men Parker secured. Marion Armstrong with his wife and two small sons, Tom, three years old, and Mel, six weeks of age, left Wise County, Texas, in October, 1878. Their destination was Fort Elliott in the Texas Panhandle. At Fort Sill, by prearrangement, they were to meet Mr. Armstrong's brother Sam, who had been living in Arizona but desired to be with his relatives again. The Armstrong family, after the usual difficulties of frontier travel, finally reached Fort Sill and met Sam. Then they set out for Fort Elliott. Just after leaving Fort Sill, they passed a camp of several hundred Kiowa Indians. A large group of Indian boys, the oldest not more than fifteen, riding their ponies, charged the wagon. Mrs. Armstrong clutched her children to her and waited. As the boy who was the leader dashed up to the wagon, he found a double-barreled shotgun shoved into his face. He spoke little English but managed to make the Armstrongs understand that the boys were just playing at attacking an immigrant train. Nevertheless, the fright received by the family made a lasting impression.

The trip on to Fort Elliott was one of hardship and danger. Lack of food and water became a serious problem. Wild turkeys and a wildcat killed near the wagon helped keep the family alive. The rowdy frontier town of Mobeetie, with its rush of government contractors, saloons, and shooting scrapes, did not appeal to them; therefore, they started to Adobe Walls. They bogged in the quicksand of the Canadian River, and after unloading their wagons and extricating themselves, they returned to a sheep camp to spend the winter. Their horses were worn out; moreover, the Armstrongs believed that they could live off the land and find protection in the camp. However, one of the horses died during the winter, and the Armstrongs found themselves sixty miles from the nearest post where food, horses, or anything else could be bought.

Under these circumstances the visit of Rack Capland one cold winter day was most welcome. He was trying to establish the mail line from Fort Elliott, Texas, to Las Vegas, New Mexico, and needed help. He proposed that Marion Armstrong and his family go to Red Deer Creek, near the present town of Miami, to build and operate a stage stand. He wanted Sam Armstrong to stay on White Deer Creek. Everyone agreed to the proposal, and Marion Armstrong completed the dugout, which was to serve as a stage stand on Red Deer Creek, in eighteen days in November. While he was preparing the dugout, Sam and Walter Dyer stopped for a meal, for which they paid one dollar, the first money received at the mail station.

The family would have died of loneliness, Marion Armstrong wrote in later years, if it had not been for the excitement which occasionally came their way. A Pueblo Indian cowboy, who spent a night with them, and Mr. Armstrong killed a buffalo from a small herd that had drifted to the creek for water. That assured the family of food for the winter. Then the mail contractor failed; and the Armstrongs, borrowing one of the contractor's mules to replace the horse that had died, made their way to Bonita Creek on the LX Ranch. This trip, like the others, was filled with danger and interest, including the finding of the charred remains of a wagon train that had apparently been burned some years before. They arrived at Bonita Creek on March 6, 1879, and there they made their home in a small rock dugout which had formerly been used by a gang of robbers. Mrs. Armstrong was the first white woman resident on the LX Ranch

PAT GARRETT

JIM EAST

JOHN S. CHISUM

KID DOBBS

From a photograph taken in the early eighties

EARLY DAY TASCOSANS

Standing, left to right: W. S. Mabry (surveyor), Frank James (merchant), C. B. Vivian (county clerk), I. P. Ryland (attorney)

Seated, left to right: Jim East (sheriff), James McMasters (county judge), and Pat Garrett (captain, Texas Rangers) and thus the first in Potter County. The LX employed Mr. Armstrong to put in a garden on the fertile, level land on Bonita Creek where the Willinghams joined them soon afterwards. Mrs. Willingham and Mrs. Armstrong on one occasion had the terrifying experience of seeing a band of Indians coming to their home. The two women barricaded the doors and fired rifles at the Indians. This turned them aside; but as soon as the women could slip out of the house, they took their five children and hid near the river until the return of their husbands at nightfall.

While working on the LX, Mr. Armstrong found that a new organization was pushing the mail line on through the country. These men took the mule he had borrowed at Red Deer. Shortly afterwards the Armstrongs and the Willinghams, having found conditions hard and trying on Bonita Creek, moved to Tascosa, arriving in East Tascosa on August 10, 1879. In that part of the town there was a store and hotel operated by Cone and Edwards. One-half mile away was Upper Tascosa, where the Kimball, Rinehart, and Howard and McMasters stores and one or two other firms were located. The town boasted a doctor. Here was the important key point through which the mail line was pushing its way west to Las Vegas from Fort Elliott. Armstrong and Willingham readily found employment with the mail line.

Advertised as "Lightning Express—Daily Mail," the mail line had a schedule of fifty-nine hours on horseback for the 200-mile run from Mobeetie to Fort Bascom. The remaining few miles from Fort Bascom to Las Vegas were made by hack. The first stop after leaving Mobeetie was the North Fork of the Red River, thirty miles distant, and the next was at Dixon Creek, another thirty miles away. It was approximately thirty-five miles from Dixon Creek across the open plains to Bonita Creek, about fifteen miles from there to Leahy Creek, and fifteen miles from Leahy Creek into Tascosa. The first stop west of Tascosa was Trujillo, thirty miles up the river, while the second stop was Red River Springs, eighteen miles from there. The next stop was twenty-two miles away at Huney, just west of the mouth of Ute Creek, and it was seventeen miles from Huney into Fort Bascom. The entire route was a difficult one through much wild country. A frontiersman with an average amount of experience could follow the trail fairly well except for the tragic route across the open plains between Bonita Creek and Dixon Creek. This stretch of level prairie with only an occasional rolling break was extremely difficult to follow in a storm, at night, or when snow covered.

Marion Armstrong rode the mail line from Tascosa to Dixon Creek (sixty-five miles) in the winter of 1880–81 and earned thirty dollars per month, boarding himself half of the time. On occasion he had to ride on to Mobeetie, sixty miles farther. This entailed riding day and night on horses not always the best—Armstrong referred to his mount as a "condemned cow pony." The prospects of winter weather, and especially of snow across that thirty-five miles of unmarked, uncharted plains between Bonita and Dixon creeks, were not pleasing to Armstrong. On a return trip in which he had been delayed, he met the contractor, P. G. Reynolds, between Dixon Creek and the North Fork of the Red River. Reynolds roared at him for being behind schedule, and when Armstrong explained that he had broken through the ice on the Canadian River on the way down and had been forced to spend half a day getting out, Reynolds became abusive. Immediately Armstrong asked for his pay and quit his job. As the two closed their relationship, Armstrong warned Reynolds of the danger between Bonita and Dixon creeks and predicted that unless the road across the plains was staked off or marked in some way before heavy winter weather, men would lose their lives on it. Although the estimated cost of staking was only ten dollars, Reynolds did not heed his warning.

John Cannington then took over Armstrong's route and on his second trip over the line was lost on the plains for three days in a bad storm. When he finally reached his destination, his feet were frozen so badly that they had to be amputated.[1]

Cannington's successor, Tom Wilson, rode the route for only a few days before he, too, became lost; with his feet frozen, he was rescued only to die at the army hospital at Fort Elliott. On this trip he was carrying two passengers in an old buckboard pulled by a pair of mules. Although one of the worst snowstorms of the season was raging, the trio started from the North Fork station and headed for the Dixon Creek stand thirty miles away. When they left early in the morning, it was extremely cold and the snow was as much as twelve inches deep with occasional heavier drifts. Midway between the two stations they became stuck in the snow, and the mules in their struggle to pull through broke the tongue of the buckboard. As their tracks had been covered by drifting snow, the men were afraid to try to return to the North Fork station and decided to attempt to reach the Dixon Creek station, using the wind as a guide. But the wind changed directions and their course changed with it, so that they missed Dixon Creek and traveled on west, south of the mail-line trail.

They struggled on for three days and nights, with little protection from the elements. A buffalo robe and a tarpaulin proved of some help at night, but one passenger was so badly frozen that he could not walk. The other man and Wilson put him on the mules and carried him to about where Amarillo is now located, forty-five to fifty miles from where they had mired in the snow and about twenty miles southwest of the Bonita station. That night the mules ran away. In the morning the two still able to walk covered the sick

---

[1] Citizens of Tascosa made up a purse of $200 with which to buy Cannington artificial feet. He took the money and started a monte bank.

man with the buffalo robe, pulled the tarp over him, and told him that they would try to find the camp and then return for him.

They set out in the direction they thought was that of Bonita Creek and traveled only a few miles to the north when they came across a fireguard which the LX outfit had plowed on the head of East Amarillo Creek. By following this fireguard, they reached a ranch road leading to the river opposite the LX headquarters. The other passenger, starved and frozen, was unable by this time to go farther, therefore, he halted on the road while Wilson went on to the river valley. Jack Daugherty, who was down on the river hauling in driftwood, spied him across the river. He unhooked his team, rode across, put Wilson on the horse, and took him to ranch headquarters. After telling Daugherty of the man left exhausted on the trail, Wilson collapsed. Later he was taken to Fort Elliott, where he died.

As quickly as possible Daugherty hitched a pair of horses to a light wagon, loaded some food and bedding, and started out to search for the unfortunate fellow. Darkness fell before he could find him. A search the next day was also futile. Likewise, no trace was found of the man left with the buffalo robe and the tarpaulin, although years later a cowpuncher found a skeleton in a small depression near where the man was supposed to have been left. Armstrong's prediction to Reynolds had come true with a vengeance. Because of the lack of a marked trail, the cost of which was a pittance, three lives were lost.

Kid Dobbs worked on the mail line in 1879 and 1880, spending thirteen months riding and blacksmithing under Cape Willingham, who had charge of the line and was stationed a part of the time at Trujillo. Dobbs rode the line between Trujillo and Fort Bascom, a distance of sixty miles. In the early period the mail-line route was on the south side of the river, and the first stop west of Trujillo was Red River

Springs, eighteen miles away. If the river was up, the rider put the mail sack on a wire stretched across the river and sent it sliding down to its destination. Then Mrs. Lackey, wife of the owner of a ranch with headquarters at Dripping Springs, about eight miles north of the original route, wanted the mail to come by that ranch, and after much correspondence with Washington authorities got her request approved. This meant that the riders had to cross the river twice. From Red River Springs it was twenty-two miles to Huney and seventeen miles from there to Fort Bascom. Dobbs usually left Trujillo at six o'clock in the morning and reached Fort Bascom about six o'clock in the evening. If the mail was on time, he would ride his horse in a walk or trot, but if behind schedule, he would ride the horse in a gallop or a run. On one occasion when the mail was nine hours late at Trujillo, he made up the time. On another he rode 170 miles in one stretch, going from Fort Bascom to Tascosa, where he found Bud Babcock, another mail rider, ill and unable to take the mail. Therefore Dobbs turned back and rode on to Trujillo before he stopped.

Kid Dobbs rode two horses to their deaths on the mail runs and in each instance he got a five dollar a month raise for his work. One of the horses which Dobbs killed had been Tom Coffee's horse, Spider, a high-spirited chestnut sorrel, had been a favorite of Tom's, who had taught him many tricks. Tom would ride him on the streets of Tascosa, apply the spurs just right, and put on a bronc show for the assembled men and women. When Tom quit the line, no one else wanted to ride Spider because all were afraid of him. As Kid thought highly of the horse and did not fear his bucking, he asked to ride him. The horse's death demonstrated the dangers of the route. Kid and Spider had fought the elements all day, and it was the early part of the night before Dobbs attempted to cross the river five miles below Red River Springs. The water was frozen hard for several feet from the banks but in the center was an icy mush. When the ice broke as Dobbs tried to force Spider into the river, the horse became frightened and whirled back out of the water a number of times before Dobbs forced him across. Both horse and rider were wet and covered with ice, and Dobbs realized that he would have to act quickly to keep from being frozen. He dropped the reins across the horn of the saddle and began beating his arms across his chest to keep the circulation going while Spider ran at full speed to Trujillo. When they pulled up at the stage stand, long icicles were hanging from the horse's nose. Kid led him into the shed, pulled the bridle off but left the saddle on, and ran into the house, where there was a roaring fire in the stove. After a few minutes by the fire, he went back to the shed and found the horse lying down. The next morning Spider was dead.

Dobbs rode Big Grey to death in a 120-mile ride with but one purpose in view—that of getting the mail through on time. The contractor had told his riders that he was under a $4,000 forfeit bond and that no horse was worth that much money.

Old-timers in writing or recalling the early-day mail service invariably mention "that notorious mail-fraud case," which concerned the star route established between Mobeetie and Las Vegas. It was a part of the line from Vinita, Indian Territory (now Oklahoma), to Las Vegas. The company which owned the line was headed by S. W. Dorsey, one-time carpetbag senator from Arkansas, who organized a ranch near Springer in 1878. This organization had contracted with the federal government for the star routes over many states of the Southwest, and when it was investigated, it was charged that Dorsey had established lines to places where the towns on the maps were myths. The population of towns actually having only two or three adobe houses was reported as several hundred. One of the fictitious cities was Silver City, which was supposedly located on Leahy

Creek where Scotty Wilson kept the stage stand, but Scotty's sole companion there was a woman of extremely dark hue, although Silver City was represented as a city of 10,000 persons. In the same manner, Wheeler, the post office at the LX Ranch headquarters, established August 17, 1879, was reported to be a large town.[2]

The Post Office Department, acting on information given by someone in the Panhandle, conducted an investigation and preferred charges against Senator Dorsey. During the trial it was alleged that a high official in the Post Office Department in Washington was a partner of Dorsey's and had connived at the deception. Dorsey employed the famous orator and agnostic, Bob Ingersoll, to defend him and was acquitted of the charges in a trial that forms one of the epic chapters of the West. The payoff to Ingersoll, however, was the climax to the entire episode. Ingersoll's fee was heavy—one-third of the Triangle Dot Ranch in New Mexico. When the attorney demanded payment, including in addition to the land 10,000 head of cattle, Dorsey's men branded the cattle by the cold-brand method. This meant that they burned the hair on the cattle but did not burn the hide. When the animals shed the next spring, there was no brand by which to identify them except the original Triangle Dot brand! There was no way, however, to "cold brand" the land, and the ranch earned as a legal fee was long known as "Bob Ingersoll's Infidel Ranch."

One of the most interesting stories of the mail line concerns also the foundation of the LE Ranch and the man who was the moving spirit behind the LS Ranch, W. M. D. Lee. When Lee, in partnership with the Reynolds brothers, was organizing the LE on the open-range country west of Tascosa, he bought out a number of nesters and improvements

[2] Winnie Davis Hale, "Scandal, an Invisible Passenger, Rode the Old Stage Lines," *The Amarillo Sunday Globe-News*, Golden Anniversary Edition, August 14, 1938.

of small plazas. He needed $35,000 in currency to pay off a large number of the men whose ranges he was buying. Therefore, he asked the mail line to bring the cash to him through a bandit-infested country. The money was wrapped in an ordinary gunny sack and Marion Armstrong tied it to his saddle along with the mail bags. As he occasionally carried packages for the cowboys, this gunny sack attracted no undue attention. He delivered the mail to the post office in the Sperling brothers' store and took the sack to the stage stand where Lee was waiting. Armstrong in his memoirs recalled the experience with amazement that he had gone through without being robbed and possibly killed. Lee apparently felt, with reason, that the simplicity of the idea would be the factor which would insure the safe delivery of the money.

Thus the mail came through to inland Tascosa—sometimes late, almost always under difficulties, but invariably it reached its destination.

6. Billy the Kid

LINCOLN COUNTY, NEW MEXICO, in the sixties and seventies was like the sprawling state of Texas. It was big and lusty, raw, untamed, and picturesque beyond imagination. It comprised about one-fifth of New Mexico, and its county-seat town of Lincoln, a crude pioneer village, hardly deserved a place on the map for size, but for loudness and deadliness it stood out like a big star. Lincoln served an area two hundred miles square, which to the east contained the rich and wild valley of the Pecos River, into which flowed the small mountain streams, the Bonita, Ruidoso, Hondo, Feliz, Penasco, and Seven Rivers. These arose near the western and northern boundaries of the county from among such mountains as the Capitan, Jicarillo, White, Sacramento, Guadalupe, Organ, and San Andreas.

California Volunteers, Texans—some good, some bad and wanted—and men who made up the backwash of the Civil War were thrown together in this rich region and mixed with the native Indians and Mexicans. The country

75

and its resources were there for the taking. Hardy, adventurous men seeking more elbow room and fortunes were not long in staking their claims.

Among the strong characters was John Chisum, Texas cattleman, who, with his brothers and his straight-shooting cowboys, had vast herds and lucrative contracts for all the cattle he could breed or trail into his cattle paradise in the Pecos Valley. He was lord of all he surveyed except for the political power and business influence of Major L. G. Murphy, who had come to New Mexico with the California Volunteers of the Civil War and stayed to grow rich with his partners, John Riley and James Dolan. Murphy's enterprises included a cattle ranch, a flour mill, a hotel, and a saloon. He was a power to be reckoned with in the crude politics of the day. He had a group of cowboys and other men as his allies who were as accomplished with firearms as any of Chisum's Texans.

Trouble started when Chisum charged Murphy with stealing his cattle. Recourse to the law was a mockery as Murphy controlled the courts. It was this fact which caused Alexander McSween, brilliant and highly ethical lawyer, who had come to Lincoln County as Murphy's attorney, to refuse to defend the Murphy men he knew to be cow thieves. Murphy discharged McSween, and Chisum hired him immediately. Within a short while J. H. Tunstall, a jovial Englishman, arrived in Lincoln, liked the country and the people, and bought a ranch. He and McSween, attracted to each other through their common background of education and culture, opened a store in Lincoln in competition with the one owned by Murphy. Their business flourished, and the two, in partnership with John Chisum, then opened a bank in one end of the store.

This brought affairs between Murphy and Chisum to a showdown. Murphy stood every chance of losing his profitable position of leadership, and McSween's activity against him in court in connection with a contested will had just about sealed his fate. Desperate action was necessary. The first step was taken when a sheriff's posse, made up of Murphy's henchmen, killed Tunstall in a drunken, ribald orgy of murder. This act marked the opening of the Lincoln County War. Few men could or did remain neutral, and the town and the country about it were soon divided into two armed forces of about fifty men each. The war raged through several engagements, culminating in a three-day fight and starting feuds which still exist. Many men were killed, much property was destroyed, and a few persons on both sides were arrested. Governor Lew Wallace, commissioned by President Rutherford B. Hayes to end the war, pardoned the participants on both sides who were not charged with crimes, but the fight broke out time and again as a result of the forces of hate and revenge.

Most notorious and colorful figure to rise out of the blue powder smoke of the Lincoln County fight was Billy the Kid, who had become the real leader of the McSween-Chisum forces. Born William Bonney in Brooklyn, brought to Kansas and then to New Mexico in his early boyhood, Billy the Kid earned his reputation the hard way. He killed his first man because of an insult to his mother. However, his reputation as a gunman was not secure until he became involved in the events in Lincoln County. There, in the pay of Chisum, he killed to avenge the death of Tunstall, the only man who had ever treated him as if he were a human being. Billy's gun, Little Angel, was an impressive factor in the war. He used it expertly.

With the good pay of the Chisum job cut off following the removal of the Chisums to Texas, Billy had to look to other fields for profit. He gathered together a group of other men in the same circumstances and collected, without too much attention to previous ownership, approximately 125 head of horses and mares. With his friends and the horses he followed the Chisums to the open ranges of the Canadian River Valley in the Panhandle, believing that there would be an excellent place to trade the newly acquired property. Tom O'Folliard, Henry Brown, Fred Waite, and John Middleton were members of his party. Middleton was a man in his forties and had been an outlaw for years. The others were young men. Bonney himself was only eighteen, exceptionally well built for a small man, with a smooth face, wavy brown hair, and piercing eyes. He smiled most of the time except when angry. His most noticeable facial characteristic was a slight projection of his two upper front teeth.

The first recorded meeting of the Kid with any Panhandle resident was his encounter with Dr. Hoyt, who was then carrying the mail for Roy Copeland between Tascosa and Fort Bascom. Returning from Fort Bascom on his route in the early fall of 1878, Hoyt found himself one day at sunrise some ten miles from Tascosa. As he jogged along, he met five men, strangers to him and to the country. They stopped to ask many questions about the location of ranches in the vicinity and told him they were bringing over a herd of horses to sell. That afternoon the horsemen rode into the frontier town, and it was not long until everyone knew that Billy the Kid and some of his men were present.

There was not a semblance of government or law in the Panhandle; consequently, it was a mecca for the outlaw, the gunman, and their kind. While Tascosa consisted of only two stores, a blacksmith shop, and an adobe house, it was even then the center of supplies for the big cattle ranches in the Panhandle. The news of Billy's arrival was of immediate interest to the cowmen, and they called him into a meeting. He came smiling, with as much poise as anyone present. C. S. McCarty, LIT boss and the spokesman, asked the young killer some pertinent questions, and Billy was frank in answering them. He told the cattlemen that he had heard that they were short of horses; therefore, he had gathered a bunch and had come to supply them. McCarty replied that the ranchmen had not sent for Billy and were not looking for him but that as long as he behaved himself and pulled no tricks, they would let him alone. Billy smiled his best when he assured the cowmen that he and his men wanted only to be left to themselves.

Billy and his gang were soon a part of the town, selling and trading, drinking, gambling, racing horses, and shooting at targets. Temple Houston, son of the famous General Sam Houston, outshot Bat Masterson, sports writer and United States marshal, and Billy in a money match that drew a great round of applause from the audience and congratulations from Billy himself. The Kid was an expert at all Western sports and dissipations, except drinking. Hoyt said that he did not know of Bonney's taking a drink while he was in the Panhandle. His men, however, made up for his abstinence.

Billy the Kid commanded a loyalty from his men which was demonstrated on more than one occasion. They loved him and were devoted followers apparently because of the magic charm of his personality. However, their loyalty caused them to be social outcasts at one time in Tascosa. There was an unwritten law that no one was to attend the *bailes* armed, and guns were usually left at Howard and Mc-Masters' store. The Kid's men were told that they were welcome at the dances so long as they left their arms at the store and complied with the same rules of conduct as everyone else. They promised to abide by the regulations.

One beautiful moonlight night as a *baile* at Pedro Romero's was going full tilt, Bonney and Hoyt stepped outside and strolled across the plaza to Rinehart's store, about one hundred yards from the Mexican home where the dance was being held. Hoyt challenged the Kid to a foot race back to the dance. Bonney was fast, but Hoyt led him all the way. As the runners neared the house, the doctor slowed up, and Billy raced full speed through the door, tripping and falling full length on the floor in the center of the ballroom. In a flash his prostrate form was surrounded by four of his gang, who stood back to back, guns cocked, ready for all comers. They thought that something had gone wrong. How or where they had hidden the guns was a mystery, and they were penitent and disappointed when they were barred from all future *bailes* at that home.

Hoyt and Billy the Kid became close companions. In fact, the Kid and his men made friends with many of the Panhandle cowpunchers whom they were to meet again as enemies. Many of Billy's friends remained steadfast even after he had become a confirmed thief and killer, and one old-timer declared that there was little difference between the Kid and his gang and most of the other men around Tascosa. All were young men of the Wild West, and all had seen a great deal of high adventure, exciting gunplay, and uncontrolled violence.

Dr. Hoyt thought enough of the outlaw to urge him to go to Mexico or South America and live honestly. He gave the Kid a lady's gold watch which he had won at poker and which Billy wanted to present to Senorita Lolita, a dainty New Mexican beauty. It had a long chain of braided hair, and in the only known picture of Billy the Kid the watch chain shows.

In late October, 1878, a Mr. Teats, who had contracted to carry the mail between Fort Bascom and Las Vegas, visited Tascosa, and Dr. Hoyt decided to leave the Panhandle with him. On the day of his departure, Billy the Kid rode into Tascosa leading Dandy Dick, a fine race horse and the best animal in his remuda. He presented the horse to the doctor, who had ridden the animal several times and had admired him greatly. Then Billy suggested that, in order to protect his friend in case the ownership was questioned, he should write out a bill of sale. He stepped to the counter in the Howard and McMasters store, rapidly wrote out a formal bill of sale, had it witnessed by the proprietors, and presented it to Hoyt.[1]

Many years later the full story of the horse was revealed. In 1921 Hoyt sent a photostatic copy of his bill of sale to Charley Siringo, who showed it to James Brady, court interpreter at Carrizozo, New Mexico. When Brady read the description of the horse, he cried out: "My God, it was my father's horse. He was riding it when killed by the Kid!" William Brady, James's father, had been a brave and honest man and a sheriff of Lincoln County. The horse, which was of Arabian stock, had been presented to him by Major Murphy.

When Billy the Kid and his gang had sold most of their horses and left Tascosa in late 1878, they knew the people, the brands, and the country. They also knew where the cattle would drift when they turned their tails to the heavy storms of the unfenced Panhandle, that the next spring they could gather in herds of Panhandle cattle on the Pecos and around the watering places of eastern New Mexico. Their camp at Black Springs Draw near present-day Portales was situated at just such a spot. Billy had made connections in New Mexico where the cattle he delivered could be promptly butchered and sold to the army at Fort Stanton near Roswell.

Billy not only disposed of his horses but also lost members of his gang at Tascosa: Henry Brown, destined to be one of Tascosa's first peace officers and later to meet an outlaw's death, and Fred Waite and John Middleton, who decided to forsake the life of outlaws. They argued in vain with the Kid and O'Folliard, trying to persuade them to do likewise. Waite and Middleton went to Indian Territory, but Brown stayed at Tascosa. Most of the men who had been in the Lincoln County War with Chisum had come to the

[1] The bill of sale is now in the Panhandle–Plains Historical Society Museum at Canyon, Texas.

Panhandle, either with him or with Billy the Kid, and other members of the groups left the two separate organizations on the Canadian. One said that he had a good home in the Cherokee Nation and was going home while he was able. He made this statement immediately after one of Chisum's men was killed at Salinas Plaza. This fellow had charged through the little plaza town on his horse, whooping loudly, and as he had slowed at a dance hall, three Mexicans with Bill Dukes or Bowie knives had cut him to pieces. Charles Reasor stayed in Tascosa, and also for a time well-educated, Tennessee-born Mortimer, another of Billy's men, remained there, working for McMasters and Mabry at the princely salary of $125 a month. He finally ventured into politics in a campaign against C. B. Vivian for county clerk. When Vivian defeated him, Mortimer decamped with the horse and buggy which the one-armed Vivian had used in electioneering against him.

Billy was not long in adding reinforcements to his group, and he rounded up a sufficient number of Panhandle cattle to cause much concern among the ranchmen. He already had the big ranchers of New Mexico after him because of his thefts and murders. One of the hard-hit outfits in the Panhandle, which had cause to want to rid itself of the Kid, was the LS Ranch. Its headquarters were a few miles south of Tascosa, and its herds, since they were on the south side of the river, drifted badly. The LX Ranch down in Potter County was also a victim; and the Torrey and LIT outfits had lost cattle, if not to Billy and his crew, then to others who took advantage of the long drift drags to add to their herds.

In March, 1880, a group of Panhandle cattlemen, including particularly those of the lower Panhandle, met in an informal session at Mobeetie and organized the Panhandle Cattlemen's Association, which was more formally set up the following year. Leaders in this group were Colonel Charles

MR. AND MRS. MARION ARMSTRONG

EDITOR C. F. RUDOLPH
The Tascosa Pioneer

REV. JOSEPH THOMAS BLOODWORTH
METHODIST CIRCUIT RIDER

MR. AND MRS. H. A. RUSSELL

MRS. CAPE WILLINGHAM AND CHILDREN

Goodnight, Colonel T. S. Hughes, Hank Cresswell, and O.
H. Nelson. The association dealt with trail-herd and quarantine problems, agreed to post a reward for the arrest and
conviction of cattle thieves, and desired to put an end to outlawry as rapidly as possible. Goodnight, who was one of
the founders and the first president, was also a prominent
leader in the Southwestern Cattle Raisers Association, which
was organized at Graham, in Young County, in 1877, for the
primary purpose of dealing with cattle theft.

The first expedition sent out by the ranchers to scout
for Billy the Kid and Panhandle cattle was headed by Frank
Stewart, the detective for the association, and included four
other men: Kid Dobbs from James Campbell's outfit, Lon
Chambers and Lee Hall from the LX Ranch, and Charley
Reasor of the LIT. Taking two pack horses, they left Tascosa in the fall of 1880, mounted on the best horses in the
country and well armed. Their destination was White Oaks,
a booming town in New Mexico, which had several stores,
saloons, and gambling dives catering to the miners who were
busily blasting and working the surrounding country. Here
Billy the Kid and his gang were selling cattle and running
wild on occasion, much to the disgust and fear of some of
the storekeepers.

The scouting party found the corral at White Oaks
covered with hides. The first six hides examined were branded "LIT" on the right side and "U" on the left neck. The
Panhandle men needed no further evidence. Showing his
officer's commission and explaining that he was working for
the Panhandle Cattlemen's Association, Stewart ordered the
butcher to stop butchering Panhandle cattle. The butcher
replied that while he did not doubt that Stewart was working for the stockmen, nevertheless he had bought the cattle
in good faith and had a clean bill of sale with two witnesses.
He had money invested in his business, and it would take
more than a verbal notice to stop him from butchering.

As Stewart could do nothing further with the butcher, he and his men then returned to their camp. Within a short time two merchants of White Oaks visited them. They told Stewart that Billy the Kid and ten of his men had been in White Oaks three days earlier, taking everything they wanted without paying for it or asking that it be charged. It was the opinion of the merchants that if the two groups clashed, the Kid and his gang would whip the "river men," as the Texans were called. Kid Dobbs reflected on the incident and declared that he was not afraid of any harm coming to him if Billy the Kid recognized him, but he was fearful that the Kid would not take the trouble to renew old friendships under such conditions. Therefore, Stewart and his men decided to go back to the Canadian River.

Upon their return they reported to the cattlemen, and new plans were discussed for ridding the country of the outlaws. C. S. McCarty, manager of the LIT, took the initiative in mapping out a campaign to retrieve as many cattle as possible and to wipe out the outlaw gang. Action was hastened when Pat Garrett, former Panhandle buffalo hunter and for a time a resident of Tascosa, returned to his old camping ground from Lincoln County, New Mexico, to ask their cooperation. After working for John Chisum as a cowpuncher and then operating a restaurant, Garrett had been drafted by New Mexico to run for sheriff of Lincoln County. He was elected by the cattlemen, whose one demand was that Billy the Kid must be run out of the country. Billy the Kid, who had once been Garrett's close friend, had many loyal friends and followers in Lincoln County. Garrett needed help badly, and he realized that men such as those from the Texas Panhandle—cold, fearless, quick-shooting frontier cowboys and buffalo hunters—would be of the greatest assistance to him in this dangerous job.

The Panhandle cattlemen and representatives from the little committee which had met at Mobeetie decided to give

Garrett the help he wanted. The necessity for quick action and for secrecy was impressed upon all. It was agreed that each of several outfits would send a crew of men along for the cattle. The men were to be told that they were going to get drift cattle in eastern New Mexico and not primarily to get into a war with Billy the Kid. Some of the ranchers cautioned that not all of the men would prove to be the fighters and resourceful individuals Garrett wanted, but all agreed that he could get a sizable posse out of the group. Frank Stewart, ostensibly a cowhand on the LIT, was to be the main contact with Garrett once the crews got into the Kid's country.

A colorful cowman, Bill Moore, foreman of the LX Ranch, was given the responsibility of fitting out the first wagon and its crew to join the trek to New Mexico. Charley Siringo, one of those picked to make the trip, declared that Moore selected the men he feared and wanted to be rid of on his ranch. Be that as it may, the LX boys, joined by men from the LIT, the LS, and Torrey's ranch, with possibly others represented, left Tascosa on November 16, 1880. The LX wagon had Siringo, Cal Polk, Lon Chambers, Lee Hall, and Jim East. The LIT sent Tom Emory, George Williams, Louis Bousman, and Bob Robinson. A Mexican cook accompanied the LS wagon. Frank Clifford was another member of the crew, and that mysterious and colorful character known as Frank Weldon, or the "Mongolian Monster," was said to have been a member of the group which left Tascosa with enough food and feed to last until they reached the Pecos.

On the first night after leaving Tascosa the expedition camped near Sperling's store and on the second at San Hilario above Fort Bascom. Then they drove across the divide to the Pecos. At San Lorenzo, Siringo, who had been given three hundred dollars with which to buy food for the LX horses and men, instructed the rest of the party to go on to

Anton Chico while he rode into Las Vegas in a buckboard to buy the supply of corn, food, and ammunition, thus saving about seventy-five miles of travel for the party.

In Las Vegas Siringo, who had also taken with him about one hundred dollars of LIT expense money, found dance halls, saloons, gambling places, and other tempting amusement spots. He lost all his own funds and the expense money as well, and had it not been for a big-hearted merchant who took an order on the LX Company, the group would have been without food. At least, that is the version given by Siringo in his book, *Riata and Spurs.* Jim East claimed that Siringo came "wandering down the Pecos without any grub" and that the men "had to tighten up their belts and postpone a few meals."[2]

The two wagons left Anton Chico and pulled up at Llewellyn's Wells. At daybreak the following morning Pat Garrett and Barney Mason, his deputy and brother-in-law, rode into the camp of the Tascosa posse.

After a discussion among Stewart, Robinson, Siringo, and Garrett on the problem of stolen cattle and the Kid, and with some of the plans still not revealed to the entire group, Garrett and Mason left with six volunteers—Williams, Bousman, Emory, Stewart, East, and Chambers. Robinson, who was traveling under a "consumed" name, turned tail and declined to go. Cal Polk was excused on account of his youth and inexperience. Siringo refused to go at all and took the LX wagon to White Oaks to establish winter headquarters.

At Anton Chico, Garrett picked up a few of his own men, and the posses started on the trail of the notorious gunman. Each man carried a six-shooter and a Winchester. The wagons had been left behind, and Garrett and the Texans traveled all day without eating. About five o'clock they had supper at Puerta de Luna, the "Gate of the Moon."

2 J. Evetts Haley, "Jim East—Trail Hand and Cowboy," *The Panhandle-Plains Historical Review*, Vol. IV (1931).

Meanwhile, members of the Kid's gang, hearing that men from the Panhandle had come for a showdown, dropped out of the pack one by one until there were only six left, including the Kid himself. The five loyal outlaws were Tom O'Folliard, Charlie Bowdre, Dave Rudebaugh, Tom Pickett, and Billy Wilson.

Garrett led his Texans to Fort Sumner, because he was sure that he would have the opportunity of meeting the outlaws there. He had learned that the Kid had gone to his old camping place on Portales Lake and believed that on his return to Fort Sumner he would ride along the Fort Sumner–Portales road. Therefore, the Texans quartered themselves in a house along this road to ambush the outlaws.

One evening Lon Chambers was on guard behind the long, low fence of crumbling adobe beside the road, and another man was detailed to guard the horses. A poker game was started inside the house, and Jim East rolled up on the floor to get some sleep. Behind the fence Chambers watched a small pattern of gray in the distance on the Portales road. It grew larger and finally focused into a compact group of horsemen, riding quietly in the snow, whom Chambers recognized as the Kid and his pack. He gave the alarm, and the card players rushed to the fence. The six horsemen were almost on the group about the house before they could see them. Garrett yelled a challenge, and the man in the lead clawed for his pistol. Shocking impacts drove him backward and almost out of the saddle as two forty-five slugs tore through his body. A volley of rifle and pistol shots caused the other horsemen to wheel and disappear in the gloom. The lead horse kept coming toward the posse, but a hand waved feebly from the saddle. It belonged to Tom O'Folliard, the boy who had followed almost every trail the Kid had ridden. Had not the Kid sensed the danger and ridden to the rear, ostensibly to get a chew of tobacco, he would have been in the lead and might have received the withering blast.

The cowboys carried O'Folliard inside and laid him down on Jim East's blanket. East sat down by the fire and began warming his fingers. The others went back to the poker game. The dying man, cursing, paid his last respects to Pat Garrett before he turned in his chips.

Twelve miles from the adobe house where O'Folliard had died, the posse the next morning found the body of a horse shot through the stomach. It had belonged to Dave Rudebaugh, who doubled with Billy Wilson until the outlaw gang reached the Wilcox ranch.

The snow had drifted and a fresh fall started that afternoon. Garrett's force lost the trail they were following, but about noon of the second day they learned from Wilcox that the Kid and his gang had headed for a deserted rock house on the Taiban. They rode for it and just before daybreak came upon the house. Garrett left Stewart, Bousman, and Williams with the horses, and in company with Emory, Chambers, Hall, and East—all Panhandle men—crawled up the arroyo to within thirty feet of the building. Three horses with reins leading inside stood just outside the door; the Kid's racing mare was inside the small rock house.

As the sun cast its first reddish glow over the landscape, Charlie Bowdre walked out of the door carrying a *morral,* or feed bag.

"Throw up your hands," yelled Garrett.

Bowdre dropped the *morral* and reached for his gun. Hall and Garrett drilled him. Bowdre staggered back through the door. The men in the arroyo heard Billy the Kid say, as he pushed Charlie back out the door, "Charlie, you're done for. Go out and see if you can get one of them before you die."[3]

Bowdre floundered toward the hidden enemy, his eyes blurred and his fingers too weak to cock a gun. He stumbled

[3] *Ibid.,* 55.

to the spot where East and Hall lay and pitched over on Hall, who took the outlaw's gun from his numb hand and laid him on the snow, where he died in a few minutes.

A full day of heckling between Garrett and the Kid, of taunting threats, occasional shots, and constant watchfulness followed. Garrett shot a horse through the heart, and it fell in the door of the house. Since the Kid's mare was inside, it was thus virtually blockaded by the dead horse. The officers shot the rope which held another horse, releasing him.

It was bitter cold. Inside the stone hut the hunted men had neither food, fire, nor liquid. Late in the afternoon Wilcox, the rancher, sent down some food to the posse. The Texans began cooking it. The aroma was too much for the Kid; he surrendered along with Rudebaugh, Pickett, and Wilson. He had lost two of the most fearless and valued members of his gang to the good aim of the Panhandle men and their leader, Garrett. He asked only assurance of protection against mob violence.

Three days later he and his friends were in the Las Vegas jail, and it was with extreme difficulty and dramatic maneuvering that Garrett, East, and Emory, the officers detailed to take the prisoners to Santa Fé, were able to prevent a mob from taking them as they were placed aboard the train. The officers offered to arm the prisoners if necessary to hold off the mob. The Kid welcomed this prospect, but J. F. Morley, inspector for the Post Office Department, saved the day. The fireman and the engineer had been pulled from the engine by the mob; but Morley sneaked into the cabin and, just as the temperature of the mob was at its highest, jerked the throttle wide open and the train sped down the tracks. The engineer managed to hang to the back coach, whence he worked his way to the engine and resumed control.

The prisoners were delivered in Santa Fé, a reward received, and the posse released.

Hall, Chambers, and Bousman had already returned

to the winter camp of Siringo and Robinson at White Oaks. After Emory, Stewart, and East returned from Santa Fe, Siringo decided to stay until spring and gather up stray LX cattle that might drift in during the winter. East wanted to return to Tascosa, and Siringo gave him permission to go. In January Lee Hall and Cal Polk also went back to the LX. Tom Emory stayed in New Mexico with Siringo until June, when they returned to the LX Ranch after an absence of seven months.

Thus for a time the Kid had met more than his match. Two of his gang had been killed, many had been forced to desert him, and three were with him in prison in Santa Fé. Garrett's reputation and that of the Panhandle cowboys, the ranchers, and the infant Panhandle Cattlemen's Association who financed them, spread far and wide. Their success had a wholesome and chilling effect on the outlaw world and definitely placed everyone on notice that the large cattle owners were not going to tolerate wholesale thievery, outlawry, and mass murder.

One of the classic stories by an outlaw hunter about his experiences on the man hunt, and one which gives some idea of the hardship many of the men were forced to undergo in their long trek, is that told in late life by Jim East.

His wife asked him one day, "Jim, what was the meanest thing you ever did in your life?"

"Well, I hate to tell you," replied Jim, "but I guess the meanest thing I ever did was on our hunt after Billy the Kid. We had almost starved out in the raw cold and one night I got so hungry that I went out to my horse and took some of the corn out of his *morral* and ate it."[4]

Peace on the range did not last long, for on April 28, 1881, Billy shot two of his guards and escaped. Again the cattlemen of the Panhandle sent Garrett help, this time in the

4 *Ibid.,* 61.

person of John William Poe, who had lacked but one vote
of being elected sheriff of Wheeler County in 1879, because
the saloon and gambling element had voted solidly against
him, while McCarty had failed to vote fifteen of the LIT
cowboys, so sure was he of Poe's victory. The sadly disappointed Poe prepared to go elsewhere, but the Panhandle
Cattlemen's Association immediately hired him as a cattle
detective. One of his tasks was to attach himself as deputy
to Pat Garrett's staff in Lincoln County and render what aid
he could in that hotbed of trouble.

When he went into New Mexico, he carried with him
a letter from Charles Goodnight, who was the strongest factor in the Cattlemen's Association, which gave him entree
into many places that otherwise would have been slow to
receive a stranger.

Poe had already searched to the ground one Pat Cough-
lin, who had found a market at Fort Stanton for the Panhandle cattle that Billy the Kid and his gang furnished. Poe
found an occasional animal or a small herd which bore Texas
brands. Garrett often worked with him in arresting the men
or chasing them out of the country. The main effort of both
men, however, was the recapture of Billy the Kid.

Early one morning in July, 1881, someone knocked
lightly on Poe's door at White Oaks. The visitor, a Texan
whom Poe had befriended, brought the message that the
Kid was hiding in the house of his sweetheart at Fort Sumner. Poe hastened to Lincoln to tell Sheriff Garrett. At first
Garrett refused to credit the story and chided Poe for believing it. He expressed the opinion that the Kid was in
Mexico. The two argued until Garrett became convinced
that the tip was worth checking. They went to Roswell for
Special Deputy Kip McKinney, and the three rode to Fort
Sumner.

Failure seemed to stalk the trio. They did not find Billy
where they had expected him. As one last chance it was

agreed that Garrett would talk with Pete Maxwell, wealthy land and sheep owner, who lived in one of the large government buildings.

On the night of July 14, 1881, the three moved up to the long, one-story adobe building which Maxwell occupied. Poe and McKinney stood in the shadows outside while Garrett went indoors to talk with Maxwell. The two deputies were conversing in guarded whispers as Garrett disappeared inside the room. Less than thirty seconds later Poe noticed a man walking along the inside of the picket fence in front of the building. He walked almost noiselessly. The two men crouched in the shadows, and the man walked within three feet of them before he saw them. Springing to the porch, he whipped out a six-shooter and demanded to know who they were. As he repeated the short Spanish term, "*¿Quién es? ¿Quién es?*" he was backing through the door which Garrett had just entered. Poe assured the excited figure that he need not be afraid, they would not hurt him. This seemed to excite him more, and he backed into the doorway and disappeared. Poe heard him ask Pete Maxwell who those fellows were out there on the porch.

There was a momentary hush and then two gunshots broke the stillness. A groan and some gasps were heard. Garrett, smoking gun in hand, ran out of the room, brushing against Poe.

"I killed the Kid!" he cried. "I killed the Kid!"

Thus Billy the Kid went off the stage in the same blazing way he had entered the feuds of the cattle country. With his death went the last and most able leader of the notorious gunmen and cattle thieves of the West. Others came to ride briefly across the stage. Some perhaps stole more cattle, but no one made open warfare in the bold, audacious manner of the Kid and his men.

As the Tascosa country had played such a big and final part in the career of Sostenes l'Archevêque, it has also taken a climactic place in the life of the Lincoln County bad man. There, as in bloody Lincoln County, he became a legendary figure. A group of daring, shooting Tascosa cowboys had been the main cause of his successive failures, and while the problem of cattle stealing was not solved by his death, it was greatly alleviated.

Garrett, who had brought the Kid to justice, was destined to play another important role for the cattlemen at Tascosa, while members of the Panhandle posses were to distinguish themselves in many fields as peace officers, for a war almost as bad as the Lincoln County War was even then brewing in the Panhandle.

7. Outlawry and Boothill

THE FORCES out of which a settled culture emerges are disparate and sometimes brutal. Tascosa had perhaps more than its share of brutality. Law had not come to Tascosa when the rocky, windswept knob of a hill that overlooked the town and the valley witnessed the first burial of a man who had met death "through violence," as the Eastern newspapers of the period euphemistically reported. It was in the fall of 1879, one of those hazy somnolent autumns which make Indian summer enjoyable in the Panhandle, when the incident occurred which jarred the serenity of the little valley.

Bob Russell, a thirsty cowpuncher, who had come to town and started a saloon and was generally said to be his own best customer at the bar, married Lizzie Rinehart, Ira's daughter and the only available single lady in Tascosa. Miss Rinehart, reared on the frontier, could speak Mexican like a horse trotting and was ready for any reasonable experience. Her father was known for his bravery and resourcefulness, and she was no less capable.

Her conduct is reported to have brought some public comment from Jules Howard. Other reports were that Howard was enamored of the girl rather than critical. Still other rumors were that there was intrigue by enemies of one or all of the three persons involved. Be that as it may, Russell became angry and began to fret and talk about his troubles, all of the time he was drowning a certain amount of them at the bar. It took two or three days of this behavior before he got nerve enough to "go jump old Howard out."

Early one morning he started to Howard's store. Howard was expecting him and watched his every move as he wobbled along the street. Russell darkened the store door, took a step inside, and through bleary eyes saw Howard standing there as cold as steel, his six-shooter pointed straight at him. Howard gave the pistol a slight up and down motion, fingering the trigger.

"Lay 'er down, Bob! Lay 'er down there on the counter," Howard ordered as he leaned over and patted the counter.

Russell slowly and confusedly complied. Howard straightened up and began talking.

"Now, Bob, to show you I don't want to take any undue advantage, I'll lay mine down by yours—and step back."

Both men knew that the real showdown had come and that it meant death for one or the other. Howard braced his feet. "If you want to pick your gun up now, let's go."

Russell was slow to get into action. He made a pass for the gun. He never reached it. Howard raised his own gun slightly and fired. Russell clutched at his breast and crumpled limply to the floor. His shirt absorbed the blood like blotting paper, but it welled through in a great splotch. Howard turned to the silent group that had congregated in and about his store and asked them to take the body outside.

Someone sent for Russell's wife, but the body had been taken away before she arrived. She asked some questions but appeared coldly indifferent to Howard and to the blood which soaked into the sand outside the store.

Imitation, the sincerest form of flattery in more sophisticated society, could not but be highly regarded by Mickey McCormick, who suggested that since Dodge City had a famous cemetery called Boothill, why not start one of the same kind in Tascosa?[1] The widow with bitter determination selected a spot in sight of Howard's store for the burial ground. Thus Boothill Cemetery was born atop one of the many knolls that reach down like fingers from a giant hand to the Canadian River.

The story of Fred Leigh, second man who died with his boots on and was buried on Boothill, gives a fairly accurate picture of some of the difficulties of maintaining order and establishing law. Oldham County had just been organized, and a small group of men had declared themselves to be for legal justice, established preferably by the courts; but by revolver, rifle, and sawed-off shotgun if necessary. There was little law anywhere in the Southwest in 1880 except the law of self-preservation with Judge Colt as the customary arbiter.

Leigh, foreman for the company which brought the first cattle to the Panhandle for the LS Ranch, pointed his herd over the ridge of breaks south of Tascosa and meandered the cattle to the Canadian. The valley south of the river and Tascosa had plenty of knee-high grass on its spacious *vegas*. It was a great spot to loose-herd cattle. The stream was too high to swim a herd across, but not so high as to keep Leigh and some of his men from swimming it on their horses when they wanted to "belly up to the bar for Red Eye" in Tascosa or to enjoy the gambling and the women common to early-day trail and cattle shipping points. These cowboys were a surly lot. Sometimes liquor, women, and gambling kept them corralled, but often these served only to make more opportunities for trouble.

[1] Jack Ryan is also credited with the suggestion.

Marion Armstrong, first justice of the peace, and Henry Brown, lately of Billy the Kid's party of expert gunmen but now Tascosa's first constable, had crossed the river from Tascosa to see about some horses. Brown was telling Armstrong of his background as they herded the horses along a narrow trail, and he said that he could handle a gun as well or better than Billy the Kid. Just then the two had their peace jolted severely in a meeting with Fred Leigh and his cowboys, who were coming back to camp after a round of drinks in Tascosa.

They had been told in town that they should not wear their guns there and were protesting among themselves. One of the cowboys cautioned Leigh as they rode toward Armstrong and Brown, but Leigh, surly under the influence of liquor, looked down on the two with contempt as he rocked in his saddle, cursing the town and its varied assortment of citizens. Brown did not care to use his gun against such odds and had to delay a chance to prove his marksmanship. Armstrong told the men that Tascosa was a peaceful, law-abiding community and asked for respect of law and maintenance of order. Then the cowboys forced Leigh to ride on; and the two Tascosa men, stung, abashed, and angry, walked down to the river, got into Armstrong's boat, and rowed across.

A few minutes later a group of angry men in Tascosa were exchanging stories of their experiences. In addition to Brown and Armstrong, among the lot were Henry Kimball, Cape Willingham, Judge J. E. McMasters, and John Rinehart, one of the nerviest men on the side of law and order in Tascosa. They agreed to watch every move Leigh and his men made in order to avoid trouble, if possible. They also decided upon a signal that would summon aid if trouble did develop.

Later that same afternoon Leigh and his men decided to risk driving the herd across the river. When the cattle were across and turned loose on the other side, the cowboys decided to go to Tascosa to get on a hilarious drunk. The men were not exactly sober when they came riding into town from the north, coming down Spring Street toward Main. Some ducks were preening their feathers on a pool of water in the street, and Leigh shot the head off one of them. A pregnant Mexican woman standing across the street screamed and fainted. Leigh and his men, who had guffawed that afternoon, laughed again.

Cape Willingham, Armstrong, and a Mexican were in the stockade back of Howard and McMasters' store. They rushed to the street; and Willingham, who did not have a gun, demanded that Leigh give up his weapon. But Leigh had the drop on the sheriff and defiantly refused. Then Willingham signaled Armstrong and the Mexican to spread the agreed alarm. He walked back of the hotel to the rear of the saloon where he had left his double-barreled shotgun—no one would have expected him to get anything else, for Tascosa had the reputation of being "hell on sawed-off shotguns." The Mexican eased off to McMasters' store, gave the warning, and then went to Kimball's blacksmith shop as others took up posts at vantage points in town.

Leigh had taunted and insulted the law twice that day. His men had more or less tacitly approved his action, although one of them had probably prevented a showdown with ghastly odds on the side of Leigh when they had met Brown and Armstrong across the river. Willingham had been helpless when without his gun he sought to disarm Leigh. Now, however, Leigh and his men were meeting on home grounds as determined and dangerous a crew of men as ever stood for the law.

Leigh and his comrades did not realize this when they turned west on Main Street and rode half a block to the saloon. Leigh was very angry. He was also cocky over his second successful bluff of the day. As he approached the

FIRST LX RANCH HEADQUARTERS IN THE EARLY EIGHTIES

LIT HEADQUARTERS IN 1939

BRANDING AT THE LIT IN 1898

Left to right in the foreground are: Mel Armstrong, Frank Mitchell,
John Morris, and Emmett Gardner

MULLIGAN STEW AT THE CHUCK WAGON

saloon, Willingham came on a half-trot from the rear of the building, his sawed-off shotgun in the crook of his arm.

Leigh dismounted, holding his reins and a cigar in his left hand. His right was free. He touched the ground without seeing the sheriff. Willingham stepped into the street, raised the shotgun, and with his finger on the trigger commanded Leigh to surrender the gun. Leigh did not reply but turned, put his free hand on the horn of his saddle, and leaped into it without using the stirrup. As he hit the saddle, his right hand flew to the holster, his fingers closing around the handle of his six-gun. That was as far as he ever got.

Both barrels of Willingham's gun emptied buckshot into Leigh's side and chest, blowing him out of the saddle. The horse bolted; as did Leigh's companions when the other men circled into a knot around the scene. Brown jumped to the saloon door. McMasters and Kimball came up from the store and the hotel corner. Armstrong and Rinehart strode across the street, Winchesters in hand.

The inquest was held by Armstrong, then and there. The coroner, Brown, and the Mexican carried the dead man into the room adjoining the saloon. Fred Leigh was resident number two of Boothill.

Brown let few opportunities pass to corral those men who thought they could ride roughshod over the law. One disagreeable individual with too much whiskey inside him caused considerable trouble about Tascosa and finally shot up the town. Brown told him to go to the court and pay his fine. The man pretended that he was on his way, but instead mounted his horse and rode to Rica Creek. Later in the day Brown asked a cowpuncher who was going that way to tell the man to come back and pay his fine or the constable would kill him.

The offender understood the finality of the command and returned to Tascosa. He paid his fine and an extra one for contempt of court. He protested and criticized the community, saying it was little else than a pile of adobes. Brown, angered at this statement, slammed his pistol on a chair and stepped back the same distance from it as the protesting cowboy. He suggested that the two grab for the gun. The offender stood, first sullen, then red-faced as his nerve failed him. Finally, after what seemed an eternity to the court, Brown picked up his gun and told the cowboy that if he was not going to grab for the gun to shut his mouth and get out of town. Another small victory was won for the law.

Tascosa early secured a wide reputation as a trading point and as a spot where liquid refreshment, gambling, ladies of the evening, and general good fellowship and conviviality prevailed. This pleasant oasis was sometimes upset by brawls, but on the whole it was attractive to the men and women of the frontier. Roundup crews and trail-herd cowboys found it especially favorable for an evening or a few days of rest and good times. The ranches prospered, and more people moved across the cattle and Indian trails of the West. Hogtown had some growth and attracted more persons of dubious character. Tascosa, now that it was the county seat with nine other counties attached to it for judicial purposes, became not only the county town but the judicial empire of an isolated world of considerable area. It was definitely the liveliest town in the West, and one officer of wide experience stated that it was the worst.

Much of the new population at Tascosa about 1882 came from Mobeetie and its Fort Elliott hangers-on. A general cleanup was held in Mobeetie under the direction of Texas Ranger Captain G. W. Arrington; and large numbers of fancy women, gamblers, and men accomplished in robbery, cattle and horse theft, "con" games, and similar practices left and made their way to Tascosa. They brought new and colorful frontier names such as Frog Lip Sadie, Gizzard Lip, Rowdy Kate, Homely Ann, Canadian Lily, Panhandle Nan, Slippery Sue, Midnight Rose, and Box Car Jane.

About this time W. H. Bush arrived in Tascosa in time to witness a shooting scrape in a saloon. Bullets were flying everywhere. Two men were wounded, and there was great commotion. One person, however, retained his presence of mind. A bullet cut a hole in a barrel of whiskey and the cowpuncher plugged it with his finger while he disregarded the fight.

Henry Brown went to an outlaw's grave after rendering the law yeoman service; and Cape Willingham traded for a "herd of horses," described as "the meanest critters that ever went unhung," and established himself in New Mexico. Before retiring, however, Cape with his sawed-off shotgun did much to establish law and order. Most noteworthy of his deeds was the arrest and conviction of Mexican Frank, a tough monte dealer. Frank was responsible for grave number three in Boothill. If marked, it would have carried the name of Henry McCullar, who died defending the law rather than taunting it as had been the case with Fred Leigh.

McCullar came to Tascosa with the tough bunch that had been run out of Mobeetie. He was a holy terror when he landed in Tascosa and became so mean that he could not get along with his own kind. He gave one fellow a "cowpuncher's shampoo," that is, he beat him over the head with a six-shooter, cutting big gashes in his scalp. Marion Armstrong helped sew up the wounds.

McCullar continued his rough actions until a cowboy gave him a whack with a gun from which he did not recover for three months. He had been found unconscious with one side completely paralyzed. He lost his memory and did not know what to call a hat or a horse and had to learn to talk all over again. The beating also changed his behavior; he became a respectable citizen and was appointed deputy sheriff. Perhaps contempt for his reform caused Mexican Frank to shoot him when he sought to arrest the Mexican for a gambling irregularity. The gambler did not have time to take his gun out of the holster but merely lifted the holster and fired, shooting McCullar through the stomach. Some persons insist that the killing was inspired by members of the underworld.

The deputy sheriff crawled from Hogtown, where the shooting had occurred, to the home of Jenny, a sporting woman with whom he lived. Jenny appealed to Mrs. Marion Armstrong for help for the wounded man, but he died after several days of intense suffering. He was buried in Boothill, although he had died with his boots off.

Mexican Frank left for the New Mexico line the next afternoon about four o'clock. Delegating Louis Bousman as his deputy, Cape Willingham took his sawed-off shotgun and followed Frank, both men on horseback. Mexican Frank ate breakfast at the Alamocitos Ranch headquarters and felt sure that he would be able to get to Salinas and across the border before anyone from Tascosa could overtake him. However, he had reckoned without the speed of Willingham's horse, and as he rode away from the ranch headquarters, Willingham rode close enough to see him leave.

The sheriff put spurs to his horse, took advantage of a superior knowledge of the country, and rode around the Mexican. He tied his horse in a small arroyo and hid in some bushes beside the trail. As Mexican Frank approached, Willingham stepped out of the bushes with his sawed-off shotgun resting across his arm. It was pointed directly at the midsection of the Mexican. The gambler knew the man behind it and hurriedly surrendered, giving up his gun and riding back in sullen but respectable protest.

He was convicted of murder and sentenced to twenty-one years in prison. Temple Houston, district attorney, prosecuted Mexican Frank, W. H. Woodman defended him, and Judge Willis was the trial judge, with C. B. Vivian district clerk.

Many of the men who died in Tascosa with their boots
on were not, however, buried in Boothill. The two victims
of a double-barreled killing in Hogtown in the Edwards
Hotel, which was also a store and saloon, were probably
buried somewhere on the prairies or hilltops with no marking
on the mounds of earth. A group of buffalo hunters still seeking the scattered animals at large in the Southwest stopped
at the hotel for the night. A big poker game was underway
in the lobby and continued well into the next morning. A
number of visitors watched the game. One of the players
was Louis Keyes, cowboy and former buffalo hunter. Playing opposite him was a Mexican. An argument developed,
and the Mexican drew his gun and shot Keyes dead. Bill
Yandell was standing behind Keyes while he watched the
play. As the Mexican fired, Yandell raised his gun, and shooting between Keyes' body and arm, drilled the Mexican
through the stomach. He died in a few minutes.

In 1882 the fourth body was placed in Boothill—that of
Bill Gibson, whose name was used for convenience sake.
When he was in town and drinking, he went to the room
of one of the dance-hall girls and fell asleep. There he was
found several hours later shot through the back of the head.
His pockets indicated that he had been robbed. Although
suspicion rested on Johnnie Maley, bartender in Captain
Jinks' saloon and dance hall, after the burial on Boothill the
incident was apparently forgotten. However, one man, Ed
Norwood, brother of the unlucky cowboy, did not forget.
He stayed away from town for a couple of months and then
came in with a tremendous thirst. He spent money as if it
were water, courted the girl in whose room his brother had
been killed, and made a big display of his money before
Maley. Then he feigned drunkenness and asked to be allowed to sleep in the bed in which his brother had been
killed. After waiting impatiently for several hours, hoping
someone would come to rob him, he moved quietly into the

saloon and shot Maley dead. The bartender was buried on Boothill.

Norwood was arrested and held in the small rock jail to await the meeting of the grand jury. He languished in the rock room for several weeks, but proved a popular inmate, as he had many friends. Finally on a holiday, when an unusually large crowd of celebrants was in the town, the cowboys staged a mock battle in East Tascosa. This drew the attention of Jim East, sheriff, and Deputy Pierce, who found no dead or wounded as a result of all the shooting. Then they rushed back to the jail to find a hole knocked in it big enough for a horse to walk through. Ed Norwood's friends had put him on one of the best horses in the Panhandle to make his escape from the country. East gave pursuit the next day; but there are those of his friends who say he did not have much desire for the job.

The Pioneer, Tascosa's only newspaper, had its say about the dastardly murder by the Catfish Kid of the Dutchman, one of the occupants of Boothill. The editor, C. F. Rudolph, did not stutter when he wrote out his report and opinion. Here it is as it appeared in the June 25, 1887, issue:

"Just before 3 o'clock Wednesday morning of the twenty second there was heard a single shot and then a cry 'Help! Help!' Jim Thurber and Alize Lynch, two young men who stop here only part of the time, were spreading down a bed or pallet in the rear lot to Cone & Duran's store. One of them drives a stage and sometimes sleeps by his team. A Dutchman came in from Springer and asked if there was any chance for him to sleep on any spare hay. John Gough, who is known as Catfish Kid, came in. He dropped down by them for just a few minutes and while they talked heard a noise over in the corner. Gough asked what was the noise and one of the others said: It is only a Dutchman who went back there to sleep. The remark was overheard by the Dutchman and he took offense. He walked forward in the dark and said something about if anybody wanted anything out of the Dutchman or Dutchy he could get it. Thurber and Lynch became frightened and ran, but Catfish Kid stayed. They said the Dutchman was carrying something swinging down in his hand. It was probably his coat which he was carrying on his arm as no weapon was found on him.

"Thurber and Lynch said that as they ran out of the shed they heard the Dutchman say: 'Let me out of here! Let me out of here!' and they said the Kid fired the fatal shot. It was done with a .45 caliber six-shooter and the weapon could not have been more than a foot or two from the victim when fired, for the clothes and flesh around the wound and the entire side of the neck and face were badly burned by powder. The ball entered the left shoulder and came out at the back. From where he was shot the man ran out the gate and shouted as he went with his hand pressed over his breast: 'Help, Help!' and then in a minute, 'Help!' He staggered along the buildings, fell and died. Thurber and Lynch say the Catfish Kid told them to keep quiet about who did the shooting. It was cold blooded murder and Catfish Kid should be dealt with. He has done enough meanness around here already."

Thus another victim, whose name is listed as Pete Fulton, was buried. A Mexican woman and two children, victims of a smallpox epidemic, were also buried on Boothill. Tom Nolan was killed by a fall from a wagon and was buried there. There were other burials, too, many of them not now recalled by early-day residents.

One of the last gun battles in Tascosa was that between Jim East and Tom Clark, the gambler, in 1889. They shot it out in a saloon. East was not hit. A move was started to bury Clark on Boothill, but the owner, Tom Smith's widow, who had bought several acres of land and moved several Mexican families there, refused to permit it. She put a notice in *The Pioneer* that she would permit no more burials on Boothill.

The refusal to allow Clark to be buried in Boothill Cemetery was a blow to the finer sensibilities of many Tascosa and Panhandle citizens, who were sensing then something of the glamour and romance which was destined to grow about the West. They resented it. A three-strand barbed-wire fence was put around the graves, and people began to argue whether there were seventeen or twenty-seven bodies buried on Boothill and how many actually died with their boots on.

8. The Cowboy Strike

As THE BIG CATTLE OUTFITS settled down to business in the Tascosa country and got control more firmly in their hands, the cowboys began to lose something of their early position. They became, as Eugene Manlove Rhodes describes them, "hired men on horseback."[1] Previously they had been independent workmen, often belonging to a partnership or having the right to run a few cattle of their own or to keep some horses. Conditions gradually changed as more cowboys came to that part of the country and as the big outfits took firmer grasp. The struggle between the old methods and the new led to the first cowboy strike in American history and was one of a series of conflicts between the big outfits and the little men in the Panhandle.

Up and down the Canadian River Valley the large ranching outfits were extending their ranges by one manner or another. In many instances they were merely buying the squatters' rights or water claims and headquarters of small outfits. For instance, the LS brand was started in 1880 when Gunter and Munson sold the owners their first herd of 1,000

[1] May D. Rhodes, *The Hired Man on Horseback, ix–xii.*

steers. They bought the TS (connected) or Torrey brand in the winter of 1881 and kept on buying until they became one of the largest outfits in the country. This group wanted to get rid of the Mexican plazas and a certain nester element in one part of their range. W. M. D. Lee, who was in charge, was notorious for high-handed, roughshod methods of dealing. As soon as he bought out a Mexican, he forced him to move and tore down and burned his improvements.

Much land in the public domain was held by the ranchers, who took advantage of a provision in the lease laws which stated that if a lessee had built as much as one hundred dollars' worth of improvements, he might hold the land without danger of being bought out or having the land leased by someone else. Many ranchers held great areas of land by the simple expedient of throwing up hastily constructed corrals and building an occasional dugout. Most of these improvements were put up on land which was never leased at all; but the ruse was effective, because most nesters either did not know how to obtain correct information on the status of the land or found it impossible to go to places where that information could be obtained. Many dared not interfere with or question the practices of the large operators who were seeking to corner great areas of grassland.

Regulations for cowboys working for these big outfits became more stringent. The ranchmen were getting together through their Panhandle Cattlemen's Association and making it exceedingly difficult for the cowpuncher to be anything more than a "hired man on horseback." Privileges which were formerly accorded the cowboy, such as keeping a brand and running a few cattle and horses, were gradually denied. Mavericking, formerly practiced by everyone, began to be frowned upon by the large ranch owners. Other concessions which had been freely given were denied, and the cowboy soon began to feel that there was a strong combination of forces moving against him.

As organization of one force brings about organization of an opposing group, the little men began to hang together. Their loyalty to new bosses, especially representatives of large corporations and foreign ownership, was not as strong as to former pioneer owners. As Bones Hooks, old-time Negro cowpuncher, has often said, "It wasn't considered any crime to brand a syndicate calf." The little men also began to hang together and take advantage of the processes of law and to exercise their power at the ballot box.

It was something of this feeling of brotherhood which resulted in Jim East's defeating Cape Willingham at the polls for sheriff of Oldham County in 1882. Although Jim admitted that he got the office by the skin of his teeth, it was the vote of the cowboy—who felt they were being mistreated and that Jim, having been one of them, would understand and help them—that elected him. He had given a good account of himself in the Billy the Kid trouble; but then Cape Willingham had also handled some bad men. Thus it was primarily the feeling of the cowboy for one of his kind that caused East to be elected sheriff.

An outcropping of this smoldering feud between the little men and the big interests resulted in the spring of 1883 in the first regional organization of cowboys. While not directly related to the war in which Billy the Kid was involved and out of which grew his outlaw activities, the cowboy strike which resulted from the cowboy's association in the Canadian River country was in almost every respect tied in with the struggle between big and little men that went on over a period of years on the Western range.

In the early spring of 1883 three big ranches of the Canadian River country, the LIT, the LS, and the LX ran floating outfits or wagons which followed drift cattle and brought them back to their home ranges. Tom Harris was wagon boss for the LS wagon, Waddy Peacock for the LIT Ranch, and Roy Griffin for the LX Ranch. Each wagon boss had a crew, and all three were together at the LS supply depot just above the mouth of the Frio Creek and east of present-day Hereford. They enjoyed a meal of beef, corn, tomatoes, molasses, and sourdough biscuit and after dinner got to talking about the wages, the new rules being imposed on all cowpunchers, and the possibility of a strike. They voiced the dissatisfaction prevalent over the Canadian range.

Tom Harris, brother-in-law of Jess Jenkins, Tascosa rancher and businessman, and a natural leader with a great deal of force, was selected as chairman of the association, although Harris at the time was drawing one hundred dollars a month from the LS, which was twenty-five dollars more than was being asked for wagon bosses.

The group talked at length around their hillside camp, and finally evolved the following proclamation:

"We, the undersigned cowboys of Canadian River, do by these presents agree to bind ourselves into the following obligations, viz—First, that we will not work for less than $50 per month, and we furthermore agree no one shall work for less than $50 per month, after 31st of March.

"Second, good cooks shall also receive $50 per month.

"Third, anyone running an outfit shall not work for less than $75 per month. Anyone violating the above obligations shall suffer the consequences. Those not having funds to pay board after March 31st will be provided for 30 days at Tascosa."

The ultimatum was signed by Thomas Harris, Roy Griffin, J. W. Peacock, J. L. Howard, W. S. Gaton, S. G. Brown, W. B. Borina, D. W. Peeples, James Jones, C. M. Hullett, V. F. Martin, Harry Ingerton, J. S. Morris, Jim Miller, Henry Stafford, William F. Kerr, Bull Davis, T. D. Holliday, C. F. Goddard, E. E. Watkins, C. B. Thompson, G. F. Nickell, Juan A. Gomez, and J. L. Grisson.[2]

[2] The original of this ultimatum is in the Panhandle–Plains Historical Society Museum at Canyon, Texas.

Having set the date of April 1 for the strike, the cowpunchers took the wagons to the Juan Dominguez canyon
place west of Mitchell Canyon and camped. Bob Robinson
of the LIT's offered the men thirty-five dollars and sixty-
five dollars to continue their work. The wages for cowboys
had been around twenty-five dollars a month, and for wagon
bosses they varied with the skill and length of employment.

The LS boys pulled their wagons into headquarters on
the Alamocitos. McAlister tried to compromise and offered
to pay the men forty dollars a month. When the strikers stood
firm in their demands, McAlister sent word to Lee, who was
at Leavenworth. Lee rode to Dodge City by train and took
an ambulance out of Dodge City to make the run to the LS
headquarters in two days and one night. When Lee arrived
at the headquarters, there were eighty men camped there.
He spoke cordially to them and went into the ranch office,
where he censured McAlister because he had not paid the
men their demands and stalled them off for a time. He said
that he could get carloads of men later at his own price.

Lee sent word to Harris to come up to the house and
talk with him. Instead of going alone, Harris took seven or
eight men with him. When they were about midway between their camp and the house, some of the men fired their
six-shooters. If this act was intended by the men as intimidation, it did not have that effect. Lee, by interrogating Harris, gained the information that Harris had set his own price
when he went to work for the ranch and had not asked for
more money. Harris also admitted that many of the nester
boys working as cowpunchers were not worth fifty dollars
a month. Lee then offered him one hundred dollars a month
to keep the wagon and agreed to pay fifty dollars a month
for every man Harris would designate as a top hand. Harris
refused the offer, saying that he would stay with the boys.

Jim Mays replaced Tom Harris as an LS wagon boss,
and some of the better cowhands continued to work for the

ranch. At Liberty a few days later McAlister was seeking cowboys and offered Kid Dobbs seventy-five dollars a month to go to work for him. Dobbs conferred with his boss, Jim Campbell, who said that he did not have enough cattle to justify that salary and advised Kid to take the job with the LS Ranch.

The LIT boys had to stay around the wagon because they were afoot, and the LE manager promptly discharged his cowboys.

The news of the strike soon spread all over the range and every ranch had demands for higher wages, even if some of the men did not join in the strike. There was, however, a fairly general acceptance of the strike ultimatum by veteran cowpunchers of the Canadian River range. The cowboys, after the Harris-Lee interview, established a camp and base of operations above Tascosa. Lee stopped feeding them. However, they had money in their pockets and time on their hands, a bad combination for any group of cowpunchers in a lonesome ranch country. Then there was the attractive oasis of Tascosa. Tom Harris had the support of his brother-in-law, Jess Jenkins, the ruler of Hogtown and purveyor of liquors and entertainment. Jenkins was always sympathetic with the little men.

An incident worthy of note in direct connection with the cowboy strike occurred at the T-Anchor, where Jules Gunter, some of whose men had quit the day before the strike began, expected trouble and prepared to meet it. He was tipped off that a delegation of cowpunchers was coming to his ranch to enforce the demands. The T-Anchor headquarters house was a large log structure, and the only possible approach to it for a group wishing to keep under protective cover was by way of a smoke or meat house some distance from the main ranch house. There Gunter arranged a mine filled with black powder in the smokehouse. A fuse was concealed leading from this house toward the main ranch house.

The fuse was short. About midway a steel scraper was placed as something of a breastworks for whoever might set off the fuse to the powder mine. Gus Lee, the faithful and later famous Negro cook, was designated as the man to light it if it became necessary. The committee of cowpunchers who came to talk with Gunter stopped short, however, when a few well-placed bullets kicked up the dirt about their horses' feet as they approached. There was no further trouble.

The only effort at intimidation of cowboys who continued to work or who went to work on the ranches after the strike began ended in abrupt failure. It involved Kid Dobbs and Tom Harris. While Dobbs was running an LS wagon, Harris sent word to him by Uncle John, Irish saloon-keeper at Liberty, that he could get work elsewhere on the river at the same price the LS was paying. He suggested that if Dobbs did not quit the LS, he would get into trouble. Dobbs replied that he would work for whomever he pleased, a brief frontier declaration of independence. He challenged Harris to name his weapons and his ground if he wanted trouble. When Dobbs and Ed King met Harris two weeks later at Trujillo, Dobbs was ready for trouble; but Harris dropped the matter with an exchange of pleasantries.

The cowpunchers at Tascosa, restless under the forced inactivity and growing short of funds as a result of drinking and gambling, gave up the strike. Its inception and failure had come within a thirty-day period. Many men were coming into the country wanting work, and since no form of force was used against their own men who might become strikebreakers or against the cattlemen, the cowboy strike failed. Many of the cowpunchers returned to their homes in lower Texas, or drifted farther west into New Mexico, or left for the ranges in Montana and Wyoming. Others established small ranches of their own in the Tascosa country, while some found work at Tascosa or other frontier towns. Some, angered by the many incidents and changes, and conscious of the opportunities offered, decided to go into the game for themselves and to get what they could out of the situation by fair means or foul. The strike gave impetus to strong opposition to the big cattlemen and further stimulus to developments which followed.

9. Mavericking

THE COWBOY STRIKE of 1883 was a complete failure, and the spring roundup and the trail herds went along as usual. The LS sent several trail herds to Dodge City and were able to find enough men to handle them, although not all the cowpunchers they employed were top hands. The T-Anchor easily found several men willing to take the places of cowboys who quit to join the ill-starred venture. The LX and LIT ranches, while shorthanded for a time, had no difficulty in getting along. The labor problem was never a big one on the ranches of the Panhandle because young men were riding into the wild country every day seeking opportunity or fleeing from troubles and disappointments at home "down in Texas." Many of them were no more than nester boys, but most of them already knew the fundamentals of riding, roping, and branding and were accustomed to long hours of work and hardships. Most of the great cowboys of the West were born on small farms or in country towns. They were always responsive to the lure of the open ranges and cowboy life.

The labor problem, however, was only a small part of the troubles of the Panhandle ranchers in those years. Practically every ranch was in possession of land on which it paid no lease and no taxes and which belonged to the public domain. Squatter ranches might control watering places through strategically placed leases and, by the prior law of possession and by force, thousands of acres of land. This was common practice in an open-range country just then coming under the control of land and lease laws of Texas. The nester cattlemen wanted a place in the sun in this grass bonanza, and even the cowboy had the ambition to burn his brand on a few cattle and start a herd of his own. This desire had been one of the reasons for the strike of April, 1883, and it was a source of trouble on the range until after 1900. The rancher found that after the strike he had sullen and sometimes dangerous nester neighbors in his former cowboys, who loved the country, recognized the opportunities, and did not want to leave. They had as much right to the land as the big ranch operator, and each of them knew these rights.

The situation on the Canadian River was further complicated by large herds of cattle drifting into the valley from the Colorado and New Mexico plains to the north and northwest. Although the cattlemen had built drift fence from the New Mexico line to Adobe Walls in 1882, it did not prevent the cattle from reaching the Canadian River. As a matter of expediency these cattle were let through the drift fence when they herded behind it during storms and consequently remained on the Canadian for months. Many of them were branded, but great numbers were not branded and consequently were maverick cattle. Maverick cattle belonged to no one and became the property of the first person able to brand them. The cowboys, who had been let out because of the strike, had long branded these cattle for their owners, usually branding cattle worth far more than their salaries on their jobs of riding line or working with a floater wagon. It was as much a practice of the big ranchers to brand the maverick cattle as it was to round up the cattle in the

spring and distribute the animals to their respective owners
and ranches as the brands designated. Thus mavericking was
not in any sense of the word considered theft but was the
common practice of the open-range world; and the cowboys,
who had long engaged in it as a part of their routine work
for the ranches, now turned it to work for themselves. The
hard storms sweeping across the northern plains drove great
herds of cattle to the Canadian. The cowboys had all winter
and until late spring to seek out the unbranded of these cattle.
It was only a matter of a short dash, an expert flip of the rope,
and a small fire; and the round iron carried on the saddle
had registered the ownership of the cow or calf for a cowboy instead of one of the big ranches.

This practice was aggravated when the ranch owners
took steps to outlaw or blacklist the cowboys who went out
on strike and any cowpuncher who started to work for his
own brand. The information on a cowboy who had been involved was quickly sent to all ranches in the Panhandle, with
the result that the cowboy found it impossible to get work
even if the ranch to which he applied was in desperate need
of men. Some of the ranchers ruled that any man whom they
hired who had cattle must keep his herd at least two fences
away from the ranch on which he was working. Since there
were few fences in a country of such vast distances, this regu-
lation virtually eliminated hiring any nester rancher or any
cowboy who might be trying to settle on land or endeavor-
ing to build a small herd of cows or horses. The ranchers,
who were determined to hold the country as their own,
drew up stringent rules and soon classified mavericking as
cattle rustling.

Mavericking in its earliest stages was an outgrowth of
the Civil War and had its beginning in South Texas. Great
herds of cattle had grown wild during the years when men
were at war and in the years following the war when there
was no market for cattle. They were public property on the

public domain. Some men took the trouble to butcher them, while others began capturing them and putting their brands on their tough hides. The first industry to grow out of this practice was the hide and tallow business—the cattle were killed for hide and tallow and the meat was wasted.[1]

One of the methods the poor man used to collect a herd of cattle in the early stages of mavericking was to "moonlight" the cattle.[2] Kid Dobbs relates his own experiences at moonlighting cattle in Houston County. In co-operation with a neighbor and by using a few old tough but gentle oxen, Kid Dobbs and the other cowboys would make camp near a water hole where the cattle came to drink at night, hiding their horses in the brush near the water hole. The wild animals would drink until their bellies bulged. They could not run as fast as usual when heavy with the water. With this advantage and also that of bright moonlight, the cowboys would rope and hog-tie the cattle, getting as many as three or four animals on each run. These wild cattle were then yoked to the gentle steers or oxen and herded together until the hunt was over. When brought back to the moonlighter's home, they were gentle enough to be left in his herd. They were branded, perhaps hobbled, as a precaution against their straying away, and were soon adapted to their new range. This was a slow and laborious but effective way for a poor man to accumulate the foundation for a herd.

When the trail blazers found a route to trail the cattle to market and the railroads reached points in Kansas, cattle became more valuable. Mavericking increased, and shortly there were few unclaimed and unbranded cattle anywhere in Texas. Moonlighting was a thing of the past.

When that state was reached, mavericking changed; and in this changed form it was practiced in the Panhandle. The mavericks which were branded in this area were usually

[1] Paul I. Wellman, *The Trampling Herd*, 62–72.
[2] Some called this practice "moonshining" cattle.

weaned calves, one and two years old, and an occasional cow or steer without previous brand, or with blotched or unknown brands. They had drifted into the Canadian River Valley for shelter and grass, usually with severe blizzards and snowstorms. The great distances from which some of these cattle came are almost unbelievable. Sometimes the branded ones did not have owners at the next spring or fall roundups and consequently were cut back on the range. Calves weaned from their mothers or lost from them in storms grew into large animals and roamed the range unbranded. These animals were public property and were usually branded either by the cowboys working for the big ranches, by nester cattlemen, or by cowboys working on their own account. While the numbers were not so large as in the early days of mavericking in South Texas, a hard-working, enterprising cowman could brand a good many cattle during the winter months. This practice came to be called mavericking. When done in this manner, it was accepted on the range and was not cattle theft nor cattle rustling, and there was no law or custom against it. It was practiced by almost everyone in the region, from the big ranch operator to the small boy who began at ten years of age branding maverick calves with his own brand. This youngster, riding horseback and ill-clothed for such work, soon learned to run the maverick until it was virtually exhausted before roping it and applying the branding iron. He also learned to leave the two- and three-year old mavericks to older and stronger boys and men.

It was an easy matter to change from legitimate mavericking to cattle stealing and the nefarious practices in which dishonest cattlemen engaged. It was also easy for cowpunchers, angered and seeking revenge, to brand every unbranded and weaned calf belonging to big outfits or foreign-owned syndicates that they could lay their hands on without danger of detection. Some of the methods used by the more unscrupulous were cruel; others involved underhanded dealing and required long experience on the range to detect. Sometimes a cowboy working a section of the country after the fall roundup would find a likely calf, perhaps about ready to be weaned, drive it away from its mother into a little canyon hide-out, where the cowboy could throw up a pen of rocks and logs into which he could put the calf. He would chase the mother into another part of the range and keep an eye on the calf for several days until he was sure that it was weaned. He would then turn the calf out of the pen and herd it to water in a part of the range which he could watch and where the calf was not likely to find its mother. Some time in midwinter or early spring the cowpuncher would find the calf again and place his brand on it. This practice, of course, was simple cattle rustling, because the cowpuncher had created the maverick. It was difficult, however, to detect or convict the offender in a case of this kind. The cowboy could easily salve his conscience by recalling his treatment by the big outfits or by remembering the branding of mavericks he had done for them. This loose construction of property rights naturally drew retaliation.

The cowboys, once they had broken over to rustling, burned and altered brands to their own ends. Many of them designed and registered brands which could easily be made by burning over existing brands. There were a dozen ways, for instance, of altering the XIT brand. It was also claimed that one of the brands of the Canadian River Valley could be used to alter almost every ranch brand of the region. Experienced cowboys who were given to rustling soon became adept at this art and had keen knowledge of brands and cattle in the country. They were masters at finding mavericks where none existed before. Sometimes at a roundup or on other occasions when there was some argument about the ownership of an animal or its brand, a man would be called on to "pick" a brand. This was done by throwing the animal and pulling out the hair over the raised welt formed by the old brand until it could be distinguished. One cowboy was so expert that he could quickly, easily, and without detection "pick" his own brand on the animal, although it actually had not been there at all. The stories of cowpunchers' burning the feet of calves, slitting their tongues, or pinching their hoofs with a pair of pliers in order to keep them from following their mothers were greatly exaggerated. These barbarous mutilations were seldom made and never by real cowmen, who would not stand for such cruelty. Old-timers unanimously agree that instances of cruelty were rare.

That the cowpuncher engaged in mavericking and rustling needed to have an intimate knowledge of cattle is best illustrated in one of the many fine stories Colonel Jack Potter has told. He related that two cowpuncher rustlers, one a comparative greenhorn and the other a man who really knew the range, roped an XIT calf and prepared to place their brand on the animal. The inexperienced cowhand was getting ready to slap the brand on the calf's hide when the other cursed him, ran to the calf, lifted up its head, and smelled its breath. He turned the calf loose and explained to his partner that you could always tell when a calf was sucking its mother by the odor of milk on its breath. If the calf had showed up alongside an XIT cow with some cowpuncher's brand on its hide, it would have been strong evidence of cow theft against the rustler.

Another practice often misunderstood by the present-day greenhorn was "sleepering." This was one of the sharpest and most daring practices of the range. The first steps were usually taken during the spring and fall roundups. One pioneer cowpuncher who knew the range from heel flies to blizzards declared that many cowboys engaged in sleepering, including some of the "outside men" or "reps" for big cattle outfits.[3] He explained that a roundup crew working out a

[3] A "rep" or "outside man" is a cowboy who represents his brand at outside ranches during a general roundup.

section of the range might have a nester cowman helping in the roundup. As the day's work was done, he would leave, ostensibly to go home for the night, ten to fifteen miles across the country. He would ride in the direction of his shack until out of sight and then would carefully thread his way into the herd which had not yet been worked, drifting a large number of cattle down a draw or over a hill behind the cattle which were to be worked the following day. He would note the number of unbranded calves and mix them among the cattle which had been freshly branded and worked. The next morning he would show up at the chuck wagon apparently none the worse for wear. Some time in the next few months he would check the cattle he had thrown behind the roundup crews and put his brand on those the cowboys had missed. Throwing cattle behind the herd could be done in daylight, but it was far more dangerous then. One pioneer nester cattleman said that he could take his brother and a friendly boy and throw more cattle behind a herd than the average group of cowboys could round up in a day's time. The cowboy actually was branding mavericks the next fall or winter when he completed his job. It was not generally known, however, that these mavericks were of his own creation. Often the outside men or reps engaged in sleepering would leave the roundup herd to go to town to mail a letter or to get supplies or to make a report. They might be gone for two or three days, but during the nights, in the meantime, they might drive many cattle behind the roundup workers.

Before mavericking grew into rustling, most cattlemen and cowboys had quit the practice. In the process of change men were killed by hired gunmen or by angry cowmen. All rustlers eventually faced the great danger of the courts, and the cattlemen were inexorable in their charges against them. The actual practice of rustling, meanwhile, was made much more difficult by fencing and development of the country. Then, too, the job was one for strong, active, courageous young men who knew how to work in a wild country under open-range conditions. That breed of men, among the most colorful in history, was created by conditions and forces which have not existed since the days of the open range.

Tom Harris and others among the top hands of the Canadian were not willing to be blacklisted after the strike and leave the Tascosa country. Some of them already had claims or leases of their own. Others were eager to get into the cattle business while there yet seemed opportunity for land and cattle at a fair price. Harris went to Liberty, New Mexico, just across the state line, and established a ranch. Then, with the co-operation of Jess Jenkins and Jess's brother, Lon, he organized a cattle pool or syndicate. Jim Gober referred to the venture as the "Get Even Cattle Company," but the evidence does not support his appellation. Some cowmen say Harris had an excellent opportunity to make his pool or syndicate pay handsome dividends because he was a good cattleman, had an excellent range, and had associated with him men who knew cattle. He sold shares in his syndicate and registered the Bar WA (connected) brand for his company. Among his stockholders were J. E. McAlister, his old boss on the LS ranch who had $2,500 invested, and Bill Ruth, who invested $2,000 in the venture. Many cowboys over the Panhandle also bought shares in the pool.

This led to complications, however, and soon when any of the large ranch outfits learned that a man working for them had bought an interest in the pool, he was discharged and blacklisted. This action intensified the feeling between the two factions.

Whether McAlister was ordered by the LS owner, W. M. D. Lee, to take his money out of the syndicate or realized that trouble was brewing has not been ascertained, but McAlister quit the syndicate and asked Harris for his money. His withdrawal brought about extremely hard feelings between the two men, as was evidenced in a Tascosa saloon some time afterward when Harris showed the intensity of his anger by insulting McAlister. Friends intervened and probably averted a killing.

Bill Ruth, one of the best cowmen in the country, drew out his interests about this time, too. Soon Harris and Jess Jenkins were heavily involved in the pool but still had a large number, perhaps as many as eighteen to fifty persons, holding shares in their venture. The Bar WA (connected), or Tom Harris Syndicate, however, found the going rough. One man after another withdrew, and finally control passed largely to Jess Jenkins, who became the power behind the pool brand. The quarrel which he and his brother-in-law, Tom Harris, had when the syndicate was finally closed out lasted for two or three days and might have ended in tragedy had not Bill Ruth intervened. The two men had drawn pistols, but Bill Ruth stepped between them, grabbed their guns, and talked them into turning the weapons loose. He then urged the men to get off to themselves on the prairie and settle their troubles without hurting each other. They finally reached an agreement, but Jenkins lacked seventeen head of having enough cows to settle all accounts.

Jenkins and Harris were both courageous men, and neither backed down easily. The courage of both was tested many times on the frontier and no one doubted their bravery. Harris committed suicide some years later; and Jenkins, after serving for seventeen years on the directorate of the Panhandle Livestock Association (which had evolved from the old Panhandle Cattlemen's Association), owning several great ranches, being president of a bank at Dalhart, is today in his eighties and actively operating his fine ranch at Corona, New Mexico. In 1942 he asserted that the quest of the big companies for land and for control of the range was the primary cause of the cowboy strike and the trouble which followed.

Many of the nester cowboys and ranchers settled on

land as neighbors to Harris in New Mexico and put in small herds of cattle. The part of New Mexico along the Texas line was more than one hundred miles from the county seat at Las Vegas, and it was a difficult country in which to travel. The Las Vegas element, largely Mexican, cared little for what happened near the Texas line. As a result the nester ranchers and cowboys who worked in that region, if they cared to do so, could steal cattle or horses in the Texas Panhandle and smuggle them into New Mexico, or they could steal in New Mexico and dispose of the cattle to certain elements in Texas. Bill Moore, at the Double H, and formerly foreman of the LX Ranch, would buy anything wearing any brand. This traffic soon presented a more serious problem for the big cowmen than Billy the Kid had in his day, because these rustlers were a part of the range in which all lived and worked.

In addition to the Harris pool, many small cattlemen and cowboys registered their brands and started herds. Some of them were bona fide and legitimate. Others were ventures in the field of mavericking, while some were a combination of plain rustling, sleepering, and other questionable and punishable offenses.

Perhaps the most notorious and mysterious of these brands was the Tabletop brand. This brand, which was made in the form of an open table top with four legs, was a classic for masters of the art of burning brands to use. It was said that almost every brand of the Canadian River Valley except the LIT could be covered by the Tabletop. It really had the appearance of the spider-like Mexican brands common to the country. The Tabletop, owned by Bill Gatlin and Wade Woods, was considered one of the maverick brands by Oldham County.

Another maverick brand, the Hondo, belonged to several different men at various times. One of these became a famous peace officer. Another, who became a prosperous rancher, was boss for the Frying Pan Ranch, and the Hondo brand cost him his job. This brand was on the left hip and was first called the Steeple Bar, then the Hackamore, and finally the Hondo.

The Pipe brand was owned by Joe Dyke, who ran hounds for the LIT. The K Triangle was owned by Bill Gatlin. The T-48 was short lived. Tom Harris recorded this brand, which counterfeited the LS, and McAlister tried to confiscate it but could not. He then bought the brand for fifty dollars and retired it.

The brands discussed above were generally regarded as the maverick brands around Tascosa when the Oldham County Commissioners' Court stepped out of its jurisdiction and into the cattle business by outlawing them.[4] At this time the big companies in the same region included the LX, LS, LIT, Frying Pan, Turkey Track, T-Anchor, and LE. The PPP and the Bell brand of the Waddington Brothers in New Mexico were also big company brands.

In 1883 a group of Tascosa men smuggled seventy-nine head of cattle out of New Mexico on the roundup and into the country near Tascosa. A boy working for the LS saw the men working the cattle up the Rita Blanca and followed them. One of the men with the small herd of cattle dropped behind and told the boy that as there were no LS cattle in the herd, consequently there was no need for him to follow. The boy, having sensed danger if he continued trailing the cattle, turned back. That night he worried about the experience and early the next morning rode thirty miles to the LS headquarters to make a report. En route he found a steer that had dropped out of the herd. It carried an LX brand which had been burned into a Spider X, an X with four wings. This made him positive that the group he had followed were rustlers.

[4] This is the first time in Western history that a commissioners' court put a county in the mavericking business.

McAlister selected Kid Dobbs, Ed King, Dunk Cage, Charley Reasor, Tobe Robinson, Lon Chambers, and three others to go with the boy in pursuit of the herd. Robinson, named spokesman for the group, told McAlister before they left the ranch that all nine of the men would go to the end of the rope to protect LS property but that they did not want to work for other outfits or to fight for them. On the north plains they ran into a large herd of Triangle Dot cattle, and after eating breakfast, they were told that the cattle had not been thrown into the herd or picked up by it. Hall, the Triangle Dot wagon boss, showed the group their one maverick animal, a black Mexican cow that looked as if not another brand could be put on her. Hall said that every time the cow got off the Cimarron someone branded her, and some Mexican claimed her. Therefore, his boys decided to brand her so heavily that no one would know to whom she belonged.

The LS men found the maverick herd drifting west toward New Mexico north of the drift fence. The cowboys bunched the cattle and finally found a two-year-old heifer McAlister thought might be examined more closely. He decided to kill the heifer and skin her so that the hide could be stretched and the burned brands more easily read. Just before McAlister prepared to shoot the animal, Robinson, speaking for the cowboys, warned him that he should appraise the animal.

McAlister realized the logic of this warning and appointed two men to put a value on the animal. They appraised her as worth sixteen dollars. Then McAlister killed the heifer, and when the hide was prepared, it showed that she wore the holding brand of MC, which belonged to a Mexican, and the K Triangle had been burned over it. Bill Gatlin claimed the sixteen dollars.

The story is told that one cowpuncher who kept a large number of hogs on his claim near one of the big ranches fed

the hogs almost exclusively on butchered cattle, whose ownership was believed to be the XIT. Friends of his finally began to grumble, declaring that it was a shame to waste good
beef on hogs even if it did belong to a foreign syndicate.
Their consternation at this act was no greater, however, than
their amazement at the cowboy who, starting his herd with
a yoke of oxen, soon had a hundred calves carrying his brand.

It was obvious to even the most unimaginative of the
cowboys and small nester outfits that conditions of this sort
would draw retaliation. Mavericking at one time and under
a certain set of conditions had been approved, but in the
present circumstances it was not permitted because it had
degenerated into something closely related to cattle stealing.
The big ranchers of the Panhandle proved themselves able
to cope with outlawry beyond the mavericking stage when
they went to New Mexico and ran down and eliminated Billy
the Kid and his gang. The little men, good and bad, in the
Canadian River should have known that it would not be long
before the big outfits took care of the situation at home.

10. Pat Garrett and the Home Rangers

THE BIG RANCHERS of the Canadian River country, alarmed at the threat to their security from mavericking and rustling and fearful of the disorder likely to break out again, decided on united action.

This time they sent for Pat Garrett, with whom they had worked successfully a few years before in New Mexico. Garrett, who was none too popular among friends of Billy the Kid, had been succeeded as sheriff of Lincoln County by John William Poe. Garrett agreed to work for the ranchers for a year provided that they got permission for his appointment as a captain of the Texas Rangers and furnished him with sufficient men. The ranchers took the matter up with Governor Jim Hogg, who gave them permission to hire Garrett and put him in charge of a company of Home Rangers, if the ranchers paid the wages and expenses of the men.

Garrett came to the Panhandle in the spring of 1884 and brought with him his brother-in-law, Barney Mason, who had assisted him in the fights with Billy the Kid and George Jones. He established his headquarters at the LS Ranch and began the organization of a company of rangers. Ed King, Charley Reasor, who was half Cherokee Indian, Lon Chambers, Bill Anderson, John Lang, and Albert E. Perry were among the first men to be employed as rangers. Perry, who had been working as a cattle detective, was made first sergeant of the group.

The first move Garrett made, after his company was organized and his men commissioned, was to tell the big companies that he could not do anything without legal papers, warrants for arrest, and search warrants. He emphasized that the cattlemen must have the letter of the law on their side before he and his men could be expected to get action without bloodshed and without overwhelming odds against one company of men. He suggested that the rangers could follow the roundups, keep down trouble, and look for burned brands and evidences of cattle stealing, but he insisted that legal action was necessary before they could make arrests and disarm the cowboys.

One of the first steps taken by the cattlemen was to persuade the Governor to issue a proclamation making it illegal for civilians to wear six-shooters and other firearms. The proclamation stated that the reasons for carrying firearms— frontier conditions and danger from Indians—no longer existed and ordered the practice stopped. It endeavored to include Winchesters carried on saddles, but the protest to this provision was so great that it could not be enforced. Therefore, only the part of the proclamation referring to the six-shooter went into effect on April 17, 1884.

Garrett and his men went from wagon to wagon and saw as many as two hundred men in one day. Some of the cowboys protested the disarming order; but the rangers quietly read them the proclamation or asked the cowboys to read it and then told them that it was the law and they must comply. If the men were reluctant, the rangers simply suggested that there were attorneys and judges in Tascosa to whom they could go to investigate the new order. That usually sufficed. However, the cowpunchers immediately

FRYING PAN HEADQUARTERS IN THE EARLY EIGHTIES

ALAMOCITOS (FIRST) HEADQUARTERS OF THE LS RANCH

SECOND LS HEADQUARTERS

Built about 1885 on the head of Ranch Creek; the background design and
architecture were copied by Jim East from a picture
on the Arbuckle's coffee sack

LS HEADQUARTERS USED TODAY

Built in 1896–97, about four miles south of Tascosa

ordered arm holsters and scabbards and carried their six-shooters under their arms instead of outside on a belt. Only two men forced the rangers to take guns from them, and both of these incidents occurred in drunken brawls. Kid Dobbs had the unpleasant experience of handling both cases, which he did expertly.

Lee and Scott loaned Oldham County $25,000 with which to build a rock courthouse and jail at Tascosa as a step preliminary to controlling the situation. Lee followed this action by buying about half of the townsite and deeding to each of his trusted LS cowboys a lot in the town. This gesture made each of the cowboys freeholders in the county and the state. There was much comment on the generosity of the LS people for giving their men lots and for loaning the county money for the buildings. One man, more far-seeing than his neighbors, warned the cowboys and nesters that a county did not have a fine courthouse unless it had a grand jury.

His prediction proved true when the grand jury, which convened in the fall of 1884, passed 159 bills, virtually every one of them for theft of one kind or another. These grand jury indictments were the legal papers Garrett and his rangers had been waiting to receive before they tried to make arrests and to clear the country of men whom the big ranchers thought improper citizens for that area. That there were instances where the charges could not possibly be substantiated was generally understood. Prior to this, Garrett and his men had been taking life easy, following the roundups, scouting the country, and acquainting themselves with every individual and almost every cow up and down the Canadian River.

As the rangers worked in the Tascosa country, the cowboys, small cattlemen, and townspeople took sides. Those opposed to the big outfits and the rangers flocked to the leadership of Tom Harris and Jess Jenkins. Upper Tascosa was split into factions, and even the men working on the big ranches were not in agreement on the question of bringing the rangers into the country. Garrett found scores of his old friends arrayed against him. Members of his ranger force faced the same situation. Lee was causing much enmity, and at times he was as overbearing in his way as Tom Harris was in his world. A great many persons felt that the rangers were unnecessary. Some believed that their presence in the valley was not only to help the big outfits gain possession of the open range but to run the little men out by fair means or foul. Some felt that possession of the range was the only issue. The cowboy strike had been the first open break on the part of the cowboys and little men, but the opening salvo of the big ranchers was the organization of the rangers and the coming of Garrett. The LS got full credit for the action, and the rangers were largely known as LS men.

J. E. McAlister, manager of the LS Ranch, was also county judge of Oldham County. He had a Commissioners' Court which was in thorough agreement with his actions. When the time seemed appropriate, the court declared certain brands on the range outlaw or maverick brands, and Pat Garrett and his men were given orders to round up the stray or maverick cattle on the range. Those wearing the outlaw brands were to be considered the property of the county. The rangers strictly enforced the rule against six-shooters and rounded up the strays and the cattle wearing the maverick brands. In this they had the full help of McAlister and his LS cowboys.

Bill Gatlin and Wade Woods, who owned the Tabletop brand, one of those declared maverick brands by Oldham County, hired Attorney Wallace to look after their affairs in connection with the brand as the maverick roundup began. Wallace was then known as the little man's lawyer, and the companies would not hire him for any of their legal work. Wallace employed one-eyed Green Reagan to follow the roundup and take care of the Tabletop cattle. Kid Dobbs, who was an LS wagon boss, got two letters, one from his boss, J. E. McAlister, and another from the three county commissioners, both authorizing him to cut and hold all Tabletop cattle. Reagan, who was camping with the Turkey Track wagon, had thirty-three head of Tabletop cattle with him. Dobbs told his boys before visiting with Reagan that if Reagan did not want him to take the cattle, he would quit the LS Ranch before he would carry out his orders. Then he went to see Reagan and read the letters to him. Reagan promptly asked for time to consult Wallace.

Reagan returned in two days and reported that Wallace had instructed him to turn the Tabletop cattle over to Kid Dobbs. Dobbs took the thirty-three head to Tascosa, where they were thrown in with other maverick cattle. Some eighteen or twenty head of the Tabletop cattle as well as some carrying other brands were turned over to Scotty Wilson, Tascosa butcher and justice of the peace. Scotty butchered the animals and later when the County Commissioners' Court sought to collect for them, he snorted, "The boys steal 'em, the county steals 'em, By Gad! I eat 'em." He did not pay but canceled the county officials' meat bills.

Wallace intended to file suit against Oldham County for $25,000 damages on behalf of his clients and threatened to seek criminal action against McAlister and the commissioners for the maverick order outlawing the brands. It was the opinion of many that the men could not have escaped criminal responsibility nor have defeated the damage suit against the county. The big cattlemen called Wallace into a conference and settled for $800. They then became friendly with him. After this new friendship with the big outfits, he announced for county judge against Theodore Briggs and won the election.

The commissioners sent one herd of maverick cattle, some three hundred head, to Springer, where they were sold by the two men who had driven them there. Then the cowboys put the money in their pockets and left the country. Thus Oldham County never realized anything but trouble out of its illegal dealings in maverick and outlaw cattle. The roundup and the charges against some of the worst offenders among the maverickers and cattle rustlers did, however, clear much of the Tascosa country of men whose honesty was open to question.

The second biggest fight in the history of Tascosa grew out of the troubled conditions in 1884. It was the habit of some of the men in Tascosa to slip LS horses out of the pasture and ride them while they hustled mavericks, turning the horses back into the pasture afterwards. Most of these men were hangers-on in Lower Tascosa. A Mexican, Jermo Martínez, who had charge of the LS horses, caught some of the maverickers in the act of returning animals which they had ridden without right or permission. He sought out Gene Watkins and others involved and told them that if they did not quit using the horses, he would report them to headquarters. His threat stopped them for a short time, but one night Gene Watkins and another cowboy took two LS horses and rode them to a frazzle, angering Martínez, who "jumped out" Gene Watkins and warned him for the last time. A bitter quarrel ensued between the two men, but friends prevented a fight.

A few hours later when Jess Jenkins was dealing monte in the northwest corner of his saloon and gambling hall, Sally Emory was paying off, and Watkins was tending bar and watching the game, Martínez walked into the saloon and stopped across the table opposite Watkins. Gene renewed the quarrel. Martínez reached for his gun, but Gene drew and fired first. The powder burns blinded the Mexican, but his shot killed Gene. Then someone shot Martínez. The lights were snuffed out by the explosions. Two men, apparently friends of Watkins, ran outside the saloon where they dis-

covered Jermo's drunken brother and shot him five times
while he was lying in a stupor. Mr. and Mrs. Sam Dunn witnessed this phase of the shooting but would not testify before the grand jury, although they did tell Kid Dobbs about
the affair.

A witness to the murder inside the saloon was an Indian, Pisquah, who could speak English well and who had
the habit of hanging around the saloon begging drinks. He
was not intoxicated that night and plainly saw the killing of
Martínez after Watkins had blinded him. Apparently the
men involved in the shooting affair did not wish any eye-
witnesses. A few nights later they bought the Indian drinks
until he was drunk. He stumbled out of the saloon and fell
into a mud puddle where some workmen had been making
adobes. Two men followed him and filled his body full of
bullets as he lay in the adobe mud.

Watkins was buried in the Cheyenne Cemetery and the
Martínez brothers in Casimero Romero Cemetery. The Indian was buried somewhere in the sandhills near Hogtown.
Kid Dobbs always believed that a group of men "voted"
Watkins to kill Martínez. He said that the charge that a
group of men voted by lot for one of their number to kill a
person who was in their way or jeopardizing their welfare
was often placed against one element in Tascosa, that was
organized originally to protect itself against the rangers and
the big ranchers but had strayed from its first purpose.

Dobbs believed that the same group voted the death of
John Brophy in another fight in 1884. Brophy was a deputy
brand inspector and had made several calls to the Harris place
to inspect some hides. Harris had been selling meat out of a
wagon and off his corral for some time. Brophy, tired of making calls without Harris's being present, threw the hides off
the corral fence and examined them. Although the hides
were in good order, this action caused much hard feeling
between the two men.

When Brophy was at a dance in Liberty some time later, a man suggested to him that they go outside. Sensing danger, Brophy let the man go out the door ahead of him and saw him draw his gun as he stepped outside. Brophy immediately "threw down" on him. Tom Harris stepped from the shadow of the building, grabbed both guns, stepped between the men, and cautioned them against trouble. They would not agree to any of his compromises. He quickly said that he would turn both guns loose, get out of their way, and let them shoot it out. The other man shot at Brophy as he stepped back, the bullet hitting his heavy watch case and turning it into a saucer shape. The force of the shot knocked Brophy down, but he fired and killed his opponent while lying on the ground. He then turned to seek the protection of the light and the group on the main dance floor. Out of the dark and from behind a Mexican outdoor oven a fusillade of shots poured in his direction. It seemed that at least four men were shooting at him. One of the bullets struck him in the back, giving him a wound from which he later died.

The capture of Bill Gatlin, who was charged with theft, was one of the most dramatic assignments the rangers had at Tascosa. Garrett had warrants for several men, including Wade Woods, Charley Thompson, and Bill Gatlin. Garrett and Jim East, Tascosa sheriff, worked as a team, and both agreed that they would have to await a bad storm to catch the men in their camps or at their homes. The two officers had used the same kind of weather to good effect in their quest for Billy the Kid. As winter reached its worst days, a terrific snowstorm backed by a howling wind gave them their opportunity. After a night and a day of storm they left the LS headquarters just after a heavy evening meal and, mounted on the best horses in the country, rode into the storm. Kid Dobbs led the party because he knew the country as well or better than any of them. Their destination was the old rock house, at Red River Springs on the Canadian, which had been built by Dobbs' father-in-law, Jim Adkins. It was believed that all the wanted men would be found at this place.

The posse stopped at Trujillo, fed their horses, and ate lunch at two o'clock in the morning. They rode to the icy Canadian before daybreak. Dobbs warned Garrett that if the horsemen topped the hill, the wanted men could see them from the house. Garrett then asked him how far it was up the river bed, and when Dobbs told him it was only two and one-half miles, Garrett ordered, "Put the steel to that horse and lead the way." The group raced up the river. When they were four hundred yards from the house, Garrett ordered them to get their guns out of their holsters and be ready for battle. They drew their guns and rode to the corral. There they were told to get north of the house because there were no openings on the north side and they would be safe from gunfire from within. The men sprinted for the north, and as Dobbs ran he saw Bob Bassett, whom he knew well, gathering an armload of wood. Dobbs got within ten feet of him, and when Bassett saw the officers, he ran for the house, throwing his wood in every direction.

Dobbs heard him yell to the men inside that Pat Garrett was outside with the rangers. Tom Harris promptly stepped out to ask if the rangers were there for him again. He had just been acquitted of a charge in which they had been involved. Garrett replied that he had no papers for him but was there to arrest Wade Woods, Charley Thompson, and Billy Gatlin. Harris said that Woods was not in the house but the other men were, whereupon Garrett demanded that they surrender. Nine men obeyed his orders, but Gatlin refused. Thompson did not have on his coat when he came out of the house, and since it was extremely cold, he asked to be allowed to go back for it. East extracted a promise that he would go in, get the coat, and come right out, but he was no sooner inside than he opened the door slightly and told East he was going back on his promise to stay with Billy and make a fight of it. East pleaded with him, telling him that he was throwing his life away and that it was foolish for him to be killed when he might be judged innocent of the cow-theft charge against him. His pleadings were so effective that Thompson began crying and walked out with his hands in the air.

·The house was built in the side of a hill, and the back part of the lean-to roof was scarcely more than three or four feet off the ground. Garrett wanted to take Gatlin without a killing if possible; therefore he bantered with him through-out most of the day. Finally his patience was exhausted. He then ordered Charley Reasor and Ed King to go up on the roof and start jerking off the roof poles. They had pulled off about three poles when Gatlin yelled for Sheriff East. He asked the sheriff to come in and talk with him for five min-utes, promising that at the end of the time one or the other would die.

When the door was opened, Jim East rushed in with his Winchester pointed at Gatlin's stomach. Deputies Pierce and Dobbs crowded in behind him, while the other officers were seeking every vantage point. Bill Gatlin was standing with a gun in each hand, his elbows well back against his belly, one hand crossed over and resting on the other and both guns pointing at Jim East's chest. In this tense position he drew a promise that East would not let him suffer at the hands of a mob. After East promised, Gatlin handed him his guns. Then the crowd built a fire, cooked some bacon, and made coffee.

This was the last big case the rangers handled. There were few if any convictions on the many grand jury charges, but much of the tougher element left the country before the cases came to trial or left soon thereafter.

Garrett served out his year. The ranger company, as such, was disbanded in the spring of 1885. Most of the Home Rangers, however, continued to work for the LS in camps up and down the river and spent a great deal of time in Tascosa. With Garrett gone, discipline in their ranks disappeared. Ed King was unruly, a heavy drinker, and extremely arrogant and quarrelsome when under the influence of liquor. The rangers enjoyed life to the fullest. It became more and more convenient for them to drop into Tascosa, where they soon became known as "barroom gladiators." There, around the saloons and gambling halls and among the women of Tascosa, they became embroiled in trouble. Against the background of the cowboy strike, the maverick situation, and the old feud between the ranch owners and the cowboys, these idle former rangers were destined to play a big part in the life of Tascosa. Despite the presence and vigilance of the rangers, mavericking and actual cattle stealing continued. Bad feeling in Tascosa and on the ranges ripened for the climax of the big fight.

11. The Big Fight

W. M. D. LEE, head of the Lee and Scott Cattle Company, had been having trouble on his range. The nesters and the little cattlemen who had been there before the country was fenced felt rightfully that they had squatter's rights.

Everyone in the country was well acquainted with the mavericking situation. It was difficult to find many without sin in the strictest sense of the word. The use of a long, loose rope and a hot running iron and certain other questionable practices of the range were not unknown to the old heads, big and little men, in the Canadian River Valley country.

When the LS and the other large outfits undertook the task of putting such an open, free-grass country under fence and under their domination, there was bound to be trouble. One way to settle it was to hire cowboys who knew how to shoot straight and did not mind doing it. Another was for the big outfits to buy out the squatters or nester cowboys and tear down or burn down their shacks and camps. The big outfits did a good job of this at Salinas, the old salt-mine Mexican town above Tascosa near the New Mexico line.

Sometimes the good citizens of the Panhandle resorted to vigilante committees.

Many persons were guilty of the practices which existed in the country in the early days, but there came a time when law and order were necessary for self-preservation. It took strong, determined men to establish them. Many resented the movement, naturally wishing to continue the life of the open range. And many law-abiding individuals, who knew the life and times of these men, did not always condemn them.

Many incidents, open to question from a strictly legal point of view, accompanied the beginning of law and order in the free-grass empire of the Panhandle. Vigilante action was followed shortly by the legal form. True, the established variety at first had to be backed up by plenty of nerve, diplomacy, and occasionally bullets. Every town of the West was a chapter, separate in itself, each an exciting part of the big story of law. Each story usually involved a woman in what was proudly proclaimed a "man's world." That was true at Tascosa in the spring of 1886 when the law received its greatest test. Here was written one of its most violent chapters.

The LS outfit started riding bog about heel-fly time. Flies usually begin to be ornery about March 1. They give cattle unshirted hell. Cows head for the nearest water or mud. Heel flies go for the heels of cows. The cows go for the river, where quicksand and bog are an even greater enemy. Life on the range is tough.

In the LS bog camp at Jerry Springs, about eleven miles above Tascosa, were Fred Chilton, Frank Valley, Ed King, John Lang, and a Mexican cook. These men covered a lot of LS territory up and down the river. They were regular cowboys and also gunmen. Former Home Rangers, they were among those termed "barroom gladiators" because, it was said, most of their fighting was done around the bar.

Ed King went to town and got a bit in his cups. He was

ever quarrelsome when drinking. He had taken over that spot in the heart of Sally Emory formerly occupied by Lem Woodruff, who went to Rocking Chair Emma for solace and understanding. This quick swapping of attention miffed Sally no end. She asked Ed King to "get" Woodruff for her, and he was easily persuaded to go gunning for him. He was in the mood.

Woodruff, Rocking Chair Emma, and Captain Jinks, the owner of the Hogtown dance hall, were sitting inside a building fronting Main Street when they heard hoofbeats and yelling outside. Woodruff looked out the window. Ed King, Frank Valley, and Fred Chilton were riding by. King, half-intoxicated, was taunting, "Where is that ── ── pretty Lem?"[1] "Pretty Lem" was a cognomen he had manufactured on the spot for the purpose of humiliating Woodruff. Woodruff knew his purpose, and as he came back and sat down at the table, he burst into tears. He told his friends that the trio were out to kill him but that he would not leave.

The gods of war, however, saw no trouble that night.

There was more than just "woman" trouble behind the fight. Lem Woodruff and Ed King belonged to two different factions in Tascosa, and some behind-the-scenes manipulators wanted to see one side or the other wiped off the map. The "woman" trouble was a good spark to set off the flames.

Spring was coming up from the south and reaching long fingers of warmth over the caprock. The weather was rather warm on March 20, 1886, when a Mexican rode into the Jerry Springs bog camp and handed Ed King a note from Sally Emory. If anyone ever knew what was in that note beyond the promise of a good time, notice of a dance, the fact that there was a new girl at one of the dance halls, or some word of personal endearment, it has never been discovered. Felix Martínez, the Mexican cook for the rangers, however, sensed

---

[1] Edward M. Dealey, "Story of Old Tascosa, Once Famous Panhandle Cowtown," *The Dallas Morning News*, Magazine Section, 1922 (n.d.).

trouble and with a shrug of his shoulders warned Ed King, "Meester Ed, I would not go to town tonight. Maybe so you find mucho trouble tonight." His singsong voice raised on the last word, "tonight," as if it were the crack of dawn on doomsday.

The sun was splashing purple shadows over the river valley along the little arroyos and sending them running far out beyond clumps of sage, mesquite and bunch grass as King, Frank Valley, Fred Chilton, and John Lang, on fresh horses and in clean clothes, trotted from Jerry Springs toward Tascosa, ignoring the cook's warning.

As the four rode along, a large jack rabbit jumped from behind a tuft of grass, hopped a few feet, and sat erect, his forefeet raised in the air, his ears pitched forward. Frank Valley pulled out his six-shooter and shot the rabbit dead. He dismounted, cut off the rabbit's left hind foot at the joint, put it in his pocket, and remounted. "That's a sure sign of good luck," he said. "Now I've got my rabbit's foot."

It was typical of such a troupe of men that there was little comment on the prospect of impending trouble. Ed King had a date with Sally Emory or someone Sally had provided. Fred and Frank wanted to play some poker, and John Lang was in for anything the evening offered. The immediate reason for the trip, however, was the Mexican *baile* in the hall of Casimero Romero's home.

The early part of the evening was spent in dancing or talking and watching the dance as it progressed. As the hours passed, the men drank an occasional beer, but not to the state of drunkenness. That would have been decidedly bad manners and entirely too dangerous for real fighting men.

About ten o'clock that evening Boss Neff, who was not nearly so superstitious as Valley, had reason to scoff inwardly at the LS cowpuncher. Valley was standing at the bar in Jack Ryan's saloon, holding Rocking Chair Emma in one arm and with the other was brushing the bar with his rabbit's foot, telling the glamorous woman that he knew his rabbit's foot was going to bring him luck but had never dreamed such luck as having her in his arms.

"I don't believe in a rabbit's foot bringing anybody luck," Neff muttered to himself, a bit envious of the progress Valley was making with the dance-hall girl.

It was shortly after two o'clock in the morning when the four swung into their saddles and loped the dusty half-mile up to Tascosa, passing Hogtown to their left. The town was only partially alive at that time of the morning. Fred and Frank had heard there was a poker game in Button Griffin's saloon on the north side of Main Street. They agreed with the others to stop for a hand at cards before going to camp. Too, Ed wanted to see Sally Emory again.

As the four slowed to a trot and entered the east end of Tascosa's Main Street, several eyes were turned in their direction. In Jenkins and Dunn's saloon was Lem Woodruff, who had a mixed feeling of fear and hate for the men, a feeling that had been fanned by Sally Emory. On the low wooden porch and in the shadows about the place were Tom and Charley Emory, the Catfish Kid, Louis Bousman, and perhaps others. Nigger Bob was asleep between the woodpile that jutted into Spring Street and a small adobe back of the saloon.

The woodpile had been replenished that very day by Boss Neff, who had been boarding at the Sheets' restaurant. He had returned from India Creek with a load of cedar late in the afternoon. Going into the back door of the saloon after his work was done, he had passed Lem Woodruff and the Catfish Kid, who were cleaning and oiling their guns.

Jesse Sheets, on this of all nights, had decided to sleep in the room back of the saloon next to his cafe to keep a watch on a cook he suspected of holding out on him. At least that was what he had told his family. The restaurant extended beyond the rear wall of the saloon.

The men in and about Jenkins and Dunn's saloon were cowboys who sided with the nester ranchers and the little men or else were town hangers-on who were allies. The four LS cowboys trotted to the front of the Griffin saloon or Equity Bar that was farther west and on the opposite side of Main Street from the Jenkins and Dunn establishment. Fred and Frank dismounted and handed the reins of their horses to John Lang, who agreed to tie the horses in the stockade back of McMaster's store. Lang and King rode back east a few yards until they were in front of the Exchange Hotel. Then Sally walked north out of Spring Street into Main and greeted King, who dismounted, handing the reins to Lang.

King slipped his arm around Sally's waist, gave her a light spank, and started arm in arm with her to her building down Spring Street. They were nearing the corner of the porch of the Jenkins saloon and had not yet turned off Main Street when one of the men on the porch made a remark which King apparently resented. Telling Sally he would come to her place in a minute, King stepped up on the porch. No one has ever reported what was said to him or what his reply was. Not all of the men about the place could be seen. It is evident that King did not see a move, for he was a gun-man, and if he had seen so much as the shifting of a hand, his gun would have been blazing.

However, suddenly there was a gun flash in the deep shadow. The impact of the bullet spun Ed King half around, and he fell face up, his head to the east, close to the saloon door. He never knew what hit him.

As he lay there with his face turned to the moonlight, blood rushing out of his mouth, he made an easy target for Lem Woodruff, who rushed out, placed his Winchester barrel close to King's throat and pulled the trigger. The powder burned King's neck and chest and his hickory shirt. Then Woodruff and his friends scattered back into the saloon, barred the doors, and turned out the lights.

John Lang, who was taking the horses to the stockade back of Howard and McMasters' store, opposite the saloon, heard the remark made to King and turned in time to see the fight start and the men scatter. Puzzled, he watched for a moment and then ran to Button Griffin's saloon. There one of the punchers was standing on a table top, whiskey glass in hand, singing "Down by Narraganset Bay," while the other was beating on the table as if it were a drum.

"Boys, they've killed Ed. Come on!" he yelled breathlessly to Fred and Frank.

This call to battle brought the two to instant action. They grabbed their revolvers, unwound belts, and began strapping them across their hips as they charged out of Griffin's saloon, less than fifty yards from where Ed King lay. They found him dead.

They raced south down Spring Street to reach the back door. The next few minutes saw a blazing, smelly inferno of bullets, smoke, and blood in a small, almost enclosed space back of the saloon. What actually happened in five minutes would take many witnesses and several days to tell. Most of the witnesses are dead. Many of the men were shelling the woods without effect, but the noise was terrific. Here is most likely what happened, although the account is subject to the usual errors and omissions in any reconstructed action, and there are those who disagree.[2]

Woodruff, Bousman, Charley and Tom Emory, the Catfish Kid, and probably others were excitedly conferring back of the saloon. Valley, Lang, and Chilton were on them before they realized it, and guns began to spit fire as everyone ducked for cover.

Lem Woodruff and Charley Emory took the brunt of

[2] This is the reconstruction which Mel Armstrong, John Snider, and others (including the author) have made on the ground; and in this account most older witnesses concur. Obviously some would disagree, as there were two strong factions involved.

THE EXCHANGE HOTEL

Photograph by T. M. Caldwell

OLD CASIMERO ROMERO HOME

Erected in 1876 or 1877, this adobe house was occupied in 1941 by
Al Morris, when this photograph was taken

FRENCHY AND MICKEY MCCORMICK'S HOME

from a photograph taken at the time of Frenchy's death in 1941

HOWARD AND MCMASTERS' STORE

with Scotty Wilson holding an old Spanish freight wheel

the first volley of firing. Woodruff was shot twice. One bullet performed a perfect appendectomy, penetrating his bowels; the other plugged into his groin. Emory received an ugly leg wound. Bullets were kicking up dust and flying into doorways like a den of mad rattlesnakes striking.

Valley charged into the middle of the space as he threw lead right and left. Woodruff half stumbled, half fell back into the saloon and closed the door. Whether there was someone else in that back room has never been ascertained, but if there was not, then all the more tribute must be paid to Woodruff's gallant fight for his life. Valley fired several shots into the door after the retreating Woodruff and then opened the door just enough to peep in. He probably thought Woodruff was dead. A bullet smashed under his left eye, fired from a rifle. He fell forward with his head on the doorstep.

As Valley charged into the door, bullets ripped from every side. Chilton and Lang dropped behind the corner of the saloon where there was a shadow and a stack of plaster boards. Bullets were plunking into the adobe walls. Chilton rested his gun against the corner of the saloon and took dead aim as Jesse Sheets, in his night clothes, stepped unarmed into the doorway of his room. The gun bellowed and Sheets fell face forward outside the room, a great hole in his forehead. The gun flash disclosed Chilton's position. Two rifle shots, apparently from the woodpile, drilled his chest. John Lang was loading his guns for him, and he handed his gun to Lang, who clutched it with both hands.

John Lang, left alone, splattered shots into the woodpile and began a dangerous retreat up Spring Street toward the main part of town. Every step he took was to the accompaniment of stinging lead. Many bullets plunked into the wall of the Cone and Duran store on the west side of Spring Street as he dashed for his life, firing as he retreated. His guns were soon emptied. He turned the corner in front of the Cone and Duran store. In all the fight and the retreat he had not been hit, probably partly because he was a moving target. A bullet did tear into his coat sleeve, and the fact that his gun had kicked his arm upward after he had fired no doubt saved him from a bad arm injury. His escape was miraculous. One of the bullets with Lang's address on it splintered the window of the Exchange Hotel across Main Street, and a woman near the window fainted.

As he rushed back to Main Street, Lang was joined by friends from the poker game. An occasional shot was still sending lead flying into the night. Four men were dead, two wounded, and others were scattered to points of vantage or better hiding places.

One of the wounded, Woodruff, stumbled out of the back door of the saloon, around the pool of blood in which Frank Valley lay, over the body of Jesse Sheets, and on into the night. As he supported himself with his rifle, pulling his wounded body along, he ran into Mrs. Sheets, her mother, Mrs. Dunn, and some of the Sheets children who were huddled into a frightened group about the front door of the Dunn home. Mrs. Sheets and her mother grabbed the wounded man, as they thought he was Jesse, the second case of mistaken identification of Sheets that night. They discovered their mistake but because of Woodruff's condition got him a glass of whiskey. Woodruff gulped it down, told them Jesse Sheets was all right, and hobbled into the darkness.

As he faded out of sight, a block away Sheriff Jim East and his deputy, L. C. Pierce, as brave and able as any officers wearing badges in the West, came running to John Lang and the little group about him on Main Street. Lang immediately volunteered his services. Hurried orders resulted in an instant start on the roundup of those fighters yet living. Pierce ran toward the woodpile. A stooping figure fled toward the river.

"Halt!" yelled Pierce.

The man did not stop, and in an instant the deputy's gun

boomed, its noise resounding like a cannon. The Catfish Kid, none too well liked by either officers or townspeople, owed his life then and there to a small depression used by an adobe maker to mix his mud. He tripped and began falling just a second before the discharge from the gun whizzed over his head. He feigned the part of a dying man, rolling his eyes, groaning, gasping, and choking, as Pierce ran up to him. Since it seemed evident that the Kid would die in a few minutes, Pierce went elsewhere to continue his work. He was considerably chagrined later to discover that he had not shot the man and that the Kid was on the loose.

East rushed to Louis Bousman's house. Bousman was in bed with his clothes on, and near the bed was his Winchester, the barrel too hot for comfort. He offered no explanation. Charley Emory was found suffering terribly in the doorway of Kimball's blacksmith shop. Nigger Bob was in the thick of the early seconds of the fight, and although generally known as a "tough hombre," he left the scene in a hurry. He reported to officers later: "I'se sleepin' on a hot roll between that cord wood and the little adobe there. I didn't mind the noise but when that lead started kickin' chips from the woodpile in my face, I done left there."

There are persons living today who will tell you that it would not have been impossible for Nigger Bob to have done some firing on that night. Several did put in a few shots who have never been mentioned as participants.

There are two stories about Lem Woodruff's escape. One is that he crawled and pulled himself over to Theodore Briggs' home, almost two miles from Tascosa. Another is that he went to the home of Mrs. Dunn in Hogtown, left his coat and hat there, and made his way to Briggs'. A more likely explanation is that friends helped spirit him to the Briggs' home some time after he had left the Dunn house. Jim Gober wrote that Woodruff told him that a friend had put him on a horse and carried him the distance. However he managed to reach the Briggs' home, he hovered between life and death for many weeks. As events cleared up, people came to sympathize with him, and he became somewhat of a hero.

Every home in Tascosa was deeply concerned with the fight and the trouble expected to follow it. Mel Armstrong remembers what happened at his home that night with a vividness of detail that is astonishing. His mother, awakened by the shots, stood in the door looking into the night, wringing her hands and crying. Her lamentations awakened Mel, who was almost nine years old, and he went to stand beside her, asking what was wrong. She explained that something terrible had happened downtown.

When Marion Armstrong did go downtown a short time later, his son Mel went with him. The morning light was beginning to reveal the scene. When the Armstrongs reached the battle site, it was in the same condition as when the fight ended, except that the chill air was causing those who were standing about to dig their hands deep into their pockets. The victims were lying where they fell. Officers had warned bystanders not to touch the bodies pending the arrival of the doctor and E. Goodwin-Austen, justice of the peace, who was to render the coroner's verdict.

On the arrival of the officials, the positions of the bodies were noted. King was stretched out face up in front of Jenkins and Dunn's saloon. Jesse Sheets was lying face down in the rear doorway to his restaurant. Frank Valley, lying in a pool of blood, had been found at the rear doorway of the saloon, his head partly in the door. Fred Chilton was slumped face downward over the plaster boards at the corner of the saloon. Woodruff and Emory had left trails of blood.

Dr. Shelton examined the wounds on the bodies. He probed into Ed King's mouth, flipped out several teeth, and finally brought out the small-caliber lead slug, the first bullet to hit him. The bullets, which were of soft lead, had torn great holes wherever they had struck any bone or resistant gristle.

Marion Armstrong kept telling his young son to stay back; but Mel, curious and anxious about the men he had known as friends, saw everything. After a while he ran up to get his little Mexican friend, Claudio Gomez, to come down to see the men. When he got back, they had placed sheets over the bodies. They were, in the pioneer term, "laid out" until proper clothes and funeral arrangements could be made. A stone terrace was their bier.

The day before the fight Sam Dunn and Boss Neff had been digging a well by hand for Truscott and Shinebarger. That night they were sleeping in a small adobe room back of the Exchange Hotel. Neff was tired and was sleeping heavily. It took Dunn some time to awaken him when the shooting started early the next morning, but both heard the last few shots fired, and they arrived at the scene just after the officers. They helped bring the bodies of King and Chilton out on Main Street. Neff remembers that Valley, although unconscious, did not die suddenly but lingered for an hour or more; and his feet had to be tied together to keep him from thrashing around as he struggled for the occasional breath he drew.

By good sunrise everyone in Tascosa was standing in small groups, telling each other of the fight, reporting hearsay, and wondering what would happen next. On Main Street, at the corner of the hitchrack in front of McMasters' store, John Lang told his story of the fight over and over. Mel remembers it as if it were yesterday. In one of the groups that heard Lang's story were A. L. (Bud) Turner and Tobe Robinson. They were delegated to ride north toward Buffalo Springs and search out that country for Woodruff and the Catfish Kid. Word had not yet reached the sheriff's office that Woodruff was at the home of Theodore Briggs and ready to surrender, although he was believed to be dying. The Catfish Kid later gave up to the officers in town.

Orders for four coffins and four graves on Boothill were given. Carpenters and mechanics went to work on the coffins, which were made from ordinary building lumber and fastened together with strong screws and large nails. The grave-diggers got busy, and other men began preparing the bodies for burial.

The Sheets were a poverty-laden family who had stopped at Tascosa a year before en route to Oregon. Now the mother and five children were grief stricken. Mrs. Sheets had lost her whole world in a quarrel in which she and her husband had no part. He, a lover of peace, had been the victim of fighting men. When neighbors reported to her that the four graves were being dug side by side, she asked that Jesse not be buried alongside the gunmen. This message was relayed to the men, and Sheet's grave was dug in another part of the cemetery, some distance from the graves which were to hold the bodies of King, Valley, and Chilton.

There was no wind blowing on the day the funeral services were held. The sun was splashing down with midsummer intensity. The heel flies goaded the cows, but the cattle had to make out by themselves that day, for all the cowboys were in town. Riders had carried word of the fight over the country. The men had many friends, men who were curious. There was the thought of wholesale revenge, of settling the little men versus the big men fight once and for all. In those days almost everyone went to funerals. From the time Tascosa held its first burial on Boothill it was the practice to close the stores and saloons and make a long procession to the burial of the victim, regardless of his standing while alive.

East and Pierce, with able deputized officers, were everywhere, and were exercising all the caution, diplomacy, and tact possible. Great tribute has been paid them for the outstanding work they did at Tascosa during a few days following the big fight, especially on the day of the funeral. Trouble might have come at the drop of a hat. Except for these officers and the fine mettle of some of Tascosa's best citizens, history might have recorded an Oldham County war more deadly than the Lincoln County War in New Mexico or the Johnson County War in Wyoming.

As the time came for the funeral procession to lead out of Tascosa's dusty Main Street, everyone was sad. There were friends who were grieved at the loss of the men; there were others in trouble with the law and others worried about the immediate future. The three coffins were loaded into one wagon and the half-mile drive to Boothill started.

Persons attending walked or rode in buckboards or on horseback. The riders went two and two. The old LS hack was in the line. When the front of the procession reached the top of Boothill and the horsemen began arraying themselves on the high ground above the cemetery proper, riders were still coming into sight in the winding line which was leaving the corner of the C. B. Vivian home, where the road off Main Street jogged south to make the curve to Boothill.

The caskets, placed beside the graves, were opened for friends to have a last look at the dead. That was the custom, and it was fortunate on this occasion because King's casket had been placed so that his head was facing west. The casket was turned around. Judge McMasters slipped and almost fell into the grave. Then Judge Wallace removed his hat and began reading the Episcopal burial service from the small black prayer book he used on such occasions. He selected the old-style Twenty-third Psalm used prior to the King James Version of the Bible. His voice and manner were dignified and impressive as he read:

The Lord is my shepherd; therefore can I lack nothing.
He shall feed me in a green pasture, and lead me forth beside
*   the waters of comfort.*
He shall convert my soul, and bring me forth in the paths
*   of righteousness for His name's sake.*

Yea, though I walk through the valley of the shadow of death,
I will fear no evil; for Thou art with me;
Thy rod and Thy staff shall comfort me.
Thou shalt prepare a table before me in the presence of them
that trouble me; Thou hast anointed my head with oil,
and my cup shall be full.
Surely, Thy loving kindness and mercy shall follow me all the
days of my life; and I will dwell in the house of the
Lord forever.

He closed the service by asking several of the ladies, including Mrs. Marion Armstrong, Mrs. J. E. McAlister, Molly Russell, and Mrs. C. B. Vivian, to lead in singing two songs.

Just as they finished the final song, the second caravan of the day pulled into view. This was the Sheets' funeral cortege, and by the time the wagon containing the casket pulled up to one side of Boothill Cemetery, the mounds over the three LS graves had been made.

Mel and his brothers, Tom and Mac, went over to stand by their playmates, Dave and Ella Sheets. The children were crying, bewildered and dazed before the mystery of death.

"It was a sad day in Tascosa, but nobody was afraid," said Mel Armstrong, who added that the town had enough of sadness, doubt, and worry without more trouble. They were fed up on it. Apparently McAlister and Lee felt the same way. The day after the funeral fifty-five cowboys, all of the LS men except one man, were in Tascosa and approached their boss, McAlister. Tobe Robinson, spokesman for the cowboys, offered to carry the fight further, but McAlister refused to do more than support them in money matters and law suits. It was rumored, perhaps with truth, that the men wanted to hang every member of the opposition and burn the houses in Tascosa to the ground.

The men wanted McAlister to lead them, and when he failed to accept responsibility, they gave up the idea. Lee concurred with McAlister after he had rushed to Tascosa in his army ambulance and had made a thorough investigation of the incident. He talked with his men, outlined the causes back of the trouble, and said that as far as he was concerned it was simply a drunken fight, since it did not arise over protection of LS property. "If it had, I would spend every dollar I've got to prosecute it," Lee said.

Murder charges were filed against Woodruff, Bousman, Emory, Lang, and the Catfish Kid, and the first trial was held at Clarendon. Jess Jenkins and his friends secured as attorney for the defense his noted brother, Charles Jenkins, who had the reputation of being one of the outstanding criminal lawyers of Texas and had defended John Wesley Hardin, the notorious Texas killer. He was later justice of the Texas Court of Appeals. His skill in handling the case resulted in a hung jury. The case was then transferred to Mobeetie, where Bousman turned state's evidence. There were many bitter clashes between the prosecution and the defense, and also with the judge. The trial at times reached a stage of wrangling and Jess Jenkins had to restrain his brother Charles from desperate action. However, the men were acquitted by the jury. Judge Colt and Colonel Winchester had long since spoken their verdicts in the cases of Sheets, Valley, Chilton, and King. The grass was even then covering their graves—numbers four, five, six, and seven on Boothill.

When the trial was over, Charles Jenkins, in his righteous anger, heatedly vowed to his brother and others present that when he returned to his home in Austin he was going to start a move which would give Judge Willis, who had presided, the trial of his life. He was forecasting the famous Willis impeachment trial, renewed troubles over the lease laws, and further showdowns between the big men and the little men in their fight for Panhandle grasslands. He had no way of knowing about the forces which were closing in to build a wall around Tascosa.

12. The Coming of Barbed Wire

THE FACE OF THE LAND was changing in larger aspects than the pre-emption and control of it by the large ranchers. Barbed wire worked a transformation and formed boundaries that natural barriers could not make. The long, steel strands, the invention of Glidden promoted by Sanborn, came thus first to the Panhandle of all the Western country. Here was an ideal area for its exploitation and the demonstration of its effectiveness in fencing cattle in and people out.

In the old days hard things could be heard about barbed wire, its inventors, and the curse it brought to the country. Its merits and demerits were still being debated by earnest individuals in the nineties. The changes it brought to the social and economic pattern of the Southwest, and particularly to great, open Texas, worried the lawmakers. In many localities the fence cutters' wars caused bloodshed and death. The big fight at Tascosa occurred in the spring of 1886; and even then the fate of that community seemed to be in a vise, which, although made of barbed wire, was as effective as if it had been made of a solid band of steel. The big fight was merely a local phase of the fight over the whole cattle world between the little men and the big interests. The days of the open range with free grass, full opportunity, rugged and vicious individualism, and all of the romance associated with those times were drawing to a close. A part of the inevitable change in the cattle business of the West was catching up with this little capital of the open range. Tascosa was being surrounded by barbed-wire fence, as completely closed in as any walled city of ancient times.

The slow but always decisive force of simple economics was revolutionizing the cattle business. Not far behind barbed wire, with its change, was a person sometimes contemptuously referred to as "the man with the hoe." The nester and the revision in land laws that came with a desire to settle and exploit the country changed the picture. Barbed wire helped make the nester farmer possible. Water holes and small tracts of land could be fenced off so that prowling cattle could neither reach water nor destroy crops. Then, too, barbed wire and the weather went hand in hand in the problems of ranching. The weather in the Panhandle during certain months of the year is the common foe of all men and animals. While Panhandle weather is pleasant most of the time, it is notorious for its violent upheavals and sudden changes which often endanger men, beasts, and plants alike. Long after the smoke had curled skyward from the guns of the cowboys at Tascosa and their arguments were stilled by death, Old Man Winter carried on his conflict with those who challenged his mastery of the plains. Cows fenced into upland pastures or ranges could not drift into the protective and warmer badlands of the Canadian River Valley. They drifted before the storm until they reached a fence. Unable to go through or over it, they stood, back to the wind and snow, heads dropped between their front legs, and froze to death. Enormous losses were recorded in the eighties by the cattlemen throughout the West from the unusually severe winters and heavy snows. Charles M. Russell, famous cowboy artist, made his start to fame with a graphic portrayal of a gaunt steer beset by wolves and labeled, "Last of 5,000."[1] "Nothing between us and the

---

[1] Charles M. Russell, *Good Medicine*, 21.

North Pole but a barbed-wire fence" was an expression that came into being shortly after barbed wire was introduced in the Canadian River country in the early eighties.

Until Glidden of DeKalb, Illinois, in 1874 got the idea of putting a sharp barb between two strands of wire and twisting it into one strand with the barbs spaced at regular intervals, fencing was a problem anywhere. It was especially difficult on the vast open ranges of Texas and the plains. Fences were put in at great cost when made of poles, lumber, or rock. Smooth wire was good only for tame farm stock; the cows of the open range walked through it as if it were not there. Many methods of fencing were experimented with by both farmers and cattlemen. For instance, George and John Leverton dug a ditch around a small field of theirs in Oklahoma. Some nesters plowed a furrow around their farms and with guns protected their properties and made the fence as effective as if it had been of wire.[2] A fence tried by the ranchers in the seventies and eighties was smooth wire charged by electricity. *The Tascosa Pioneer* had much to say about this fence and at one time proclaimed its success,[3] but it did not work because cows and horses coming in contact with it were so frightened that they were as apt to jump through the fence and tear it down as they were to jump away from it. One of the first, if not the first, electric fences in the country was built and tested in the Canadian River Valley but was soon abandoned.

Glidden's idea for a barbed fence went through several stages before it was finally perfected; but after it became an acknowledged success, cattlemen could fence their ranges, stop their herds from drifting, and prevent trespass and invasion by other herds. The cowboy who had been a herdsman and drover became more of a line rider, fence repairer,

---

[2] Roy Riddle, "The Two Little Men," *The Amarillo Sunday Globe-News*, Golden Anniversary Edition, August 14, 1938.

[3] *The Tascosa Pioneer*, September 15, 1888.

veterinarian, and windmill mechanic. The barbed-wire fence marked the end of the great free-grass cattle kingdoms but also provided greater security for the large operator who had possession of land. It literally bounded the cattle ranch and because of its cost virtually did away with the small open-range operator, the mavericker, and the cattle thief. Glidden and a partner and salesman in his enterprise, Henry B. Sanborn, saw great possibilities for barbed-wire fence in Texas and envisioned this state as their greatest potential market. They established a horse ranch in Grayson County and in 1881 moved to the Panhandle of Texas, where they promptly bought large blocks of land and soon controlled 250,000 acres of grass in Potter and Randall counties, south and east of Tascosa. One of the needs of their business was to test the barbed wire by putting it to use on their own ranges, and consequently they built the first pasture fence in the Canadian River sector in 1882. If it held for them, it would sell.

The wire was manufactured on contract by Washburn and Coen of DeKalb, Illinois, and was made by twisting together two number-nine wires. The wire in use now is generally number twelve or fourteen. This means that twelve to fourteen strands can be made out of an inch of metal, whereas only nine strands of the old wire could be obtained from an inch of material. This first wire was shipped to Dodge City and freighted with teams from there to Tascosa and on to the Frying Pan Ranch. Much of it is still in use today on the Frying Pan.

The new fencing job started at the Canadian River between West and East Amaryllis creeks and ran south along the western edge of present San Jacinto Heights in Amarillo to a point near Canyon City, approximately eighteen miles south of Amarillo. The course of the fence was then west almost to the Oldham County line and thence north to the Canadian. The pasture was enclosed on the north by a meandering fence line a short distance from the bed of the Canadian River, which connected the west and the east lines of the fence. It enclosed approximately forty thousand acres. It was later cross-fenced in two places, giving the Frying Pan excellently divided pastures. The cost of the fence was put on the Frying Pan books at $39,000.

One of the first jobs cowboys had after completing the fence was to kill off the mustang stallions on the range. The wild stallions had great ability at stealing tame mares from ranch remudas; consequently they were considered a nuisance by the ranchers. Mel Armstrong believed that he killed the last of these troublemakers, a small roan stallion which used the plains country above the head of India Creek as late as 1895.

The loyalty of a cowboy to his herd and his love for the animals under his charge are illustrated in one of the most dramatic incidents of its kind in the early history of the Frying Pan Ranch. Arthur Childs, a trusted ranch employee who was given considerable responsibility, was informed that the new wire fence which enclosed the forty thousand acres of prairie grass was a test fence. Its inventors and owners were eager that the fence be given a real test to facilitate sales and advertising. He was instructed that in the event of a storm the cattle must be allowed to drift against the fence and under no circumstances was it to be cut or let down.

With these specific orders emphasized, Childs one day faced a terrific snow of blizzard proportions on the range. It was one of those beast- and man-killing weather forays which occasionally caused great damage in the Panhandle. Heretofore the herd would have been turned loose to drift from the storm, to find shelter miles away in some small canyon, valley, or creek. The cowboys often moved with the animals and facilitated their drifting if it seemed feasible to do so, in order to give the herd the little natural protection in the country.

On this occasion the herd began drifting in front of the

storm and hit the strong four-strand fence with its cold, cruel, cutting barbs. They packed against it. Animals that drift into a fence in open country before a storm such as was then raging soon freeze. Arthur Childs watched the Frying Pan cattle drift in against the fence, test it, and then stand with heads between their legs, eyes blinded, and finally go down frozen and dying. His love for cattle and his unwillingness to see the dumb brutes sacrificed to the innovation of the wire fence won over his inclination to obey orders.

He cut the fence, drove the cattle not yet dead through the gap and into a drifting herd. Once he got the cattle through the fence and moving before the storm, he rode to the ranch headquarters and resigned his job. He had sacrificed his personal interest and his future with the Frying Pan outfit by deliberately disobeying orders because he could not stand by and see cattle frozen merely to test the holding qualities of a new barbed-wire fence.

The Arthur Childs incident was one which involved cattle only, but it serves to illustrate the possibilities for friction between new owners of vast herds, themselves carrying no more right, as a general rule, to the open-range resources than the men who worked for them. The trial fence of the Frying Pan was merely a symbol; so was Child's reaction to it. The test, however, was advertised as a success and the use of the barbed wire progressed.

In 1882, the Panhandle Cattlemen's Association, through the close co-operation of some of the large ranch owners, pushed to completion one of the longest drift fences in the West. The Turkey Track, LX, LS, LIT, and LE cattle companies pooled their resources for this fence. It had stout posts and five strands of wire—most of the early fences used four strands of wire, and the XIT fence used four strands of wire with three wire stays between posts, which were about forty feet apart. The north plains drift fence began in the breaks in New Mexico and ran east through the center of Hartley and Moore counties and then in a northeasterly direction until it reached deep into the breaks of the Canadian River at the eastern boundary of the Turkey Tracks. This was almost to the Indian Territory, and many pioneers in describing the fence say that it did extend to Indian Territory.

The LX followed the Frying Pan's fencing program by enclosing their John Ray pasture on the north side of the river. This fence now placed two fences, one on each side of the river, between the LX Ranch and Tascosa, and it cut the range of the LIT cattle to the east. Upon completion of the drift fence the LX Company ran a fence from the northwest corner of the John Ray pasture to connect with the drift fence at a point some four hundred yards east of the southeast corner of the section on which Dumas is now located. This fenced in the Prairie Company on the north and east. About the same time the LS Ranch built its fence south of the river further fencing off Tascosa and causing considerable disturbance among the nester ranchers and squatters in the Canadian River Valley. The LS tied on to the Frying Pan's southwest corner, extending due west several miles, and then turned north to the Canadian River. A large portion of the LS fence still stands and is in excellent condition despite the wear of more than fifty years. The LIT joined on to the north drift fence across the Panhandle, by bringing two lines of wire south to the Canadian River, one above and one below Tascosa. The Turkey Track was the fifth outfit to fence, and its action isolated the Canadian River country as far as the outside movement of cattle was concerned.

The XIT fencing job undoubtedly stands as one of the biggest tasks of all time. Work began on the XIT fence at Buffalo Springs, some one hundred miles north of Tascosa, in the winter of 1884. Bill Metcalf, a former buffalo hunter and frontiersman, had the contract for the fence; W. S. Mabry, who did much of the surveying in the Panhandle, had the job of surveying and staking out the locations of posts thirty feet apart along the fence line. The winter of 1884–85 was extremely cold, and soon after the survey and fencing job started, the ground became frozen and work progressed under great handicaps. The fence crews started at Buffalo Springs on the extreme north end of the ranch and went southward. During 1885 the workmen completed 162 miles of fence that reached to the Canadian and beyond along the New Mexico line. The fencers enclosed great bands of mustangs and antelope and a few small bunches of buffaloes as the cowboys drove thousands of cattle on the range.

J. M. Shannon, a Scottish sheepman from Mitchell County, was awarded the contract for the south end of the ranch in late 1885. He and his men met extreme difficulties that included a devastating prairie fire and lack of water and feed for their animals. The fencers by the fall of 1886 had erected 78½ miles of fence. This fence in its west line with its "jogs" was 260 miles long. It began in the northwest corner of Texas and extended south for 150 miles without a turn on its first stretch. The east line was 275 miles long. Line riders had to watch 575 miles of outside fence which had been built at a cost of $181,000 and required more than 300 carloads of material. Posts had been secured from the Canadian River breaks and at other places in the country where small amounts of timber were available. The materials were freighted from El Morro, Colorado, about six miles from Trinidad, and from Colorado City on the Texas and Pacific Railroad. The XIT by the latter part of 1886 had enclosed all of its land except 35,000 acres, which were not fenced immediately because the company expected to swap them for state land that lay inside the enclosed syndicate land. They continued their fencing until eventually the 3,000,000 acres of land was cut into 94 pastures and had approximately 1,500 miles of fence. A part of the XIT fence, usually the top wire when feasible, was used as a telephone line, which was erected from Tascosa to the general headquarters on the

Alamocitos in 1888. This was hailed as a great step in telephonic communication by *The Tascosa Pioneer.*[4]

The fencing of the XIT dominion near Buffalo Springs was incidental to two rangeland tragedies in 1885 and 1886, one of fire and the other of snow. The first paved the way for the second, as is often the case when "trouble comes double." Bill Metcalf, an early settler of the Cimarron and the man who built most of the XIT fence, was employed to plow a fire guard one hundred yards outside the XIT fence from Buffalo Springs southward. He began his work early in November, 1885, and used enormous gang plows pulled by six mule teams. One team and plow was followed by another a few rods behind; and as they set up this earthen guard designed to stop prairie fires, they, in turn, were followed by the cook with his wagon, which carried food and water.

Metcalf's cook was working about his wagon when through some mishap the grass about his campfire caught fire and flames spread rapidly out of control. The plow crews were five miles south of the camp and there was a fairly strong wind from the south. The cook got on a mule and rode to Trinidad, 135 miles away. Metcalf recovered the mule, but the cook left the country. The fire spread over an immense amount of country and in two days had destroyed the grass to Beaver Creek. Then the wind switched to the north and grew to gale proportions, driving the licking flames from the Beaver down to the Canadian River, some seventy-five miles to the southeast. A. W. Thompson and another cowboy, who were working in the New Mexico country, saw a brown-tinged cloud on the horizon toward the north and immediately guessed that it was a great prairie fire. Many kinds of wild animals were killed by the fire, including several small herds of buffaloes and many antelope, or were left in such helpless condition that they starved.

4 *The Tascosa Pioneer,* January 14, 1888; Haley, *The XIT Ranch,* 94.

The Coming of Barbed Wire

The weather was mild the remainder of November and through December after the big fire, but it was a calm before the great blizzard which struck the north plains on January 7, 1886. The blizzard raged for two days and three nights; it was one of the worst storms ever known in the Panhandle. The plains country was a swirling, blinding mass of snow. Thompson was lost twice in his efforts to get from the barn to the house of the ranch where he worked. Cattle, some of which still bore wounds from the prairie fire of middle November, fled before the storm. As they drifted toward the Canadian River before the icy gale, they came up against the stout five-strand drift fence across the north plains. So long as the cattle could travel, they managed to keep from freezing, but the drift fence proved a death trap. Thompson rode to the drift fence three days after the storm, and when within one to two miles of it he saw piles of dead cattle. "Never have I seen such a sickening and pitiful scene," he said. "I could have walked for miles on dead animals, stepping from one carcass to another."

The next spring there were thousands of dead, putrefying cattle behind that north plains drift fence; many small cattlemen were bankrupt; and the big companies were woefully short in their tallies. Thompson said, "One rancher recovered 80 out of 22,000 head as a result of that storm and the fence which stopped his cattle on the exposed plains."[5] Many a cowman's hopes for fortune ended in 1886 in a pile of bones and rotten hides behind the barbed-wire strands which stretched across the north plains country.

Jim East, sheriff at Tascosa, did not collect much in drift taxes after the winter of 1886, as he had before that time. He had claimed that the ranchers from northern New Mexico, eastern Colorado, and No Man's Land should pay

[5] A. W. Thompson, "Fire and Snow Caused Great Damage in Early Days," *The Amarillo Sunday Globe-News*, Golden Anniversary Edition, August 14, 1938.

a drift tax on their cattle, and although they made strenuous protests, he collected the tax. The drift fence put an end to drift taxes, which were nevertheless something of an innovation in the West.

When the XIT completed the fence across 260 miles of land to the north and west of Tascosa, the ranch not only had fenced in a great open range for its own use but had cut off free access to Tascosa for all persons who came from New Mexico and Arizona. Herds were no longer free to drift into the accustomed watering places and the grassy protection of the Canadian River lowlands. Gates were placed at certain spots on the ranch, but free travel was a thing of the past. This cost Tascosa some of its trail-herd business. For a time the XIT permitted herds to come through its property, but usually under escort, to be checked on the east side. W. F. Baird, pioneer cowboy of Canyon, tells of an instance when he helped drive a herd of cattle from below Roswell to Carson County in 1885. This traffic soon became a source of annoyance to the XIT, and, on the other hand, the merchants of Tascosa felt that they were losing business and traffic that rightfully belonged to them. As a result bad feeling grew against the ranch and the fence. As the fencing was underway, scores of Tascosa cowpunchers and citizens worked with the crews; but with the fencing completed and the trail herds and general traffic stopped, there was a depression in business at Tascosa.

The Potter-Bacon Trail, which passed through Tascosa and drove on to Dodge City, Kansas, and other cattle trails, largely unnamed, from the south to Dodge City, to Colorado, or to Montana and Wyoming, were later wiped out of existence by this fencing. Likewise, much business in the trail-herd center was lost. Outfits now were forced to go around the XIT, the LS, Frying Pan, and LX ranges, and had extreme difficulty in finding their way north.

Two of the large ranch outfits, the LS and the LIT, set

about moving the Mexican plaza residents and squatter ranchers and cowboys off of their ranges as soon as they had completed their fences on land leased under the law of 1883. In some instances the ranchers had to buy out the improvements of these people along with their herds, and in other cases they simply told them to move, and backed up the request with a court order, a show of their lease, and what appeared to be force. Once they had their ranges fenced, anyone inside that fence was actually guilty of trespassing. Consequently the population of the Canadian River Valley began to dwindle. Some of the families moved to Tascosa, others moved back into New Mexico, and others went north to Kansas, Montana, or Wyoming. Still others began to find school-land sections which they could buy or pre-empt, and moved out to various places in the Panhandle. The Tascosa school, which had been having some thirty-five to forty students prior to 1886, was one of the institutions hardest hit by the fencing of the ranges. Several families left to take up land at the head of creeks in Oldham and Potter counties and consequently took their children out of school. Typical of these were the Armstrongs, the Trujillos, and the Snyders.

The task of fencing Panhandle ranches was an enormous one which involved a great number of people and tremendous supplies. The XIT was probably the biggest fencing job in the world, but fencing the Frying Pan, the LS, the LIT, the LX, and the Matador were big jobs, too. They kept all the available nester cowboy and Mexican labor in Tascosa busy, and almost all of the early-day residents of that community worked with the fencing contractors or with the ranchers in enclosing this part of Texas.

Posts for the enormous amount of fencing needed for the open-range spaces of the Panhandle were obtained in the plains country. The task of securing them furnished much work. Crews of men with saws and axes were able to find posts from cedar, walnut, chinaberry, and hackberry groves in the Palo Duro Canyon, along the Canadian River, and in the numerous small canyons and creeks tributary to it. Some of the post supplies came from New Mexico, but by and large most of the posts came from the Panhandle-Plains area. There may be seen at many points in the Palo Duro Canyon today remains of strong wire pulleys by means of which the posts were snaked out of the canyon and up to the level land, where they were loaded on heavy wagons drawn by oxen or mules and freighted across the plains wilderness to the fence-building crews.

In the early stages of organization of the XIT Ranch, a large warehouse was built at Tascosa in 1885. Its building and operation kept a number of persons busy; and the constant flow of supplies into and out of the warehouse, plus the regular freighting outfits, gave the town the appearance of prosperity and industry. The XIT, however, did not buy from the local merchants but instead bought from wholesale concerns and contracted for the freighting from Springer, Dodge City, and Colorado City. The XIT headquarters were established on the Alamocitos Division, adding to the traffic and to the sense of importance of Tascosa and helping in some measure to salve the wound caused by the fences.

At this time the court at Tascosa was busier than usual because the country was increasing in population and activity. As yet Tascosa had not lost a county adjoined to it for judicial purposes as a result of county organization, but many proposed organizations of counties were being rumored.

It was well that the hopes brought by the XIT warehouse and headquarters and by the supply and court activities were alive, because the town was completely fenced in by 1887. It was not hard for the observer, regardless of his love for his community, to anticipate the inevitable depression and gradual death which must face this inland spot.

There was some promise of a bright future, however,

because as early as 1886 the Fort Worth and Denver was extending two rail lines, one from Fort Worth and one from Denver, which seemed destined to cross the plains of Texas, and there seemed no doubt that Tascosa would be an important shipping point on the railroad. In spite of their depression, the impending gloom caused by the barbed-wire fence, and the terrible winter, the people of Tascosa rallied and were happy over the prospects of the railroad. At last, they thought, they had something to offset the poison of barbed wire.

13. Life in Tascosa

LIFE IN TASCOSA was not all rowdyism, conviviality and brutal gunplay. There was a gradual forward movement of social forces in the face of almost insurmountable obstacles. Tribute is due the pioneer women, mothers who guided small broods of children toward higher ideals in a society which, if not degenerating, was at times utterly demoralizing. A few women in Tascosa, as elsewhere in any pioneer world, fought for decency, a factor over, above, and beyond law and order. Decency was a social force, the force which was working all over the West, transforming it from a country of pistol-packing cow thieves, rugged and at times dishonest individualists, and questionable characters to a place where a piano, an organ, or church singing might be occasionally heard. The struggle was hard and often saw little fulfillment in the pioneer generation and sometimes little progress even into the second generation; but gradually the roots of decency, culture, sobriety, and home bear fruit. The fruit often is richly flavored with high spirit and great strength of character and an understanding that denotes sound American foundations.

When Tom Jones and Kate McCauley were married in Tascosa, they had a larger than average wedding. Their friends who were making arrangements for the wedding went to the saloon to borrow the big swinging lamp. The saloon had not only the only big swinging lamp in town but also the finest furniture. Its highly polished mirrors and mahogany bar overshadowed even the furniture and equipment of the courtroom which served ten counties.

This incident is indicative of life at Tascosa and the centers of influence behind the community and the times. Most activity centered about the saloons and their accompanying gambling rooms and the dance floors in the parlors of the women who lived back of the business section, the big stores, the hotel, the livery stable, and the courthouse. The sphere of influence ran in about that same order. When C. F. Rudolph established his *Tascosa Pioneer* in 1886, he appraised society and life in Tascosa in this paragraph: "Society is not so rough as many have been led to believe. . . . It is true that our social regulations have been guiltless of church or Sunday school. But in general, the people of Tascosa are wholehearted, social and exceptionally civil."[1]

Early in 1887 he was able to report activity in this direction, but the school, when one could be organized for a term, the Union Sunday school, and the occasional religious service were always minor factors. People respected and attended an occasional service by a protestant circuit rider, and Catholics had a celebration the few times the priest came from Trinidad, Colorado, more than two hundred miles away.

"Father, dear Father, why don't you come?" were the keynote words in the mournful ballad which Louis Bousman sang best after a few drinks and the encouragement of friends about the bar. The well-known song, which is a little

[1] *The Tascosa Pioneer*, June 12, 1886.

girl's lament for her drunken father, was appropriate in those days almost anywhere in the West. Tascosa was no exception, for starting with one saloon established by Jack Ryan in 1878, the town eventually had seven emporiums for quenching the thirst and providing popular meeting places for the populace, visiting cowboys, and railroad men. One by one the saloons went out of business until in 1891 *The Tascosa Pioneer* lamented that the town had only one left.

The Equity Bar, which faced south on Main Street, was one of the largest and best-known saloons. It was established by Jack Ryan and passed to various owners, among whom were Jim East and Button Griffin. It was of adobe construction and had two large rooms about eighteen feet wide and twenty feet long. A cottonwood beam in the center of the room helped support the roof. A hectagon-shaped column made of finished lumber was placed around the cottonwood beam and provided protection when Jim East killed Tom Clark. The main room had a bar across its east side, and in the northwest corner was a small raised platform on which five or six barrels of whiskey stood. The back room of the saloon was reached through an open archway and was used as a game room. It contained chairs and gaming tables. Dancehall girls were permitted in this room but never at the bar in the main room of the saloon. This design was typical of most of the saloons in the West Texas region, although some were smaller and had only one room.

The Jenkins and Dunn saloon faced north on Main Street at the corner of Spring Street. It had a tin roof and the bar was on the east side of the main room that contained the small platform rack for barrels of whiskey.

The Cattleman's Exchange Bar, located near the Cone and Duran store, faced north on Main Street.

The Charley Ross saloon occupied a large building at the corner of the square. Ross operated his Barber Shop and Tonsorial Parlor, the only one Tascosa ever had, in one part of the front room of this saloon. He was both barber and bartender.

Jess Jenkins operated a large and popular saloon in Hogtown. The saloon was the scene of Tascosa's second largest killing when Gene Watkins and two Mexicans were killed and another man injured. Jenkins was also interested in a saloon in Tascosa proper.

Button Griffin's saloon was always popular. It was about two doors down Main Street from the Equity Bar, and between it and the Exchange Hotel. Griffin also had an interest in another saloon in Tascosa.

One of the best stories to come out of Tascosa had its setting in Griffin's saloon. George "Pidgeon" Ely was a kid of a cowpuncher when he came into Tascosa with a trail herd in the late seventies. Tired of the hardships of trail driving, he had ambitions to become a bartender and applied to Griffin for a job as apprentice. Griffin hired him and let him bring his bedroll and sleep in a back room. Ely washed glasses, swept floors, cleaned the place, and kept the fire stoked in the big pot-bellied iron stove that stood in the center of the room.

One night while a heavy snow and ice storm was raging, Griffin decided to go home and leave the saloon with the youngster. He left, telling Ely to keep the place open about an hour longer. The young former cowboy was happily polishing glasses and the big mirrors of the bar-display section when the door opened and a huge man wearing a bulky buffalo-robe overcoat stepped inside. He shook himself like a giant dog and flipped the snow and ice over the room. He walked over to the hot stove and hugged it. Then he commented briskly on the weather and ordered a cocktail. Ely had never made one; however he stirred up a mixture from the contents of several bottles, shook it, and handed a liberal gobletful to the big man. The customer drank it down at one swallow, gasped, bent over the stove, and pulled his coat tightly about his stomach.

"Make me another," he gasped.

Ely, happy over the success of his bartending, outdid his previous effort in the new cocktail. He walked over to the stove and handed it to the man. There was a quick movement. The surprised lad felt a gun barrel against his ribs. "Now drink it yourself and we will die together," growled the visitor.

Tascosa did not call the small two- and three-room houses that clustered in the flats behind the saloons and big merchandise stores a red-light district, nor did it always regard the dance-hall girls and prostitutes who lived there as persons apart from the rest of the town. There were a number of these women. Some had children who went to school with other children and played with them about town. There was no class or moral distinction among the children. Most every woman had a favorite sweetheart, a cowboy or gambler, with whom she lived. Some married and settled down to homemaking. Other couples asked no questions about the past and moved elsewhere to rear families of their own. Others moved to Amarillo, Raton, or Trinidad as activity in Tascosa slowed to a standstill.

"Shorty" Delaine, a clerk in one of the big general stores, more than met his match in a group of the girls and their cowboys. His friends as a practical joke put up his name for constable at an election. He took the honor and the office seriously and had the blacksmith make him a badge. He bought a big pistol and strapped it on for all to see. Pranksters in the Jess Jenkins saloon faked a charge, and the constable came down to make an arrest for vagrancy. As he walked into the gambling room, one of the girls slipped up behind him, threw her apron over his head and took the pistol away from him. She marched him outside into the street with his own gun jammed against his back. Delaine resigned his office immediately. Whenever the event was mentioned afterwards, he brought out cigars for everyone present.

One of the most notorious of the women was Rocking Chair Emma; her rival was Sally Emory. Then there were Jo Rice, Santa Fé Mol, Mustang Mae, Spotted Jack, Dolly Varden, Ole Buck, and others with even more colorful names. Some of them had come to Tascosa when Ranger Captain Arrington cleaned out Mobeetie. Some had drifted into Tascosa on their treks from town to town in the West. They frequented the back or gambling rooms of the saloons and made their entrance and exit through the back doors, which were convenient to their small homes. They bet on horse races and played a vivacious part in the seamy side of a boisterous frontier.

Joe Bowers sold three of the women—Brady, Nelly, and Buck—some drugs supposed to help a stomach complaint then epidemic in Tascosa. The medicine made the three women dangerously ill. Other dance-hall girls did not hesitate to summon the help of the wives of the leading men of the town, and these women lent their neighborly assistance without question or hesitation. There was no quibbling over moral issues when people were sick and needed help.

The houses in which the women lived had a front room or parlor, a bedroom, and a kitchen. Some of the women kept their places neat and tidy with lace curtains and flowers for the windows, but others were sloppy in their housekeeping and rowdy in their behavior.

Tascosa was famous for its gambling. Among the populace were a number of professional gamblers. Others came by from time to time from other Western towns, and practically every businessman, lawyer, official, and cowboy gambled. Every saloon had its gambling games and ran faro, monte, and poker tables. The two livery stables were the scene of many big card games, while the hotel had its share of poker. Players often backed their luck and skill at cards with great stacks of silver dollars and twenty-dollar gold pieces. Some of the games resembled the fastest and biggest play of the mining towns. Some ran for several days and nights. Mickey McCormick, Lon Jenkins, Tom Emory, Louis Bousman, and the Catfish Kid were gamblers to be reckoned with in any company. Gambling was the sport of almost every man who came to the town, and it was the business of a large number who stayed there.

Tascosa, as the county seat of Oldham County with nine other Panhandle counties attached to it for judicial purposes, was for a few years one of three important legal capitals of the great cattle-range empire. The others were Mobeetie, which had the honor of being the first legal capital of the Panhandle, and Clarendon, which was dubbed the "Saints' Roost" of the area. The same district judge, Frank Willis, and the same district or prosecuting attorney, Temple Houston, served at all three points, where court was held twice a year and lasted for about two weeks.

The semiannual meeting of the court was a gala affair. Virtually all work in the region was suspended, and the towns were crowded beyond their capacity. Horse races were arranged and other events planned. The court and the attorneys traveled together in buckboard or hack. When the court sessions were over, they drank, played poker, and engaged in story-telling bees that became traditional. Some had classical educations while others had little knowledge of law but much of human nature and the eloquence and tricks it took to sway people. W. H. Woodman, "an Englishman by birth, a Virginian by education, and a Texan by his own choice and the grace of God," was one of the latter type. He was a small man and wore his raven-black hair long, reaching to his shoulders after the theatrical styles of the day. It was rumored that he had been a Shakespearian actor. He was called "The Lone Wolf of the Yellowhouse" and won most of his cases by his persuasive oratory or by some trick pulled to influence the jurors. Once when a candidate for public office, he spoke from some planks placed on top of a pile of dry cow chips. Noticing this fact, his opponent declared, when it came his time to speak, that he had a specific platform while his adversary seemed to obscure his by standing on it.

Temple Houston was the first district attorney. He dressed in flashy clothes, often wore a beautiful, large white hat, and had courtly, graceful manners. He was a master storyteller and an orator of national fame. His oration in defense of a fallen woman at Woodward, Oklahoma, ranks along with Senator Vest's eulogy to the dog as a classic. Moreover, he was an expert marksman, a favorite with the ladies, and popular with men.

Judge Frank Willis was one of the best-known and most fearless frontier judges and the scion of a large family of Panhandle lawmakers. His impeachment trial in connection with the Texas land-lease laws was one of the big political events of the times, and he was declared innocent of charges of favoritism to the large cattlemen of the Panhandle.

J. N. Browning, who rose to the position of lieutenant governor of Texas, in connection with the land-law controversy was another picturesque character in the legal profession.

Judge H. H. Wallace, tall, stately, and polished Virginian, was Tascosa's most famous local attorney. He was typical of his contemporaries and read the Episcopal prayer service for most of the funerals at Tascosa, including the services for the victims of the big fight.

The community's importance as a court center lessened as the counties attached to Oldham began to organize themselves. Court sessions then attracted fewer persons and less activity. What had once been a gala state occasion now became a humdrum monotonous gathering of a few people involved more or less in civil and land suits.

Jack Ryan, serving on a jury in district court at one of the terms, was "hanging" a jury which wanted to convict a man of an offense. He alone had held out for a day and a night and well into the next day, when there came a tapping on the jury-room window. A messenger whispered to Ryan that a big poker game had been going on in his place during the time the jury was out and that the players were about to break the bank. Ryan demanded a retake of the vote by the jury, cast his ballot for conviction, and urged the foreman to hurry in the verdict so he could get into the game.

Tascosa was famous for its peace officers. It claimed among them such famous names as Pat Garrett, Cape Willingham, Jim East, Louis Bousman, Tobe Robinson, and John Pierce. That these men understood human nature and appreciated their fellow man was shown by the action of Tobe Robinson in releasing all the prisoners in the county jail for a Fourth of July celebration. *The Tascosa Pioneer* carried an item on the event, commenting that the prisoners did not abuse their liberty and were back at the jail ready to be locked in their cells at midnight.[2]

In 1889 under the leadership of Mrs. Cecil H. Withington, wife of the manager of the LS Ranch, donations were made to overhaul the old adobe schoolhouse and convert it into a small Catholic chapel. It was called St. Barnabas Church, a mission attached to St. Anthony's Church at Dalhart. A new schoolhouse had been erected. Prior to this, Catholic services had been held in the long, wide hall of the Casimero Romero home. On one of the first visits of the priest from Trinidad, sixteen babies, some of them rather hefty for babies, were baptized. Father Patrick J. Murphy made regular missionary calls at Tascosa in the years when the town was in its decline. In fact, the Catholic church was erected long after the doom of the community had been sealed and only when Romero had sold his home to a Protestant family. No Protestant church was ever organized, and Tascosa never had a resident pastor or priest.

<hr/>

[2] *The Tascosa Pioneer,* July 6, 1889.

Photograph by T. M. Caldwell

THE CANADIAN RIVER NEAR TASCOSA

Photograph by T. M. Caldwell

BUFFALOES ON THE RANGE

Courtesy Mel Armstrong

ST. BARNABAS MISSION

the first building erected for a schoolhouse at Tascosa, about 1885

BOOTHILL CEMETERY

showing graves of Valley, King, and Chilton about 1934

Once an immigrant preacher stopped in Tascosa because of high water on the Canadian. He lectured one night and preached the next. On the third night of his stay he got drunk and quarreled with his wife, and Mel Armstrong put him in jail. When sober again, he was released on condition that he get out of town and cause no more disturbance.

The moving religious spirit in the community was Grandma Cartwright. She came to Tascosa early in its existence searching for her son. With a considerable amount of money on his person, he had left Dodge City with a group of buffalo hunters when the hunting was at its best and danger at its height. Word came to his mother that he had been killed and his money stolen. She came to the buffalo hunting grounds to find him and his money and decided to stay in Tascosa, as she believed that he would come there sometime. She proved to be a neighborhood godsend. She did laundry work for the cowboys, helped in sickness and distress, and generally did good. One day some boys playing near her home heard a voice raised in lamentation and crept nearer. She was kneeling in her garden, praying for the return of her boy.

The Reverend J. T. Bloodworth, one of the Panhandle's noted circuit-riding pastors, was one of the first to hold services at Tascosa, in June, 1886, and he brought about the organization of a union Sunday school. Mrs. F. G. Copeland was chosen superintendent, Mrs. I. P. Ryland, secretary, Mrs. Rowland, treasurer, and Mrs. E. Godwin-Austen, librarian. Mrs. Cone and Mrs. Rinehart were the teachers. On his second trip a short time later cowboys and young rowdies sent a delegation to his room with a note soliciting money to buy liquor for one of their number. *The Pioneer* reported that the preacher took the prank good naturedly.

Mrs. Cartwright gradually became the leader of the Union Sunday school. When the schoolhouse was erected, she made it her business to see that the bell rang out for the

Sunday school every Sunday morning. After she moved with her children to the head of the Alamocitos, where they had staked out a claim, she was not able to attend regularly, and Gran Cole and her sister, Aunt Sue Jackson, conducted the Sunday school for a time. Mrs. E. A. McKinnon was a teacher and a mainstay in the Sunday school around 1911 and until the community was no longer large enough to support services.

The first public school was organized in Tascosa in 1885 and a contract entered into between the Board of Trustees, composed of Dolores Duran, I. P. Ryland, and C. W. Croft, with Clayton McCrea, teacher. McCrea in 1942 recounted in part this experience:

"The school house was not built when school opened. The trustees got a room in the old adobe courthouse. It had been abandoned as a courtroom. There were no fixtures such as desks, recitation seats, teacher's table, blackboard, no stove to heat the room, just a little Mexican fireplace of that day. We got tables like a counter, made small tables out of store boxes for the small lads. We used boxes and benches for seats. I never had 'herded' pupils like that and there was about 30 pupils. I don't recall the books used but they were scarce. School supplies were not carried by any of the stores so any books or any series were welcomed.

"The principal thing the trustees wanted to do was to get the children off the street and give them plain reading, writing, and arithmetic. There were no advanced pupils as high as the fourth or fifth grade. Most of them could neither read nor write. During October, November, and part of December, we had some 10 to 12 Mexicans from 12 to 21 years of age. They had moved in from up the river. Few could speak English but all wanted to learn to speak, read, and write in English. Mary Duran understood English well and she helped in teaching the Mexican children. I never had any trouble with the Mexican pupils. All the trouble was with the Americans scrapping among themselves. The Dance Hall 'get' and the better town youngsters just didn't mix.[3] Believe me I had plenty of headaches. The new school was adobe built, about 20 by 30, shingle roofed, plastered inside, had a good blackboard and good equipment. It was located away from the Main Street. After setting up in the new school house we had 15 American children and 10 or 12 Mexicans. The subjects I taught them were Orthography, Reading, Writing, Arithmetic and Geography, in the intermediate grades. The school funds played out and I closed school on Friday of the week the 'Killing Bee' occurred.

"There was no church or Sunday School in Tascosa up to that time. The town was wider open on Sunday than usual."

Other efforts were made to hold school, and one existed for short periods of time most years thereafter. *The Pioneer* reported several times the difficulty of organizing the school and keeping it going. One of the most discouraging events to the community was the departure of Professor Ben Lawson to the newly organized town of Hartley on the north plains.

This teacher had held the Christmas tree and school recital the year before he left for Hartley. Every school child in the community and many parents, cowboys, and friends came for the program. Al Morris, who played Santa Claus, had considerable difficulty with his costume, much to the delight of the youngsters.

Clayton McCrea commented on the pleasant relations between the Mexican and American children. Boys and girls who attended the school also attest the fine comradeship which existed between the Mexicans and Americans. Lifelong friendships grew out of those school days. The little boys during recess periods in 1888 ran to the top of the red hills near the river to look toward the horizon to the south

[3] This statement has been questioned by persons who attended the school.

and watch the railroad construction crews build the grade and lay the steel.

Tascosa's biggest wedding was that of Mel Armstrong and Miss Clishie Mitchell. He was nineteen years old and she was sixteen. The ceremony was held in the Tascosa schoolhouse on February 23, 1898. Miss Mitchell was the daughter of Mr. and Mrs. C. L. Mitchell, who were employed on the Frying Pan Ranch in 1892 when the youthful pair became acquainted. Mel had been a cowboy since his thirteenth year, when he began work for the Frying Pan as a horse wrangler. At this time he was in charge of a pack of wolfhounds for the LS Ranch.

Formal invitations to the wedding were written by Miss Lillian East, teacher at Tascosa and the sister of Jim East. Lizzie Rinehart, now Mrs. Al Popham of Amarillo, came to play the wedding march. Mrs. Marion Armstrong, mother of Mel, who had left Tascosa years before, came for a two weeks' visit and to be present for the wedding.

The crowd assembled early. Ed Payne and Marshall Price were ushers and promptly at eight o'clock the schoolhouse doors were thrown open for the entrance of the bridal party. Vince Stambaugh, LIT cowboy, and John Bouldin, LS cowboy, entering with Miss Nellie Hamilton and Miss Lillian East, preceded the bride and groom to an improvised arch made of a wagon bow decorated with evergreens and placed in the northwest corner of the room. The couple stood beneath the arch while Judge H. H. Wallace performed the marriage ceremony. Afterward they received the congratulations and good wishes of friends who filled the schoolhouse and overflowed into the yard. The wedding was followed by a dance in which old and young joined. They stepped to the music of Mac Hood, XIT cowboy, who played the violin, and Ed Payne, LIT cowboy, who played the guitar.

At midnight supper was served in the hotel by Mr. and Mrs. Bill Anderson. The dining room was equipped for the occasion with two large tables with long benches from the district courtroom. Coffee was made in the big coffeepots used on the LIT Ranch. Bread had been ordered from Frank Hassen in Amarillo. Mrs. Frank Mitchell had baked the wedding cake. Other foods for the wedding supper were home-cured hams, fried, smothered, and baked chicken, roast beef, many varieties of salad, pies, cakes, homemade preserves, pickles, and jellies. As fast as one table had been served and the meal completed, the diners returned to the dance to make way for others. The dance did not close until daybreak, and Mrs. Mitchell held open house for all who remained in Tascosa the next day.

The couple received many useful and beautiful gifts. The bride was highly complimented on her wedding dress, which was of white brocaded albatross cloth—a fine, thin woolen cloth of crepy appearance—from Sanger Brothers in Dallas. It was trimmed with soft, frilly lace. Miss East had made a wax wreath simulating orange blossoms for the bride and a buttonhole bouquet for the groom.

A partial list of the guests read like a "Who's Who" of the leading pioneers and ranchers of the plains country.[4]

[4] Guests from the LS Ranch: Walter Bliss, Hannibal Blain, Anderson Witherspoon, Raymond Witherspoon, Johnny Jones, Will Bouldin, John Bouldin, Louis Capps, Jack Bradley, Jim Whitfield, John Snider, J. W. Peacock, Mr. and Mrs. Dolph Meyers, Bob Fields, Frank Freeman, Dave Jones, Sylvester Kernen, Harry McGee, Bill Ray, Ben Mays, Joe Christy, Bob Dudley, Jack Cooper, Hamblin Hill, Walter Hamilton, Tom Goodman; from the LX Ranch: Charlie Gource, Bill Troyman, Hawley Plemons, George Hayden, Clem Johnson, Rich Crump, Jim Bell; from Amarillo: Miss Fannie Denton, Miss Martha Snider, Mr. and Mrs. H. B. Hayden, Mr. and Mrs. Hank Siders, Mrs. Al Popham, Mrs. R. H. Seewald, Miss Mayme Cochran; from Tascosa: Mrs. Sandoval and daughter, Marcellus Sandoval, Mr. and Mrs. Theodore Briggs, Mr. and Mrs. Tom Harland, Mr. and Mrs. Meeks, Mr. and Mrs. A. L. Turner and family, Al Morris, Mrs. William Reed and family, Mrs. Mary Cole, Sam Killen, Tom Jones, Mr. and Mrs. Joe Bowers, Mr. and Mrs. Steve Price, Marsh Price, Aunt Sue Jackson, Mrs. Aragon and family, Mr. and Mrs. J. H. McGee, Mr. and Mrs. Bill Blevins, Mr. and Mrs. Bill Simpson, Mr. and Mrs. Bill Anderson, Grandma Cartright, Mr. and Mrs. Cecil Withington, Mr. and Mrs. Jim

Weddings generally called for an all-night cowboy dance, and in addition New Year's Eve called for a dance. Cowboys took time off at that time of the year to celebrate Christmas and to come to town. The dances, always a big attraction, sometimes lasted more than one night. They were held at various ranch headquarters in the Tascosa country, at Pedro Romero's home, at the home of Casimero Romero, or at other places in Tascosa.

Hospitality, loads of food, a strict code of manners, and the cowboy dolled up and diked out in his best Sunday-go-to-meeting clothes were interesting features of the dances. None of them ever stopped before daybreak. A cowboy might work all year long without attending a social event, but if it were at all possible, the New Year's ball in the Tascosa country or some wedding and dance found him there "with bells on."

The people of Tascosa made social occasions out of picnics, fishing and hunting, and plum-gathering trips. These events did not come often, but a survey of *The Tascosa Pioneer* during the years of its publication reveals news items about them from time to time. C. B. Vivian, county and district clerk, made one of these picnics in the Cheyenne Grove the occasion for his wedding and had the ceremony performed at the outing site. He had issued his own wedding

May, Tom Armstrong, Mr. and Mrs. Ysabel Gurules, Mr. and Mrs. Scottie Wilson, Mr. and Mrs. Jim Swain, Mr. and Mrs. Mickey McCormick, Mr. and Mrs. Ysedro Serno, Mrs. Moore and family, Charles Russell. From other points came: J. Montgomery, Ojo Bravo Ranch, Channing, Texas; Miss Bessie Hammer, Ojo Bravo Ranch, Channing, Texas; Mr. and Mrs. Jess Jenkins, Hartley, Texas; Mrs. E. C. G. Austin and family, Channing, Texas; Mr. and Mrs. Otho Mimms, Channing, Texas; Emmit Mimms, Channing, Texas; Mr. and Mrs. J. H. East, Channing, Texas; James McMasters, Channing, Texas; E. A. McKinnon, Channing, Texas; Miss Lula Brown, Channing, Texas; Miss Maggie Eubanks, Channing, Texas; Bob Duke, Channing, Texas; Mr. and Mrs. Henry Timble, Channing, Texas; Mr. and Mrs. Celco Trujillo, Rita Blanca; Mr. and Mrs. Cruis Trujillo, Rita Blanca; Mr. and Mrs. Jim Lucero, Rita Blanca; Mr. and Mrs. Henry Kimball of Tascosa were also present.

license. Outings on the river and the creeks tributary to it were held by family groups and friends. Often a basket lunch was carried along, and fish caught in the streams might be fried to furnish the meat dish.

The Tascosa Pioneer carried several news items that tried to create interest in a dramatic club, but only one program was recorded for this group. There was a small group of singers, who displayed their talent chiefly at funerals.

Social life in Tascosa and the Canadian country was drab and outside contacts were infrequent, but a more disturbing factor to the women was the lack of doctors and facilities for caring for the sick. This was especially distressing to women in childbirth. Whereas the Indian woman might stop beside the trail, give birth to her baby, and in a few hours continue her journey, the pioneer American woman, rugged as she was, needed help. Often children were born without benefit of either doctor or midwife. Sometimes the mother had her ordeal alone. One Panhandle ranch wife gave birth to every one of her three children alone. In each instance the doctor, who had to come by horseback from a long distance, was too late.

For several years after the departure of Dr. Hoyt the town was without a doctor at all. C. W. Croft, an educated Englishman who served successfully as cook, horse wrangler, and male nurse about town, also served as doctor, and was soon called by that title. He knew something of medicine and pharmacy and rendered the community service to the best of his knowledge and ability for many years. Dr. J. M. Shelton also served the community for a few years. Tascosa, however, was without a doctor more often than with one.

The most pitiable deaths that resulted from the lack of medical attention or the failure to use it in childbirth were those of Mrs. James E. Wyness and her baby. She had come from Scotland to marry James E. Wyness, himself a native of that country. He had saved his money while she waited out the years to make the trip to America. She arrived in Tascosa after hardships both at sea and on the long journey from the seacoast to the interior of the country. The two were married in Tascosa and were supremely happy in their new home on the LX Ranch. Plans had been made to take her to Fort Dodge for the birth of the child, but there was a forced delay and the baby was born under extreme difficulties with only local women acting as midwives. She died in a few days, and the baby soon followed her.

Wyness, heartbroken, asked his friend John Arnot, another native of Scotland, to select some place on the Canadian River that looked as near like their native Scotland as possible. Arnot selected a site near the LX Ranch headquarters about one-half mile north of the river, which seemed to him a bit of country typical of their native heath. The mother and babe were buried there.

The lack of social activity and the hazards of frontier life were not a serious check on romance in Tascosa. Wherever man and maid meet, there will be love, and this picturesque little range trading center off the beaten paths had its share of romance. Mickey McCormick and his pretty girl, "Frenchy," lend an air of storied enchantment and a certain mystery to Tascosa. Mickey was a small Irish gambler and livery-stable operator. Frenchy was a dance-hall girl who had run away from a convent in Louisiana, migrated by easy stages to St. Louis, Dodge City, and then to Mobeetie, where, when she was eighteen years of age, McCormick had seen her. It had been love at first sight, and he had brought her to Tascosa with him.

Alexander "Scotty" Wilson, the *alcalde* or justice of the peace at Tascosa, loved his liquor but he was not always able to raise enough money for it. When the first book of marriage licenses to reach Oldham County arrived, Scotty and the county clerk held a conference. The next day Scotty called in the dance-hall girls and the cowboys and gamblers with whom they had been living without benefit of clergy. His language was colorful and sharp as he told the couples present that law and order were coming to the community and that it behooved them to buy their licenses and be married in legal form. His closing remarks were a demand.

Compliance with this order was prompt, and among the couples who bought licenses and were married were Mickey and Frenchy. They later were married again by a Catholic priest. Frenchy always refused to tell her maiden name or talk of her girlhood. She was a beautiful woman, and the two were ideally happy. Sometimes she helped Mickey at the gaming tables. At other times, if a woman were in the gambling room and Mickey's luck was running bad, she would order the woman out of the room. The two were constant lovers, and when Mickey died in 1912 Frenchy swore she would stay near his grave as long as she lived. She died in 1941, having lived alone for more than a quarter of a century in the home he had built for her. During most of that time she was the town's only link between the modern world and its colorful past. Her love story has attracted many writers and other interested persons. The priest who said her burial rites stressed her fidelity and paid high tribute to her constancy to an ideal against great odds. Reporters referred to her as the "last of the Girls of the Golden West."

One cattle trail, the Tascosa–Dodge City trail, is marked on the map as having its beginning on Tascosa's Main Street. While off the route of the more widely used and popularly known cattle trails, Tascosa did attract much trail-herd business. The groups of cowboys who came with herds stopped in the town long enough to restock supplies, to mail letters, and to refresh themselves if circumstances permitted. Frequent efforts were made to attract more trail-herd trade, and *The Tascosa Pioneer* carried several editorials and news stories that referred to this matter.

Tascosa, skimpy on cattle-trail routes, had its share of

freight, stage, and mail lines for an isolated Western ranch-supply center. One of these freight and stage trails was the Tascosa–Dodge City freight route, whose 242 miles were logged as follows: Tascosa to Little Blue stage station, 35 miles; Little Blue to Jim Cator's place "Zulu," 30 miles; Cator's place to Hardesty's ranch, 40 miles; Hardesty's ranch to Jim Lane's on Beaver Creek, 35 miles; Lane's to Hines Crossing on the Cimarron, 40 miles; Cimarron to Hoodu Brown's on Crooked Creek, 20 miles; Brown's to Dodge City, 42 miles. Another stage, freight, and mail route was from Mobeetie to Tascosa and from Tascosa to Las Vegas. Two freight trail routes ran from Springer, New Mexico, to Tascosa after the Santa Fé had reached that point in New Mexico. One of these routes ran from Springer by Knell's store at Tesquesquite, New Mexico, but it was rarely used by heavily loaded wagons because the long, steep descent from the top of the mesa at Knell's store was dangerous. The route most generally used from Springer to Tascosa was: Springer to Ute Creek, by Jaritis and Chico creeks, 50 miles; Ute Creek to head of the Tramperos, 16 miles; head of the Tramperos to turnoff, 4 miles northeast of García's store, Tramperos post office, 20 miles; turnoff through Charley Adams's draw to crossing of Tramperos Creek, IL Ranch, 20 miles; Tramperos Creek to Antelope Springs through Leon G. Shaw cedar brakes, 15 miles; Antelope Springs to Monia Draw, 10 miles; Monia to Entrania Spring, 10 miles; Entrania to Monilloso to Narvise Spring, south to the Canadian and thence to Tascosa, 74 miles. This made a total of 215 miles. No one had permanent residence along the Tascosa–Springer trail from the Ute Creek crossing to the Tramperos, 56 miles, nor from the IL to the Canadian, 75 to 80 miles, though watering places were available along the way.

Along these routes in the eighties one met a heterogeneous group of freighters. Some of them had one wagon drawn by only two horses or mules. Others used four and six animals. Some used wagons drawn by oxen. Some of the freighters hauled four and five tons. Their charge depended on classification and bulk of their cargoes. Freighters came from local ranches, neighboring localities, and other states. They were a hospitable but rough and ready crowd. Their fare was simple, but a traveler on horseback or in a buggy was welcome to share it with them. The favorite food of one freighter when he stopped in midafternoon to let his oxen or mules "rest and blow" was a strip of raw salt bacon placed between sourdough biscuit.

Some of this enormous freight traffic went to the big stores in Tascosa, which boasted annual sales of $250,000, and some of it went direct to the ranches. Salesmen from the Springer and Dodge City houses called on the ranches in search of their business. They came by buckboard and carried beds, tents, and camp equipment. A salesman was treated as an honored guest at a ranch. His team was cared for as were the needs of himself and his driver. The day following his arrival at the ranch no business was permitted or discussed. A ride over the prairies and through the ranch herds was made; and hunting for quail, antelope, or wolves was a sport. The ranch foreman, bookkeeper, or other trusted employees accompanied the salesman. On their return from the day's visit over the ranch, a specially cooked meal was awaiting them. The residents of the ranch then gathered around to hear the news from the outside world.

The next morning the ranch manager, bookkeeper, clerk, and other employees were assembled in the ranch office. Lists of goods needed for six months or a year were made and prices discussed. How many cars of sacked corn, how much sugar, coffee, spice, salt, dried and canned fruit, and salt pork would be needed? Included in the orders would be saddles for the cowboys, bales of rope, hardware, and other materials necessary to operate a big outfit. The bill might run into several thousand dollars.

KEY TO MAP OF OLD TASCOSA

Redrawn from a map constructed by John R. Snider and H. H. Hutson in 1937 and based on a survey made by W. D. Twichell in 1887, corrected by Twichell in 1938.

1. Wright and Farnsworth General Store
2. McMasters' store and post office
3. W. S. Mabry, surveyor's office
4. Charley Ross and wife's millinery shop
5. Shelton Drug Store
6. Russell Hotel (Exchange Hotel)
7. P. H. Sewall Jewelry Store
8. Cattle Exchange Saloon
9. Scotty Wilson's restaurant
10. John King Drug Store
11. Jim East Saloon
12. Joe Krause and Tobe Robinson's livery stable
13. Louis Bousman's residence
14. Jenkins and Dunn Saloon
15. Jesse Sheets' restaurant (North Star)
16. Henry Kimball's blacksmith shop
17. Mickey McCormick's livery stable
18. Adobe shacks
19. Cone and Duran Mercantile Store
20. J. W. Cone's residence
21. Ira Rinehart's store
22. Dolores Duran's residence
23. Ira Rinehart's residence
24. Adobe
25. Adobe
26. H. H. Wallace's residence
27. Jack Ryan's residence
28. Dunn's residence
29. Mrs. Jesse Sheets' residence
30. Drift-Wood Brown's residence
31. Byrum's residence
32. Jess Jenkins' residence
33. C. B. Vivian (later Jim East's) residence
34. I. P. Ryland's residence
35. Ysedero Sierna's residence
36. Mickey McCormick's residence
37. Miguel Tafolla's residence
38. Cruz Trujillo's residence
39. Jose Castillo's residence
40. Widow Moore's residence
41. Mark Snider's residence
42. School building
43. John Ross' residence
44. Henry Kimball and Frank Romero's residence
45. Dr. J. M. Shelton's residence
46. Bill Warlick's place
47. Marion Armstrong's residence
48. Dugout
49. A. M. Austin's residence
50. Juan Gomez, Alfonso Padillo, and Felis Castillo's residence
51. Frosty Tomb's residence
52. Mae's place
53. Josephine Rice's place
54. Emma Walker's place
55. Dolly Varden's place
56. Dan Cole's residence
57. Slats' (manager of Mickey's livery stable) residence
58. John Pierce's residence
59. Fisherman Russell's residence
60. Billy the Kid's camping spot in Tascosa

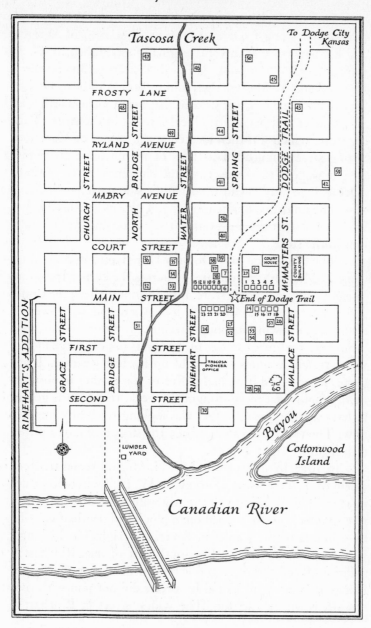

The two major stores in Tascosa were Wright and Farnsworth's and Cone and Duran's. The firm of Wright and Farnsworth was the one originally established by G. J. Howard, who later took J. E. McMasters as his partner. Howard and McMasters then sold to Bob Wright of Dodge City, who owned a great store at that place. Farnsworth was his manager and had a little local interest in the store. This big store, which was then located at the corner of Main and Spring streets, unloaded its tons of merchandise from the freight wagons at its side entrance on Spring Street. Often a great, high wagonload of salt pork side meat (sowbelly) would be unloaded in one morning. The handlers used large hay hooks to lift the meat out of the wagon and lay it in salt bins in the store.

John W. Cone and Dolores Duran operated the big Cone and Duran store diagonally across the corner from the Wright and Farnsworth store. It had formerly been the Cone and Edwards store. Although it was stocked with everything from sewing-machine needles to heavy hardware, sometimes the store ran out of certain types of merchandise when freight wagons were held up by bad weather. John Cone, when asked if he had coffee or some other important item, would then reply, tongue in cheek, that he was going to have it right away, in fact was looking for it any minute now. Then he would step outside the store and look up the trail for the freight wagons.

In 1937 John Snider and H. H. Hutson reconstructed a map of Tascosa using a survey by W. D. Twitchell, made in 1887. This map showed the townsite to be a rectangular plot six blocks wide, with about a block and one-half cut off by a bayou of the Canadian River, and eight blocks long. It was in two additions. The south part of one, Rinehart's addition, faced the river and extended north for two large blocks and one small block. Its streets did not join with the original townsite addition. The widest street in Rinehart's

addition was Bridge Street. West of Bridge Street was Grace
Street, while to the east was Rinehart Street and Wallace
Street. The addition, however, formed the south side of Main
Street, and then to the south was First Street and Second
Street, and the riverbank.

Tascosa Creek meandered through both additions, but
most of its course lay in Water Street. The main addition had
its Main Street on the south. Running east and west were
Court Street, Mabry Avenue, Ryland Avenue, and Frosty
Lane. Streets running north and south from the west side of
the town were Church Street, North Bridge Street, Water
Street, Spring Street, and McMaster Street. The Dodge City
Trail had its beginning in the business district at Main and
Spring and went a block up Spring before it curved across
to McMasters Street in front of the school building and con-
tinued north up McMasters and out into the hills beyond.

The reconstruction by these two men shows fifty-nine
business and residence houses. This just about represents the
solid, substantial Tascosa prior to the railroad boom and for
a period of years thereafter. Clustered about Main and Spring
and McMasters and Main and Rinehart and Wallace streets
in the Rinehart addition were most of the business houses and
the courthouse. They were: McMasters' store and post office,
Wright and Farnsworth's store, W. S. Mabry, surveyor's office, Charley Ross and wife's millinery shop, Shelton Drug
Store, Exchange Hotel, P. H. Sewall Jewelry Store, Cattle Exchange Saloon, Scotty Wilson's restaurant, John King Drug
Store, Jim East Saloon, Joe Krause and Tobe Robinson's livery stable, Louis Bousman's residence, Jenkins and Dunn
Saloon, the North Star Restaurant, Henry Kimball's blacksmith shop, Mickey McCormick's livery stable, adobe shacks,
Cone and Duran Mercantile Store, the *Tascosa Pioneer* office,
and I. Rinehart's store. Thirty blocks in the town plat had
no houses. Twenty had one or more houses. They were located largely between Bridge and North Bridge streets and

Wallace and McMasters streets. Besides those named above, which were concentrated in about two blocks, in 1887 there were the residences of J. W. Cone, Dolores Duran, Ira Rinehart, two adobe residences, H. H. Wallace, Jack Ryan, Sam Dunn, Mrs. Jesse Sheets, Drift-Wood Brown, Jess Jenkins, C. B. Vivian (later Jim East), I. P. Ryland, Ysedero Sierna, Mickey McCormick, Miguel Tafolla, Cruz Trujillo, José Castillo, Widow Moore, Fisherman Russell, John Ross, Henry Kimball and Frank Romero, Dr. J. M. Shelton, Bill Warlick place, Marion Armstrong, dugout, A. M. Austin, Juan Gomez, Alfonso Padillo, and Felis Castillo, Frosty Tomb, Mae's place, Josephine Rice place, Emma Walker place, Dollie Varden place, Dan Cole, Slats, John Pierce, and Mark Snider.

At its height during the railway-construction boom there were many temporary structures and tents. These included a railroad dance hall, the only public one Tascosa ever had, two lumber yards, and many fly-by-night businesses. But these were quickly moved or were torn down, leaving the squatty, rambling adobes clustered about Main, Spring, McMasters, and Waters streets and in East Tascosa or Hogtown a clump of lesser firms and houses. Many of these firms left an imprint on the history of the town and the country. Some achieved wide local and regional fame.

The one institution which did more to spread the reputation of Tascosa beyond its own borders and which worked unceasingly for its development was *The Tascosa Pioneer.* Its editor, Rudolph, crystalized opinion that he could influence and rode herd on the community. In his columns was painted an accurate and appreciative picture of a community. *The Pioneer* was a strong institution, typically Tascosa, the shadow of a colorful and capable man whose pen was as true to the life of that day as it was brilliant and bold. He seemed to appreciate the struggle for improvement at Tascosa and was one of its strongest advocates.

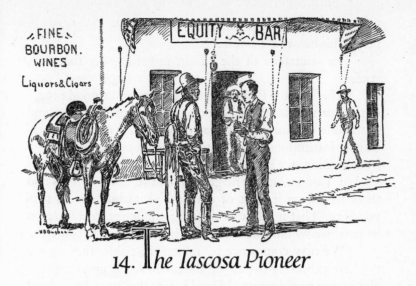

14. The Tascosa Pioneer

"THE TASCOSA PIONEER": Such was the appropriate and distinctive name chosen for his paper by C. F. Rudolph, editor of the official journal of Oldham, Hartley, Dallam, Sherman, Moore, Potter, Randall, Deaf Smith, Parmer, and Castro counties. This news sheet made its initial appearance on Saturday, June 12, 1886. Rudolph, always a brilliant booster, a strong champion of his town and countrymen, and a writer of exceptional merit, clipped the reading matter of *The Pioneer* and pasted it on the strong pages of a type-specimen catalog; thus the files of this rare paper were saved to posterity. L. F. Sheffy, secretary of the Panhandle-Plains Historical Society, found the bound scrapbooks in a fairly good state of preservation among the waste and scrap in an attic in Amarillo about eighteen years ago. Through this good fortune, students of Panhandle history have been privileged to look in on life at Tascosa during its busiest days. Files of other papers, as at Clarendon and Mobeetie, are not available to throw as much light on those communities as Rudolph's cast on Tascosa. He would have liked it that way. He was always boasting of the present superiority or the future greatness of his beloved Tascosa.

The salutatory of the editor, printed under that title, reads:

"The Tascosa Pioneer tips its beaver to the good people of the great Texas Panhandle on this fair June morning, and settles down to business, we can only hope, as one of the permanent institutions of the section. The Pioneer is among you by invitation, we might almost say by creation, of the citizens of Tascosa and its neighbors; and to those citizens and those neighbors it must of course look mainly for its perpetuality. That it realizes this fact is sufficient guarantee on its part, we would think, for watchful and efficient service.

"We may commence by telling the public that we are not here expecting to paw up the earth, to stir up young cyclones, nor to obliterate old land marks that were here ahead of us, but simply to pursue a legitimate business in a legitimate way; to publish a paper that shall be democratic so far as its politics goes, or in its criticisms liberal and considerate enough toward all men and all business; and to all labor for the good of Tascosa, the best town of its size on the continent, and the good of all the Panhandle. We have no hostility for any lawful interest or industry; and The Pioneer wishes to go on record as a champion of the idea that while the live stock interests of the Panhandle so far overshadow every other pursuit, that interest should be fostered and the farm will crowd the ranches of Northwest Texas, though that eventually is perhaps inevitable. And while the man with the hoe is destined to work out the possibilities of the children's domain, in the fullness of time, yet for the present that domain, and vast tracts of individual possessions with it, are working out no insignificant purpose. The ranges of the Western continent are supplying stores for the world.

"Between its patrons and itself, The Pioneer is led to hope for relations the most cordial, and believes that reasonable service will be reasonably appreciated. We expect to furnish more reading matter than any local weekly contemporary paper and expect that a fruit of it will be a better circulation. Those who avail themselves of our advertising space will find the investment a profitable one.

"To the people of Texas and other sections, among whom this paper has no small circulation to open with, it will be its pleasure to give each week reliable figures and factors and news of the wonderful events in West Panhandle, to which—my eyes are just turning. To my brethren of the press, and especially our more immediate neighbors we promise a rivalry for the good graces of the public that shall make everybody get up before day or see their laurels fading. And finally to Tascosa and to Oldham, the queen town and the banner county, The Pioneer this morning dedicates its future years of labor. That future of course has many changes —those years will bring strange experiences, but not until the twentieth century is fairly upon us, not until The Pioneer has become a great morning daily or has been laid away under the sod, not until Tascosa rings with her factories and her round-houses and crowded railroads and water works and national banks, or until we have yielded to some rival town, not until these things have happened will the history of The Pioneer and the progress and development have been written.

"To conclude, we have no lack of faith in the future of our section, and while we are aware that a newspaper of this size will be looked upon by many as too large for such a town as Tascosa, we trust to the pride and liberality of our people and to its own energy and endeavors, to keep it up. Thus we take the future at what it may hold, and launch out our little boat. Father Time will tell the rest."[1]

Mr. Rudolph in his first issue defined the purpose of

---

[1] *The Tascosa Pioneer*, June 12, 1886.

newspapers in the western country to be three in number: "First, to make money for the owners; second, to furnish an advertising medium for business men of the town; third, to proclaim to the world the advantages of a place and its adjacent country." He said, "to accomplish these three things a printer must issue a good paper, and the business men are pushing, wide awake and devoted to the success of the town and their own business. In a large town newspaper support can be drawn from any and all quarters, leaving all who do not advertise to the fate they invite by their own stinginess, but in small places every man who has any pride in his business and honors his town will give his paper liberal support."[2]

Under the heading "Our Advertisements" Mr. Rudolph took inventory of the Tascosa he found in 1886 and contributed a paragraph on each firm or individual that did not have an advertisement. His own description follows in part:

"The professional card of Messrs. Brown and Wallace, speaks of one of the leading law firms in the Panhandle. Mr. Wallace alone of the firm is resident here. Judge Brown, his partner, attends here when his presence is necessary.

"Vivian and Ryland are the 'oldest established law firm of Tascosa' and as attorneys, as land and collecting agents, they have a practice that is most lucrative and growing. Mr. Vivian's office of clerk of course debars him at present from regular legal practice, but that part of their business is safe in the capable hands of Mr. Ryland.

"McMasters & Mabry, the only exclusive real estate men in the city, and that means in this portion of the Panhandle, have a business that has reached large proportions.

"In favor of Dr. P. L. Shelton, our only M. D., a practitioner who certainly appears to be master of his profession, it would be difficult to say too much.

"Wright & Farnsworth's carries as large and well diver-

[2] *Ibid.*

sified a stock of merchandise as any in the Panhandle, or we had almost said beyond it.

"Messrs. Cone and Duran are the owners and managers of the other mammoth mercantile house, and the stock carried by them is no less large nor less varied.

"The single drug store, though it is only now growing into a business that is profitable, could not be in more popular hands. I. Rinehart is one of Tascosa's landmarks, and is reliable.

"Ross' millinery house, book and news stand, stationery and fancy line is winning a fair and paying patronage. It is a branch of trade that will pay better and better here, and Charles Ross and his lady are calculated to make much of it.

"Dunn & Jenkins' Saloon is a most deservedly popular resort, and has an annual trade which in the aggregate would surprise you. Particular in their selection of brands, they propose to set out no 'pizen,' and having won a big business, they mean to hold it.

" 'The Equity Bar,' which Mr. John Ryan owns and Mr. Button Griffith at present manages, was as his card tells you, the first saloon here. Many a thirsty soul comes up to the fountain here, and is refreshed, and still the liquor business at the 'Equity' gets better and better. None but superior brands.

"The 'Cattle Exchange' next door east, also owned by Ryan, is run on the same plan, and is made pleasant for the boys to lounge in. Samuel Dunn is the clever manager here.

"Michael McCormick's livery and feed stable, the only establishment of that kind here, has a business that is paying and popular. Plenty of comfortable stalls, good teams and vehicles, polite attention to his customers, have won for 'Mickey' as he is popularly called, an enviable run of patronage.

"The City Restaurant, conducted by Messrs. Dove and Lemmons, is in the right hands.

"The Blacksmith Shop, by H. M. Kimball, is one of the solid businesses.

"R. L. Marsh's Saddlery, harness and repair shop is growing into the right dimensions.

"F. G. Copeland is the only house and sign painter in the place.

"The Dairy has as paying a trade as many larger concerns, and it was built to what it is by the right kind of attention and clever management. Messrs. Shinebarger & Trescott are well liked.

"The Boot & Shoe Shop, by George Stoll, an efficient workman, is conducted on the right principles and is doing well.

"Besides those lines advertised, the town has an excellent school, a well managed hotel, the 'Exchange,' a bread establishment, a regular gardener, three barber chairs, a wagon yard, etc., but which we cannot go into descriptions of here. We will have one more saloon shortly. Sporting men can indulge their fun here too, in a nice variety of ways."

It was his custom in his editorial columns to review briefly or to summarize state, national, and world events, and often to offer his comment on them. He was just as free with his comment on local affairs and apparently was fearless in his editorial policy. In his first issue he mentioned that E. G. Ross was installed "governor of our near neighbors, the New Mexicans, on the 26th of May." Two items distantly related but now known to be of such great importance to the country were also reported in the first issue. They were: "There have been some pretty heavy drives of cattle during the spring from various sections of the Panhandle and from Southern Texas to Montana and other Northwestern territories"; and "Dirt has been broken on the extension of the Fort Worth and Denver City railroad between Harrold and Quanah which will bring the iron horse fifty miles farther toward the Panhandle."

Then in prophetic vein he began the boosting for which his paper was famous: "Two years hence you can write Tascosa down as the Queen City of the Panhandle. This is a prediction, not a threat."

Some idea of the business enjoyed at Tascosa in this item from the first issue:

"The XIT, the LX, the LS, the LIT, and other wagons from the prominent neighboring ranches have been in the past week, loading with provisions and feed, and left for the big round-up.

"The general round-up of the ranchmen of this section and farther west commences next Tuesday, the 15th, at the New Mexico line, some fifty miles from here. The work will necessarily require some time."

The editor in his first issue also told of the visit of the Reverend J. T. Bloodworth, a Methodist minister from Mobeetie, to Tascosa. The minister "preached to a small but respectful congregation on Sunday, the 30th of May, and occasionally during his stay. He was on a tour of the Panhandle, and took in the ranches on his rounds. He left again about the 7th. This was the first preaching Tascosa people had enjoyed since last summer."

Apparently Parson Bloodworth found fertile ground because *The Pioneer* reported in the same issue:

"A Sunday School was organized at this place last Sunday, during Rev. Bloodworth's stay here, which has started out, we learn, with a very fair attendance and interest. The school meets every Sunday, at 10:30 A.M., and those who have it in charge are especially zealous in their wish that it may be a benefit to the children.

"The officers chosen were: Mrs. F. G. Copeland, superintendent; Mrs. Ryland, secretary; Mrs. Rowland, treasurer; and Mrs. Austin, librarian. The teachers are Mrs. Cone and Mrs. Rinehart and one or two other ladies whose names we have not now."

The editor saved both time and labor by keeping in standing form a condensed description of Tascosa and Oldham County for the benefit of new subscribers, for information to those in distant places, and as an answer to the ever increasing flood of inquiries about the country. The text was changed from time to time, but the material carried in his first issue gives an excellent picture of the region in June, 1886, as he took over the job of boosting it to be the "Chicago of the Panhandle." A part of the standing material on Oldham County and Tascosa follows:

OLDHAM COUNTY

"So named for Captain Oldham, an early frontiersman, is situated on the west boundary line of the State, bordering New Mexico, near the extreme northwestern corner of the Panhandle. It has an area of 1,477 square miles, or 945,280 acres, being more than half as large again as either of the two other organized counties in the Panhandle, and as large as any of the unorganized except Greer. Oldham was the second county in the Panhandle to organize, assuming her own county government in the latter part of 1880.

"The general surface of this county, as of all the western and northwestern portion of the Panhandle, is high, undulating prairie, in some parts decidedly rocky and mountainous, with a diversity of fair valleys and level plains. Along the rivers and their tributary creeks are high, pebbly bluffs and deep gorges, and among many of these are to be found considerable growths of cedar, cottonwood, hackberry, wild china berry, mesquite. The plains proper set a few miles to the southwest of Oldham County, and even on these, notwithstanding the prevailing opinion that they are an arid desert stretch, there is soil that promises much for future development. Occasional tracts there are of land which is sandy and sterile, productive of nothing but coarser grasses. But much of the soil comprised in the famous staked plains will one day in the years to come be converted by the energetic wand of the actual settler. The mystic energies of the man with the hoe, into farms that shall wave with yellow grain where now stretches the unbounded level. Years will be necessary to a change like this, and there is no need to hasten it. But years will eventually tell the change.

"If this be true of those plains, how much more so of the lower plains around it? It is only rarely that agriculture has been attempted throughout the Panhandle proper, but in most of those instances the success has been fairly encouraging. The cereals will always grow better in this section than corn, it is likely, and cotton will never be a Panhandle product. But in the course of time wheat, oats, rye, millet, etc., nearly all of the fruits, and most of the vegetables, will be found to yield an abundant tribute to the grower in Oldham and many of the other counties of this section.

"The annual rainfall for the Panhandle in past years, though never accurately kept, has been estimated as ranging variously in different portions from fifteen to twenty-five inches. In Oldham County, being off from the Staked Plains and directly on the Canadian River, the largest stream in the Panhandle, there is about as much rainfall as is needed generally. During '85 there was almost a sufficiency of rain for the few patches of vegetables, roasting ears and melons without the aid of irrigation, but so far the spring of '86 has not brought specially good rains. Spring and autumn invariably bring refreshing showers. Much of the valley land of Oldham County, along the Canadian River and its tributaries, will ultimately when called into thorough test be found among the richest and most fertile soil of Texas. As a general thing it is of a chocolate and reddish colored sandy loam, generally of a superior clayey foundation.

"But the prime interest of our section, the chief industry upon which the thousands of our people depend at present and will look to for years to come, one of the main sources of supplies to a great market and even to a great State, the pride of the Panhandle and of Texas, is the colossal business of stock-raising. The Panhandle proper represents an ownership of somewhere near a million head of cattle, horses, and sheep, and the section of it in which are Oldham and adjacent counties is pasturing some two or three hundred thousand head, generally owning the land they occupy. The capitol syndicate Messrs. Farwell Taylor & Co., have their three millions of land located in the counties of this section, holding nearly half of Oldham, and they are arranging to inclose and stock their entire tracts. This will be the largest corporation of the Panhandle. There are various smaller companies in different localities. Some of the pasture lands of this section are the finest in the world. The grasses are the mesquite, gamma, sedge, bunch and blue stem. The cattle and sheep usually find good winter grazing and sufficient protection in the valleys and gorges. Running water is unfailing in the driest times in the Canadian and most of the creeks flowing into it."

Thus Editor Rudolph in his first issue set the pattern for his newspaper.

In his second issue *The Pioneer* editor had some comment on the return of President Grover Cleveland and his bride to the White House. He had sent a copy of *The Pioneer*, Volume One, Number One, to the President on the occasion of his marriage, reported in the first issue. He also expressed his gratitude for the universally kind words with which the opening number of the paper was received. In defense of Tascosa's reputation he wrote in his second paper: "Tascosa has not had a man for breakfast[3] in all the two weeks' history of The Pioneer. This will be surprising news to a good many people on the outside, who thought we kept our streets always running crimson."

[3] A killing. The expression had its origin in the fact that fights often occurred at night and the corpses were laid out before breakfast.

The Pioneer had not been in Tascosa long before its
tone of cordiality and support of the country as strictly a
ranching region cooled noticeably. In his opening editorial
Rudolph had hinted that in the distant future the country
might be settled but that unquestionably its present destiny
was stock raising. Within a few months he became openly
hostile to the lease and land laws and to persons supporting
the existing laws. He challenged the big cattle baron, Goodnight, time and again, and accused him of unfairness and
high-handed methods.[4] In one issue of his paper he assured
settlers that they could come into the country and settle on
land without danger of physical harm and molestation.[5]

This cooling of his attitude toward the cattlemen was
followed by what appeared to be an outright break. Jess
Jenkins declared it was because of a difference in politics
between Rudolph and the XIT and other large ranch owners.
"The XIT and the other fellows couldn't handle Rudolph
and his influence wasn't to their liking, so they withdrew
their support from him," said Mr. Jenkins. "Rudolph was a
brilliant man who influenced many people and when the
ranchers found they could not 'vote him' with them they
dropped him."

The strong individualism of Al Boyce, manager for the
XIT Ranch, no doubt was a big factor in forming Rudolph's
attitude. Boyce in his heydey ruled the XIT country with
a firm hand, and as counties were organized in the ranch territory, he or his men dominated the county politics. Consequently there developed a strong antagonism to the ranch.
Judge James D. Hamlin has declared in recent years that the
XIT was never able to go to court with much chance of winning suits because the people generally were against the
ranch. The desire of cowboys and ranch foremen to hold

[4] *The Tascosa Pioneer*, September 14, 1889; November 26, 1887; December 10, 1887; and January 21, 1888.
[5] *The Tascosa Pioneer*, November 26, 1887.

their jobs and their distaste for sale and settlement of the lands caused no end of opposition. A part of the ranch feeling was directed against cattle rustlers and petty maverickers, but in general the attitude was that "if you were not with the XIT, you were a cattle thief." Naturally a great many honest, industrious, and upright persons were put into the classification of cow thieves under this strict and unfair predication.

Apparently Rudolph after his break with the big cattlemen had no other choice than to boost Tascosa more enthusiastically than ever and to reiterate his predictions that the "man with the hoe" was destined to come and stay. He did, however, state many times that in his opinion the true destiny of the country was stock farming, where hundreds of stock farms would occupy the space then occupied by one large ranch. As strange as it seemed, one of his antagonists, Charles Goodnight, held the same opinion but felt that the stock-farming period was for some future date.

Despite this boosting of the country as a potential farming and stock-raising region, Rudolph apparently counted among his closest friends ranch foremen and cowboys.

The first notice of opposition to the wagon bridge across the Canadian River appeared in the second issue of *The Pioneer*. The bridge, which was a matter of controversy for years, was first noticed in this manner by Rudolph:

"In the light of recent developments, notwithstanding the existence of some active opposition from certain heavy property holders in the county, we may put it down as reasonably certain that work on the bridge to be built over the Canadian here will be begun at a very early date. There is no question but that the bridge is sorely needed."

The big fight occurred only a few weeks before Rudolph started his *Pioneer*, but his only mention of it was in the stories necessary to report activities of trial lawyers and witnesses and the progress of the wounded.

Any detailed story of the Panhandle country must of necessity include many items and observations on the weather. One item of weather which is always dramatic, impressive, and destructive is the hailstorm. The following description of a storm of this sort in the second issue of *The Pioneer* leaves nothing untold in its descriptive effect:

"Thursday evening, just before dark, Tascosa had one of the most severe and damaging storms of hail that has swept this section for years. For some time during the evening heavy, black clouds had gathered and banked up in the north, threatening a storm of some description, and gradually spreading overhead till nearly all the sky was hid. A little after 7 o'clock a single tremendous sized hailstone, sounding like a heavy stone thrown from a man's hand, could be heard striking here and there on the roofs of houses, at occasional intervals, gradually increasing in frequency, until soon the piff! bang! that was heard at first had changed to a fearful clatter. The showering on the iron roofs was deafening. Then the hail-stones began to find the windows. A sharp wind was blowing from the cloud bank in the north, and the storm fell slantingly. Windows and glass doors were just playthings for the storm. A good proportion of the hail-stones were as large as hen's eggs, and anything of that sort falling from the clouds was not likely to find much opposition in a thin pane of glass. Every house that had a window fronting the north, unprotected, lost it. Up and down on the south side of Main Street, from end to end, the wreck was thorough. In at least two houses, fifteen out of the sixteen panes of glass were shattered. In all, they were nearly all broken.

"It was a dangerous time to be out from shelter. A Mexican called Trinidad was above town coming in with a load of roofing poles for building here, and his team took fright and ran, scattering his load, throwing him off and running the wagon over him, and at length broke loose from the wagon and came on to town. Trinidad received pretty severe injuries, and the beating of the hail alone was heavy enough to be dangerous. He was unable yesterday morning to be out of bed.

"We are told that a team came up to the lower town about dark, bringing the fore parts of a wagon. A horse was seen loose a few hundred yards above the river, wearing a buggy bridle. We have not heard if it was discovered who were the owners, before going to press, and can only trust that nothing too serious may be developed. Doubtless many a little calf, an unlucky pig, or a poor chicken, had to turn its toes to the daisies."

Shortly after the hailstorm Tascosa was visited by another severe storm which *The Pioneer* described as follows:

"A wind and rain storm struck the town last Monday evening while many of the windows were still open and made itself disagreeable. Besides blowing into many houses it took a corner from the high front of Cone & Duran's store, loosening up the roofing of one or two other buildings, and for so short an acquaintance made itself generally too familiar. It is not understood just what brought about these storms, usually at this season up here, unless it was a job put up by the glass men and the repairers, or else the storms came long to get a notice in the new paper. In either case we trust now to have a let-up."[6]

Buffaloes were still being killed occasionally in June, 1886. *The Pioneer* carried this item: "A small supply of buffalo meat was brought in by our neighbor, Mr. T. Briggs, yesterday, and disposed of readily in the market. Bison steak, juicy and delicious, is a rarity in these days even in the West. It used not to be thus."

Another item gave an account of members of a hunting expedition who had been through the Panhandle of Texas recently, had returned to Garden City, Kansas, and had re-

[6] *The Tascosa Pioneer,* June 26, 1886.

ported that they had seen during their few weeks' trip about three thousand buffaloes in all, in small and scattering bunches. They killed three and captured fourteen calves for the Kansas buffalo ranch.

An idea of the traffic over the trails of the western country is gleaned from the third issue of *The Pioneer*, when the editor comments: "The number of cattle that have gone up the trail through Greer County during the spring on their way north was said to be, up to June 6th, 89,297."

Rudolph loved the picturesque language of the West and quoted the advertisement of Messrs. Jones and Wiren of Duncan, Arizona, in the Las Vegas, New Mexico, *Stock Grower:* "Whoever handles these cattle without authority will catch hell."

Rudolph early suggested the possibility of orchards, and later several were planted and were successful. In the same issue he mentioned the fact that the roundup on the other side of the river had reached a point opposite town on Thursday, and "the cowboys during the day thronged our streets numerously. Not less than forty or fifty of them were in, and many a dollar changed ownership. It was a lively but not a disorderly day."

Rudolph went to work early in the life of *The Pioneer* to serve notice on the world that Tascosa was to be a second Chicago in an incomparable country with great natural advantages. Some of these advantages were location, climate, an abundance of water, plenty of native stone, and a far-seeing, intelligent, and lively group of citizens. His favorite theme was that the city would become a great railroad center. He worded his stories and comments with such assurance as to give them the ring of absolute conviction. His logic was sound to the layman's mind. It evidently found much support among Tascosa businessmen, even if it did not appeal to the ranch owners and to others who had largely lived in an open country where the land was public domain.

There was much in the paper about the route of the Fort Worth and Denver Railroad across the plains and across the river. The surveying parties in the country in 1886 surveyed many of these routes and Rudolph offered his advice in this paragraph: "There are two ways for a railroad from the Southeast to build down to the river to a crossing here, either of which is as simple and easy a descent from the Plains as could be found anywhere; and either one of them leads directly into and through Tascosa. More than this, after the town is passed the route up Tascosa Creek leads to the Plains in the direction of Denver by a more gradual ascent again than the north side of the river shows at any point. Then the Plains afford a dead level as it did south of here and that is why Tascosa counts on it as a matter of reasonable certainty."[7]

The editor of *The Pioneer* could argue the railroad question with anyone. A typical comment presented in argumentative style in the same issue reads:

"Whether the Southern Kansas will cross the Fort Worth and Denver in Carson County, in Randall County, in Potter County, or in Oldham County is the question to which the people of the Panhandle are giving occasional thought. Otherwise papers published far away profess to have settled this problem in favor of Carson, and in Carson the intersection may be; but how can our contemporaries know so much when the railway men themselves and their surveyors have not yet settled upon it. Very much like it is the announcement in some of the papers that after the junction of the Southern Kansas with the S.K. of Texas, then a line will diverge from that junction to Albuquerque, N.M., while others just as confidently stated that it is to build straight to El Paso. Meanwhile, we are mindful of two things which we know to be facts; that the charters of the two

---

[7]*The Tascosa Pioneer,* January 26, 1887.

ADA ARMSTRONG   MR. AND MRS. MEL ARMSTRONG

TASCOSA'S SECOND SCHOOLHOUSE

also used for Union Sunday School service. Mr. and Mrs.
Mel Armstrong were married here

HENRY KIMBALL

LUCIUS DILLS

THEODORE BRIGGS

J. E. MCALISTER

lines of the Southern Kansas both call for Oldham County, and that a representative of the Southern Kansas of Texas distinctly said that at present no divergent line toward any other point is in contemplation."

In the same issue, also, he turned to the citizens of Tascosa in an editorial which summed up the entire situation:

"There is a turning point in every life, it is said, and the same may be found equally true of every town. A certain growth, a certain importance, is attained without extra effort, and then a change comes o'er the spirit of the prospect. The turning point is reached, and all else that is gained must be earned by energy and by unity of effort. If ever Tascosa is to become a railroad center, if she has any aspirations to reach the dignity of a city, if we expect to see the place which knows us now to know us ten years from now, then it is time to be getting to work. Railroad locators are on all sides of us; capital is watching for places of investment in this section, and fortune is going to smile with a very excess of favor on some Panhandle city in the near future. Will it be Tascosa? Is this fair and unexcelled location—unexcelled for the greatest of conveniences, we may say necessaries, water, soil, valuable stone, a practical and lasting bridge over a dangerous stream—is this to be the seat of a metropolis? Hardly, unless attention is invited to us in ways that will have effect. The turning point in Tascosa's history is not far off, and the aftermath is going to be a very emphatic boom, or very certain, even if slow decline. It takes no prophet to foresee this; he that runneth may read, where the signs are as plain as now. The season is fast coming and the summer [1887] will bring it, when active committee work, energetic advertising of our advantages, the offering of positive and infinite inducements, involving some outlay of time and money perhaps, will be absolutely demanded. When it comes, each man should be ready, and we believe will be, to spit on his hands, roll up his sleeves, and wade in, in earnest."

A while later he declared that "Tascosa is in the way of the Omaha, Kansas and El Paso road, newly chartered; it is in the way, or nearly in the way, of the Rock Island's projected extension from Englewood and at a convenient point for numerous other lines now building or arranging to build." Among these others much attention was given to the North Platte, Lakin and Tascosa Railroad and the Houston and Texas Central, which, with its terminus at Albany, was pointing toward Tascosa where the road owned great tracts of rich Texas land.[8] In connection with the Houston and Texas Central Rudolph wrote: "We are reminded that the Houston & Texas Central which is resting now at Albany, in Shackelford County, points toward Oldham County, and its company owns immense tracts of valuable land in the Panhandle, which they will want to see increasing in value and which it is said they are going to push their lines through in the near future. All new railroads are building toward the Panhandle and toward Oldham County." In the same issue he wrote: "The decision of the Rock Island men to build their west line from Kansas south through the Panhandle to Cisco, Texas, instead of to El Paso will throw them on a line with Tascosa. This extension of the Rock Island road is already arranged for and will be pushed early."

There was big news for Tascosa in the item *The Pioneer* copied from *The New York Times* on March 2, 1887:

"The information which comes from New York, copied by us last week out of The New York Times, showing that 'the legal papers have been drawn up for the consolidation of the Fort Worth and Denver City railway and the Denver, Texas and Gulf that a syndicate is to be formed to build the tap which will connect the two roads, making a continuous line from Denver to the Gulf, the money for this purpose to be raised at once and Gen. G. M. Dodge is to be in charge

8 *The Tascosa Pioneer,* March 2, 1887.

of the construction' is most encouraging information. It proves beyond a doubt, where there was some little doubt before, that this through line was to be completed at an early date, for the consolidation would not have been made, nor the syndicate formed, nor the construction let, unless a vigorous prosecution of the work was to be the next step. The completion of this grand trunk line which will connect the mountains with the seas, the coal fields with the pineries, the inland with the ports, Denver with New Orleans, will furnish an important, an invaluable ally in the development of the Panhandle, and will find its business unequalled by that of any railway in the Southwest. There is no question but the intention of The Fort Worth and Denver is to take a front rank, and no doubt but that they will do it."

Again on March 2, 1887, the editor of *The Pioneer* held out to his public some of the advantages which go along with a railroad boom in these words: "Once Tascosa has railroad facilities the other concomitants of a large city will rapidly follow. Among these added blessings in pretty much the order they would take, we may mention other railroads, multiplied business and population, national banks, slaughtering yards and refrigerating establishments, union depots, round houses, manufactories and founderies, colleges and churches, municipal dignity, water works, street cars, opera houses, a tremendous boom in real estate and a morning Pioneer."

Thus in 1886 and 1887 Mr. Rudolph kept his paper filled with railroad gossip, rumors, facts, guesses, challenges, and sometimes morbid fears expressed with regret but with a loophole for optimism. He never missed a detail of surveying work or railroad gossip and never failed to hold out the promise of a big boom and much development. He played down the fact that the Santa Fé system, the Kansas City Southern, which some larger papers had said would build to Carson City in Carson County, actually did extend its hungry fingers from Oklahoma across the Canadian River and over the plains to that point, to which cowboys soon were driving large herds. There the line stopped, but through agreement a short connecting line was built over to the Fort Worth and Denver railway at Washburn only to be torn up and moved bodily to Amarillo by its citizens in later years. He gradually forgot all other rail-line prospects, as they dwindled, to favor the Rock Island line, which he hoped would intersect the Fort Worth and Denver at Tascosa. He referred to his town as "Rockislandville" and argued with as much logic for the location as for other roads in the early years of railroad building.

There were many surveying crews in and around Tascosa when the route for the railroad was being decided. There were a dozen rumors for each crew. One of the routes was across the Canadian and to the plains by way of India Creek. Rudolph and others scoffed at this plan. The route proposed and boosted most ardently was across the river at Tascosa, up Tascosa Creek, and then out on the plains. Rudolph argued in support of this route, presented many reasons for its selection, and expressed full confidence in its being the final choice of the railroad men. Another route, which was advanced by some with logical enthusiasm, was across the river about two miles above Tascosa and up Cheyenne Creek on a winding course, topping the north plains grade some eight to twelve miles north and west of Tascosa. It was argued for this route that the grade was much better up the winding cottonwood valley and that the river crossing was shorter and more logical than the other routes.

Another route proposed at one time and tentatively accepted was across the Canadian River due north of the present town of Amarillo. This route, as has since been proved by the Santa Fé line from Amarillo to Boise City, Oklahoma, and Lamar, Colorado, would have missed many small streams and much country difficult for railroad construction. Decision to abandon it was reported to have hinged on the opinion of the engineer that the grade was entirely too steep to make it practical.

In the course of the surveying, Tascosa men made it a point to have trusted emissaries drive and work for the railroad surveyors and officials. These men were sound in their knowledge of the country and determined in their purpose to have the railroad line come through the county-seat town of Tascosa. One of the escorts of the railroad officials was Jack Ryan, saloonkeeper and cowboy. When a discussion of the route proposed up India Creek was underway by the railroad officials, Ryan forgot his duties as guide and driver and snorted in disgust as he utterly condemned the project.

The railroad men talked with the businessmen of Tascosa about the route and asked for a heavy sum of money to direct the road through the town's borders. The sum was so large that the Tascosa residents could not raise it, and though they reported the fact to the railroad officials, it was never mentioned in *The Pioneer*.

The announcement of the location in *The Pioneer* carried a picture of a crowing rooster above the headline, "Lucky Tascosa," and which, in decks and subdecks, went on to say: "Doubts and uncertainties are dissolved like morning mists! And the little city has only to go on to greatness! The Fort Worth & Denver is located to and through the town, and bright beams the future."[9]

The main story reads: "Glad are the tidings that The Pioneer carried forth today—a certainty of railway connections for its beloved town with all the outside world, a promise of stability that had begun to seem something of a question, and a dissipation of all doubts of coming importance. A hint of this might have been given earlier, but it was thought best to wait until the matter was settled beyond question. It is so settled now, and right well pleased is the

[9] *The Tascosa Pioneer*, July 30, 1887.

town and equally well pleased is The Pioneer that can tell the good news abroad.

"Since his return here from below, Mr. McCrickett, the locating engineer, has been giving the route up the river his close attention, evidently satisfied from his first inspection that it was much superior to the India Creek route in several prospects. Our county surveyor, W. S. Mabry, who we may add here has done more for the town in this matter than the town could ever have done for itself, devoted to the work much valuable time and labor, and by his knowledge of the country was able largely to assist in discovering the route now determined upon. The examination made of it by Mr. McCrickett was thorough and his report, which went down to his chief ten days ago, stated in simple terms that this route just run by him—quitting the other line at the Sierrata La Cruz, following the river valley on the south side to a point some two miles above here, where they bridge, and then taking up the Cheyenne—is at least two and one-half miles shorter than the other, and for cheapness of construction incomparably better. Knowing that it would be accepted and adopted, Mr. McCrickett lost no time, but proceeded with the location. He passed by here on the opposite side of the river Wednesday evening, and when the answer came Thursday night—an answer which announced the selection of this route and directed the rapid pushing forward of the work— the twelve miles which parallel the river were already located and staked. Behind him now comes the engineers; and grading parties will within the week be assigned to work along the valley, almost or quite in sight of town. The living evidences of the nearness of this road to us will show up shortly —indeed, are showing up already. Mr. Wood, who brought these instructions up, has orders to proceed at once with the building of the railroad bridge on the Canadian, and his force will come on and commence the work without any delay. The bridge will be, it is probable, some two miles above

town. The Cheyenne, by which creek the line leaves the
river, is scarcely three miles. .

"Thus Tascosa has so far in her history met with not a
single disappointment. Commencing with unparalleled natural advantages, such as a beautiful location, plenteous supplies of purest water, and her lovely groves, she added first a
splendid courthouse and jail; then a bridge that was sorely
needed, and now, greater and better than all else, she writes
down railroad number one. This is what will make our real
estate sought after; what will bring in wholesale houses, and
in time banking houses, increase our population, increase the
number of our retail businesses, multiply immigration, bright-
en the chances for other roads, better our facilities for shipping in and out, cut down prices of all commodities and the
cost of living, and swell rapidly Tascosa's volume of trade.
Great are the railroads, and especially great is the Fort Worth
& Denver.

"To Mr. McCrickett's perspicacity, to Mr. Mabry's in-
domitable energy and perseverence, and to The Pioneer's
unwavering faith this happy result is attributable. 'Natural
advantages' were of course with us, and these same natural
advantages will be in our favor it may be unnumbered times
in future when good things are passing. And now let us go
to work in only sensible ways to make the most of fine opportunities. The only one of the original Panhandle towns
to secure a railroad, there is much for us to be thankful for
and much for us to do."

He added a word of warning in another part of his
paper, saying: "A common mistake which is made in new
towns supposed to have bright futures is the holding of real
estate at too high figures. The principal result is that capital
which would be invested there, and desirable citizens who
would otherwise settle there, are frightened off. We are persuaded that Tascosa's property holders will not commit this
blunder."

This word of uncertainty, however, creeps into a paragraph in this same Saturday, July 30, 1887, issue when the editor writes: "It still looks as though Tascosa may become the metropolis of the Panhandle." The location of the road bridge two miles above Tascosa and its line up Cheyenne Creek three miles away undoubtedly brought this element of doubt.

Two weeks later *The Pioneer* went into further detail in mentioning and in answering some of the questions in the minds of the people: "Messrs. F. E. Bissell, Dan Carey and Engineer McCrickett held a conference here Wednesday and as a result the grading forces working under Mr. Carey will be assigned to work along the route by here without delay. The second line just run by Mr. McCrickett, which would have crossed the river a mile below and gone up back of town, was pronounced by both Bissell and McCrickett as being no better than the one south of the river, if equal to it, and the latter was therefore finally settled upon for the road-bed, beyond any further question. This puts the depot perhaps three-fourths of a mile from town, but the bridge places direct and first-class connection between and nobody acquainted with the two localities imagines that there will be building over there in a way to cripple this side. The depot will be convenient enough and stock pens are better that far off. The arrangements would have been hard to beat."

It took real nerve a short time later for Rudolph to keep his optimistic attitude, because there came to be some doubt that the new railroad would build a station at all across the river from Tascosa. The rail-line promoters apparently had designs on some other location, and the Tascosans hired an attorney and sent a committee to Austin and to the company's headquarters in Fort Worth to look into the matter of an injunction.[10] The railroad officials came back with a

[10] *The Tascosa Pioneer*, December 17, 1887.

statement that it was preposterous for them to refuse a railroad station across the river from Tascosa and in the statement was an assurance of friendly interest and co-operation.
The Pioneer took occasion to mention the state law which
required any railroad route that came within five miles of a
county seat to have a railroad station at the county seat.[11]

The Tascosans, keenly interested that the new location
would provide only a railroad station and stock pens and not
a site for a new town, finally bought some land about two
miles from the river on the line. The land near the river was
owned by the LS Ranch, and after considerable dickering,
the townspeople swapped their land to W. M. D. Lee of the
LS for the land on which the station was built. It was mutually agreed that no land would be sold to business firms and
no other houses would be erected here.

The station for New Tascosa was a small, two-room
wooden building and was located approximately a mile or
a mile and one-half from Tascosa. It stood a good half-mile
from Borregos Plaza where Jim Dobbs had filed on 320 acres
of land which included the old plaza houses. Kid and Jim
Dobbs and their families lived there. As news of the location
spread, a speculator made Jim a proposition for an option on
the land. Here was to be the site of a new Tascosa. He put
up one hundred dollars in forfeit money and had three weeks
in which to exercise the option. When he did not put in his
appearance, Jim Dobbs sold the plaza and the land to Jack
Ryan for three hundred dollars. Jess Jenkins and his partner,
Bill Wheeler, meanwhile bought an eighty-acre tract in the
same general area and hired a man to stay on the land for
some time.

Tascosa, with a railroad, did not bloom overnight into
a metropolis. The railroad brought with it many potential
cities at many points in the Panhandle, which promised to

[11] *Ibid.*

scatter to the four winds the supply and shipping points for
the cattle industry. The town fathers of Tascosa were also
not giving up without a fight. They were determined to keep
their status as a city and as a trading point. A taxi and dray
line was immediately organized to connect Tascosa over its
new wagon bridge with the station, which was becoming
known as New Tascosa.

Then a hint to the wise was sufficient. The railroad,
town boosters, land boomers, and landowners had ambitions
and designs for other towns on the new railroad line. The
construction of the railroad had brought Tascosa only a temporary boom and a temporary lease on life; but *The Pioneer*
of September 3, 1887, was able to say that "within the week
every empty residence in Tascosa had been occupied. Scarcely a day passes now but adds to the population of the best
little city on the border." The paper also noted enlargements
of business houses and of stocks. On September 17, 1887,
The Pioneer could list under the heading:

"*Tascosa Has*
The finest of natural locations,
An abundance of the best water,
Two of the largest and most successfully managed mercan-
tile houses in the West,
Four of the best conducted saloons in any country,
Three of the most astute and reliable young attorneys in the
state,
The best hotel in the Panhandle,
Two blacksmith shops that turn out more and better work
than any other two,
Best doctor on the frontier,
Absolutely no empty houses,
Nicest arranged drug store on the frontier,
Elegant restaurant,
Three barber shops that lay it over all others,

Millinery establishment that is not surpassed in its management nor appearance,

Two livery stables that are not beaten west of the Mississippi,

A cowboys' supply house that acknowledges no better in the
cattle countries,

A citizenship that stands shoulder to shoulder for common
work in a way to shame the average towns,

Two butcher shops that are run on the right principles and
by the right men,

Boot and shoe shop that takes front rank,

A weekly newspaper about which, perhaps, the less said by
us the better,

Chop house and lunch stand that can assure itself of a splendid business from this on,

Carpenters that don't need any word of commendation from
anybody,

Postoffice that comes nearer filling the bill to everybody's
satisfaction than one would think possible,

Dairy that furnishes better products,

As good a jeweler as any other town in Texas,

Painter whose reputation is already made and who will hold
the field against all comers,

Orderly, peaceable and social population numbering fully
half a thousand,

More visitors than any other point excepting none,

Most substantial inducements to offer to business men and
investors of all the towns on the border,

Bakery that is the pride of the city,

Tinner who is a first-class workman,

Real Estate dealers who invite correspondence and will do
the right thing by anybody,

Best school outside of the large cities,

Bravest and most conservative officers in any county seat,

Grander scenery all about it than you will find in a month's
travel,

Bridge over the Canadian River that holds this as a center of
    travel always,
Bigger trade in every line than the uninformed would
        imagine, or even dream of,
Finer building stone adjacent to town than any other place
    can show,
Book store and news and nation house that lays it over any
    of them,
Professional plasterer who is confessed the most thorough of
    his craft,
Courthouse and jail that is an ornament even to a fast place
    like this,
A little lunch counter that does a surprising business,
A system about everything that is most admirable,
The world by the tail and a downhill pull,
Her future in her own hands,
And an endless variety of lesser attractions that are not here
    enumerated.

   "Tascosa Will Soon Have
Another restaurant,
A national bank,
Exclusive hardware store,
Produce and hide exchange,
Two more saloons,
Trains running in from the Southwest,
Depot and stock pens,
Population more than doubled,
Wholesale houses,
Lumber yards,
Hacks running to and from trains,
Terminus of the Fort Worth and Denver for the winter,
Railway connections with the coal fields of Colorado,
Saddlery and harness establishment,
Building boom that will astonish the world,

And finally, everybody acknowledges that as a city she is chief."

Despite this optimism, as the construction workers pushed their work to completion and as more and more Tascosa residents sought out farms and opportunities elsewhere, it became apparent that the railroad had actually hurt the community far more than was thought possible when the first shocking news that it had missed Tascosa was relayed to the public. It soon was realized that somewhere in Potter County there would be a county-seat town which would logically develop into a trading center because of its easy access to people of the south plains and to those west of Amarillo in the plains country. Jess Jenkins had a section of land on which he hoped to build this new Potter County capital. He, along with others from Tascosa, had taken full advantage of the construction boom to establish a saloon, a store, and other enterprises in tents at Rag Town, which was located on Jenkins' section, the first water west of Clarendon. Then it was rumored that the railroad company or its land and colonizing department would build a city a few miles above Tascosa on the Cheyenne Creek, which was to be christened Cheyenne, Texas. Meanwhile, it had been rumored that A. G. Boyce and the XIT, who had long been galled by their failure to run Tascosa, would establish a city near their new headquarters in Hartley County.

All of this news was enough to blow out the spark of any boom for a town at New Tascosa and to smother the fire in the sand-covered plaza which a short while ago had entertained such enthusiastic dreams of being the capital of the Panhandle range world. *The Pioneer* recorded, almost with "I-told-you-so" enthusiasm, the birth of the new town of Amarillo and its selection as a county seat. As this was done, *The Pioneer* also carried reports from time to time of new locations, of the advent of farmers as settlers in various parts of the Canadian River country and on both the south and north plains regions.

Other news which *The Pioneer* recorded also pointed to the rapid change then taking place. The railroad took carloads of cattle to the slaughter pens and feeding grounds of the Midwest in four or five days. It took weeks and months to handle a herd of this size over the trail. Little mention was made of another factor in the changing world which had for a long time been doing great damage to Tascosa—the barbed wire fence. The fence was stopping trail herds, travelers, and other persons. It was whittling down the free grass and free range of the old days, and while giving the large ranch owners temporary advantage, it was also offering hope to the farmer. He could now fence in his plot for garden and crops and his pasture for the small herd.

Perhaps the editor of *The Pioneer* was too busy thinking of additional verbal insults for the new town of Cheyenne to notice all that was occurring about him. Perhaps, not having been blessed with eyes that could see and record forthcoming events, he was more concerned with fighting the bitterest rival Tascosa ever had, when the fight was hardly worth the effort regardless of which won. But Tascosa had been peopled with many who looked for a fight for the sheer love of fighting. So far as the future was concerned, there could have been little justification for Tascosa's town fight with Cheyenne. Rudolph, however, thoroughly enjoyed it.

W. M. D. Lee had always let it be known that he did not wish the settlement and development of the country. When the citizens of Tascosa had succeeded in electing J. E. McMasters to the Commissioners' Court and in winning the friendship of W. W. Wetzell and Quitman, a contract had been let to the King Bridge and Iron Works Company for a wagon bridge across the Canadian River at Tascosa and the county bonded for $22,000 for this purpose.

Representatives of the big interests did their best to forestall this action and to delay building once it got under way. Editor Rudolph had several caustic remarks on the subject and included an editorial blast which was a potent one for a pioneer paper. Nevertheless, the bridge was completed in 1888 and opened to traffic. The voting of the bonds, however, did not end Tascosa's trouble. In fact, the action further irked Mr. Lee and other members of the big outfits, but Lee in particular. He had been provoked to the point of exasperation by the little men of Tascosa. One of them said that Lee and the big outfits wanted to "peon" the citizens of the town and keep it only as a hollow shell.

During the arguments with the Commissioners' Court over the bridge bonds, Lee in a huff had told the court that if bonds were voted which would result in the LS Ranch's having to pay higher taxes, he would ruin Tascosa forever as a town. Lee carried out his threat, and so his name must be added to the list of factors in the death of Tascosa.

He donated LS land for a townsite three miles west of Tascosa along Cheyenne Creek, up which the Fort Worth and Denver Railroad wound its precarious way. His offer of the townsite to a group of promoters was immediately accepted by Fort Worth and Denver officials. R. E. Montgomery, general town-lot agent and developer for the railroad, began advertising a new town. The site was surveyed and then was platted by the Dallas Lithograph Company. Blueprints and advertising bills were distributed to induce homeseekers to investigate the possibilities of Cheyenne, as the town was to be called, taking its name from Cheyenne Creek. It was to have all the natural advantages enjoyed by Tascosa, plus a railroad.

The creators of copy that boosted the new town turned out a masterpiece of advertising literature. The prospectus described the location as being on the north bank of the Cheyenne Creek, 376 miles from Fort Worth, Texas, and

212 miles from Trinidad, Colorado. The creek was pictured as having never-failing, pure, free-stone water fed by constant live springs that would furnish an abundant supply for domestic and manufacturing purposes. The town proper was to lie in a beautiful valley where water could be obtained at twelve- to fifteen-foot depths, where fine building stone was available and where ample protection was afforded by surrounding hills. The promoters claimed that it was the only safe crossing on the Canadian River and predicted that other railroads would cross there in the near future. The advertisement said that a strip of land parallel to the Fort Worth and Denver right-of-way was reserved for roads expected to run out of Kansas City and El Paso. It stated that the new railroad company would fence the grounds on either side of Cheyenne Creek for a park to conserve the beautiful cottonwood trees growing along its banks. The rail line also promised to erect stock and feeding pens.[12]

The promoters added that "there will be a large city in the Pan-Handle situated as Cheyenne is, in the fertile valley of the Canadian, with the best country in New Mexico and the Pan-Handle tributary to it. It should, and will, command its entire trade that now goes to build up and has made Dodge City, Las Vegas, Springer, and other cities in Kansas, Colorado and New Mexico what they are." Mention of Tascosa was carefully avoided.

Plans were announced for a great excursion train to run to Cheyenne for a public sale of town lots on Thursday, December 15, 1887. The sale of lots would be by auction to the highest bidder. Purchases under $100 were cash, while purchases above that amount might be made on terms. As a further inducement, all persons who made purchases of more than $150 would have their round-trip fare refunded by the Fort Worth and Denver Railroad. Moreover, work was be-

12 D. A. Sullivan, "When Tascosa Had a Rival," *The Amarillo Sunday Globe–News*, May 3, 1940.

Courtesy John Arnot

MAIN STREET, TASCOSA, ABOUT 1911

Courtesy Temple Houston Morrow

MAIN STREET, TASCOSA, IN 1942

OLDHAM COUNTY COURTHOUSE ABOUT 1887

Sheriff Tobe Robinson is in the doorway. The house at the left is
that of Frosty Tomb and the child is his daughter

Courtesy Metro-Goldwyn-Mayer

BOYS' RANCH, 1945

The old Tascosa courthouse, showing movie-set barns and corrals,
from a photograph by MGM still-cameraman Bert Lynch

ing pushed on a two-story hotel. Excursion rates were granted, and excursion trains were to be run from Clarendon to Cheyenne on the day of and during the sale. Further information was available from C. C. Allen, agent; J. A. H. Hosack, auctioneer; R. E. Montgomery, general town-lot agent; and W. Y. Newlin, general passenger agent at Fort Worth.

The sale was highly successful. The hotel was completed and opened to the public. A store was built, and two or three saloons and gambling places were quickly established. Several homes were erected and occupied. The railroad company built a depot, cattle pens, and loading chutes.

The men at Tascosa remained steadfast and refused to buy lots or to aid in any way the growth of Cheyenne. They called the sale of lots a swindle. George Suddeth, an enterprising one-armed individual, instituted hack service between Cheyenne and Tascosa when passenger trains began to stop at the new station, but his activity was definitely not appreciated. There were several clashes between Tascosans and railroad officials and workers.

Within the space of a year Cheyenne had enjoyed its rise and experienced its fall as a city. When application was made for a post office, it was discovered that there was another Texas town which claimed the name of Cheyenne. The name was then changed to Magenta, after the color of the red soil along the banks of Cheyenne Creek. The Fort Worth and Denver kept an agent there for several years, but the town was a dismal failure after a few months, and it died without ever achieving even the status of a ghost town except in the memory of a very few Panhandle pioneers.

Some two years after the big townsite sale for ill-fated Cheyenne, *The Pioneer* and its editor, Rudolph, fully appraised of the work of Tascosa's enemy, Lee, had genuine revenge. Rudolph dipped his pen in vitriol and wrote a swan song for the place that once was the rival of Tascosa and Lee's method of revenge and ruin for the town:

" 'Cheyenne has been a city for over 20 years,' sings the Northwestern Livestock Journal, 'and during the greater part of that time an active business center where all trades people were prosperous.'

"Well, we clip the above to institute a comparison between that city of 20 years and of active business and its prototype, its counterpart, and at the same time its antithesis, its contrast, the CHEYENNE of Texas! The latter announced a metropolis of the immediate future, a swallower of Tascosa and everything else that should risk its ravenous maws, cannot see nor say as much from a hind-view as it did from a fore-view, and is peculiarly and distinctly not a city of years nor of business, is in fact, just about the same narrow, water-washed, unsettled townsite as nature left it. For two years it has gone from nothing steadfastly downward, until now it stands out in bold relief as the most colossal fizzle in the history of town building and an exposition of the rise and fall of Boom Town.

"Cheyenne of Wyoming, with her light reflecting over a territory, is NOT Cheyenne of Texas!"[13]

Rudolph was shortly to write the swan song for *The Pioneer* and his beloved Tascosa. The log of how a town dies was being printed in almost every issue of his paper during those eventful years. The opposition of Lee and the other big men was part of that log. Cheyenne was only one chapter. *The Pioneer*, brilliant and loyal as it was, could not win against such odds.

[13] *Ibid.*

15. How a Town Dies

THE SALTY TOWN FIGHT between Cheyenne and Tascosa resulted in a genuine victory for Tascosa, and the railroad real-estate promotion scheme at Cheyenne died a-borning. Editor Rudolph of *The Tascosa Pioneer* did a good editorial job in wiping Cheyenne off the map, exulting: "Cheyenne is no more"; but not even Rudolph's optimism could prevent the inevitable slump which came to Tascosa. More and more of her people moved to Amarillo, others homesteaded claims on the plains, and some returned to their old homes. The gradual disintegration of the town was fought by the stout heart and facile pen of Rudolph, who kept *The Tascosa Pioneer* alert to every opportunity for optimism and ahead of the times and the country in equipment and quality of content. Rudolph pleaded for many improvements for the town. He urged macadamized streets, a bridge across Tascosa Creek, a waterworks, a streetcar line from the courthouse across the bridge over the Canadian to the railway station. His picture of the future Tascosa and its greatness all but overshadowed the factual accounts his paper printed of a dying town.

One of the pathetic items covering only four lines was printed in the midst of the railway boom of 1887. It told the discerning that there were many who did not think enough of their property to pay taxes on it. He wrote: "There are some excellent real estate values open for someone in a few tax title suits scheduled for next term of court."[1]

Often in his items boosting the town there was a condition or a doubt expressed, sometimes as a challenge. Some of these statements indicated that even so bright a booster as the editor of *The Pioneer* must have felt the undertow of the tide that was pulling on the good ship Tascosa. On one occasion he dismissed the possibility of a rival town on the plains because the country was high and dry and did not have any water. He made much of this point, and when water was discovered at Carson City by well-drillers, he emphasized that they were forced to go 288 feet to get water while at Tascosa it could be had in artesian wells at the shallowest depth.

Many items in *The Pioneer* give some idea of the trend of events. On July 6, 1889, is recorded: "It was never known within the memory of the oldest inhabitant when the Canadian River remained so low nearly all the time for a year or more." In the same issue is an item relating that Sheriff Tobe Robinson released the prisoners and gave them the freedom of the town on July 4. "To their credit be it said, the boys required no particular watching and were on hand to be returned at midnight."

On July 18, Rudolph recorded: "John W. Cone is away in New Mexico, drumming up the Southwestern country which is properly tributary to Tascosa."

An unusual thought for Rudolph, one that mingled sarcasm and regret at the march of progress, is the following item: "Lon Jenkins and George Doty left Tuesday for Ros-

[1] *The Tascosa Pioneer,* February 11, 1888.

well, New Mexico, on the far Pecos. People do say that Roswell is just for the world such another town as Tascosa was when she stood far inland and the scream of the iron horse had not brought civilization and confusion and other undesirable things. It is a great thing to live way back on the frontier, where money is plentiful and good prices prevail and competition doesn't crowd every line of work and where every man can do as he pleases in every particular. Don't you know it is a great thing to live there?"[2]

Events were livelier by midsummer, 1889, and had to be condensed in the PHAT column. Here is a sample of the condensation:

"Two wounded men in town.
Got in front of guns.
Wrong ends.
Happened to be loaded.
Man behind 'em
Hand on trigger
Pulled.
'Twas in New Mexico
But that's why
Two wounded men in town."[3]

Here is another paragraph: "If Tascosa had shipping pens and were on the trail that leads from the Southwestern country to the Rock Island at Liberal, she would be doing a mammoth business this summer and would be a noble town. But the situation is not thus, and it is ours to lament it."[4]

The PHAT column said on July 27:

"Four business houses
All standing empty.

[2] *The Tascosa Pioneer*, July 13, 1889.
[3] *The Tascosa Pioneer*, July 29, 1889.
[4] *The Tascosa Pioneer*, July 27, 1889.

It won't be the case
When the ———!"

On August 17, 1889, *The Pioneer* carried this item:
"Mrs. John Ryan and the little ones took the train Tuesday
night for Amarillo, where they joined Mr. Ryan and where
they will make their home for the present. But Jack is one
man who has lots of confidence in Tascosa, and he will have
his citizenship here when the Rock Island comes, without
a doubt."

On August 24 the paper said: "the waterworks sprang
a leak last night in the middle of Main Street, and quite a wet
spot of ground this morning showed surprisingly up. An investigation discovered that a plug had become loosened, and
in an hour or two it was repaired. But for the nonce our usually quiet town was greatly excited, not having anything to
excite us so much since the train robbery at Cheyenne."

On September 14 of that dry, hot summer Rudolph
saw some hope in a rumor that Charles Goodnight was selling
out and quoted the *Fort Worth Gazette*, which thought it
presaged good for the Panhandle. *The Pioneer* commented:
"If Charles Goodnight, the greatest of all the cattle
kings, has indeed sold out, as reported in the Gazette's Clarendon specials yesterday, the greatest living obstacle to the
settlement of the Panhandle has been removed. And if he has
disposed of his cattle interests, it may well be construed as
an indication of the approaching end of the big pastures.
Charles Goodnight is a smart man, and knows when he has
enough. The man with the plow will occupy the Panhandle
—the future granary of Texas."

The week of October 18, 1889, the editor deplores the
school situation: "We have no school now. A town ought
always to keep a school if it means to convince a skeptical
public of its boast of being the metropolis city of the Panhandle. Because the other big towns have schools."

In the same issue *The Pioneer* announced it was dropping a column for the winter. "We have dropped a column, and will come forth in this slightly reduced form until one of three things takes place—until spring opens, or business improves, or the Rock Island comes."

On April 19, 1890, *The Pioneer* carried an item to the effect that J. M. Robinson and Bud Turner were putting in and operating a saloon at the "new and tolerably coming town of Grenada in Deaf Smith County."

On April 26, 1890, Rudolph reported that W. D. Twichell, E. C. Godwin-Austen, and Z. B. Hagins had left to survey a townsite at the Rivers section house twelve to fifteen miles above Tascosa in Hartley County.

On May 3 of the same year Rudolph surveyed the situation in Tascosa under the heading "Building and Realty" and listed a dozen buildings, screen doors, and other items, but no transfer of property.

On May 31, *The Pioneer* reported that "Ira Rinehart is preparing to pack up his goods some time next week, probably about the 4th, and ship to Texline where he will open a grocery. Mr. Rinehart thinks there is not local trade enough here now to give him his share, and he will hunt new fields. His family will not go now, but will perhaps go later. The Rineharts are others of the old timers, and we don't know hardly how to let them go."

In the same issue the paper reported that the well-diggers had struck water at Rivers at 288 feet and suggested that the new town "was starting out to capture the business of Hartley County, because a $5,000 hotel is to be built there shortly, and it is said a trail opened up through the Capitol lands from New Mexico to that point, which will make it a shipping town and guarantee it to down Hartley in all respects."

The hope of the editor about the future of Tascosa was expressed with as much confidence as circumstances permitted on the occasion of *The Pioneer's* fifth anniversary number on June 14, 1890. He again declared that the coming of the railroad within the year might save the paper and the town. A part of his summary follows:

"Tascosa expects and hopes for an extension of the Rock Island railway within another year; Amarillo counts on the building of the Santa Fe Line from Panhandle; the southern counties, notably Deaf Smith and Randall, are calculating in the Denver road building across them to the Southwest; Mobeetie is awaiting with impatience the pushing out of the 'Frisco'; and all over the Panhandle development and progress are halting till the railroads lay their network and mark where the successful towns and convenient markets will be."

On June 28, 1890, he chided those weak in their faith: "There may be a few people who are weak in the knees and tender in the spine over the prospect of staying with Tascosa through her travail and sorrow and days of decline; they who remain will have their reward, and establish themselves in the best town to the discomfiture of those who are weak in faith; for the time is surely coming when fortune will reverse her favors among the Panhandle towns, and the boom that will strike Tascosa then will land her high up on the dry and grassy beach, above the rivalry and safe even from the envy of the towns that are now talking so boastful. These things will be and come to pass when the Rock Island comes. Watch the prediction."

Jess Jenkins always had a strong following among the little men he championed, and when he moved from his ranch on the Punta de Agua to the new townsite of Hartley, about midway of Hartley County, a large number of men and their families followed. They filed on land in Hartley and Moore counties outside the XIT spread and formed the nucleus of a strong nester settlement on the north plains. There Jenkins was soon involved in a townsite fight. The XIT group headed by Al Boyce were determined to move the county seat to

Channing. The nesters in the upper plains area were as determined not to have this done. Jenkins lost no time in going into business in the new town and let no grass grow under his feet in electing his friends to public office.

Ruck Tanner, Tascosa cowpuncher and former member of the crowd often accused by the big outfits of being opposed to their best interests, was elected the first county judge of Hartley County. He was later indicted and removed from office because of irregularities. Tobe Robinson, another popular businessman and cowman of Tascosa, was the first sheriff of Hartley County. Dave Adkinson, Bill Wheeler, George Knighton, Britt Roberts, and a large group of other men who made their living wolfing, mustanging, running a few cattle, or picking up odd jobs and doing a little trading about Tascosa joined the exodus to the greener pastures at Hartley.

The Pioneer carried many personal items concerning the removal of these men and their families to the new town and the business firms which closed in Tascosa. Always the items wished to a departed citizen good luck but expressed regret at his loss. With every removal went an old friend of Rudolph's, one more foreign subscription to his spunky little paper, and one less advertising prospect. Undoubtedly he often longed to go with them; for there was an occasional note in his paper which indicates as much to one who reads between the lines.

The exodus from Tascosa to Hartley was typical of the development that was taking place over the Panhandle as the Denver Railway began its early business. The Santa Fé pushed across the Canadian River from Oklahoma and continued to Carson City but missed Fort Elliott and old Mobeetie in its route. The junction of the two roads, first accomplished by a spur from Washburn to Carson City but later by a direct line from Carson City (now Panhandle) to Amarillo, opened a vast country to development and furnished many shipping points. Amarillo, by securing the intersection of the two railroads, became definitely established as a rail-crossroads town. Hope that the intersection would be hers had kept the flame of Tascosa's ambitions burning. Now, as many people left Tascosa for the new town of Amarillo as had left for Hartley. Rudolph himself, attracted to the new metropolis of the Panhandle, established a daily newspaper in Amarillo, even though he continued *The Pioneer* at Tascosa. The one tie which held him to Tascosa was the possibility of the Rock Island's intersecting the Denver at Tascosa on its transcontinental route. As railroad development came, new shipping facilities were made available for cattle herds and new business firms sprang up to serve the great empire that once centered in Tascosa. The new towns were generally strongly supported. During their first few years of boom existence, they always offered business and political opportunities to the hungry pioneers of the Canadian.

As the new shipping points and rival towns were sapping away Tascosa's population and some of her fame, the fight for grasslands in the Panhandle country brought further reductions in population in the Canadian River country. When they realized that free grass and open ranges were no longer possible, the cattle outfits made every effort to get as much land in their possession by sale or lease and under fence as possible. The fenced cattle kingdoms came into being, and since it took far less men to handle cattle under fenced range than in the open-range country, a cut in population along the Canadian resulted. Out on the plains, thanks to the use of well drills and windmills, the farmers were settling on small farms, and stock farms and many small ranches were coming into existence. These, however, were being accommodated by the new towns on the rail lines. Homestead laws and liberal terms for the purchase of state lands led to rapid development in other sections of the Panhandle. These regulations had been adopted only after a long and bitter fight between cattle interests who sought free grass and the open range and politicians and citizens of the state who felt the country should be thrown open to settlement. It was merely another phase of the battle between the big men and the little men. The little men won on the face of the returns; but the laws, which grew out of the problems of the day and the change in range practices, permitted the fencing of vast ranches as well as the development of farms. The Tascosa country was suitable only for the cattle business, and Tascosa had no friends among the big outfits. They fenced the town in and carried their business to townsites of their own promotion or bought from the big houses that were being established in Amarillo. They were vigilant in protecting their fences from visiting herds trailed in from the south or the west. The XIT turned their herds out of the Escabadas to the Tierra Blanca and thence into Amarillo. The LS co-operated through its fiery and able young boss, Al Popham. He made it difficult for anyone to use the shipping pens at Tascosa because they were in the midst of LS-owned and fenced land.

Another factor that worked against the Canadian River Valley and Tascosa was the Texas tick fever. The cattlemen established a quarantine and prevented trail herds from crossing certain sections of the plains country, but they did not have any rule against the XIT's bringing in several thousand head of South Texas cattle. These cattle brought tick fever with them. Heavy loss was incurred by the ranch, but a more irreparable loss was sustained by many of the small stock farmers and nester cattlemen, who did not have the financial ability to withstand the losses of their small herds. Marion Armstrong and others sued the XIT for the loss of their cattle. They claimed that in bringing the tick-infected cattle to the Canadian River, the XIT had brought about great loss to the small herds. Jess Jenkins said that it was his opinion that the tick-infested cattle were deliberately brought into the country to bring about the destruction of the nester herds. This idea, of course, could immediately be discounted by the terrific loss suffered by the XIT. Nevertheless, there was a great amount of hard feeling over the losses sustained by the little men, many of whom held this theory. This contributed to a further decline in business, to a further loss in population in the Canadian River country, and to a wider breach between the big outfits and their small neighbors, the real citizens of Tascosa.

Typical of the bad feeling which existed toward the nesters throughout the Canadian River country was the tragic death of John Leverton on December 1, 1886. George and John Leverton, able cowpunchers and bronc riders and experienced in the rough and tumble hardships of the frontier, had gradually acquired a small herd of cattle, married, and settled down in Evans Canyon in the Blue Creek country. By a few weeks John and his wife preceded George and his mate to the canyon homestead and thus had the honor of being the first settlers in Moore County.

Through a mistake in the little-known survey lines, they built their first rock cabin a few yards inside the LX range, where they were decidedly unwelcome, as were other nester families that moved into the section. They were first subjected to court action on charges of the LX Ranch that they had trespassed on their land. The harassing experiences of the next few months put them on a keen edge. Two outlaws who later "moved West" plagued them by putting their brands on four LX calves. Someone took an LX calfhide and hid it in a prairie-dog hole near the John Leverton home. They had court action over the removal of their home from the LX range and that ranch sued them for $5,000 damages.

The culmination was the shooting of John Leverton by a posse of six men on a cold day in December, 1886. The men had a warrant for him charging cattle theft. Billy Dixon, the famous Indian scout and hero of the battles of Buffalo Wallow and Adobe Walls, refused to be a member of the posse. Rudolph's first story of the killing was a damning in-

dictment couched in bitter and resentful words. The next issue stated that perhaps his first story had been wrong or that
all of the facts were not available, and in a third story he
stated that the matter would be settled in the courts.[5] G. W.
Arrington and Cape Willingham were tried at Clarendon for
murder on charges growing out of the Leverton affair but
were acquitted.

Not all of the hazing and harassing by the big outfits
resulted in tragedies such as the big fight at Tascosa and the
Leverton shooting, but they were effective. Although the
citizens of Tascosa resented these actions wholeheartedly,
the little men became fewer in numbers as the rules and regulations of the ranchers were enforced with a vengeance and
sometimes without regard for individual or property rights,
or for the little men themselves.

In 1890 Al Boyce submitted a report to the XIT officials
in Chicago that proposed to reorganize the ranch and move
its headquarters and warehouse from Tascosa and the Alamocitos region sixteen miles northwest to a point on the
plains just out of the breaks in Hartley County. He pointed
out that this move would make management of the ranch
more efficient and would better adapt it to the new order in
the cattle industry. Some persons believe that additional factors influenced his suggestion, because he proposed to buy a
town section on the railroad near the new headquarters and
to establish at Rivers (later Channing) a ranch-headquarters
trading town and possibly county seat of Hartley County.
He was later principal owner of the Channing Mercantile
and Banking Company, and he controlled the new town,
whereas he had run into considerable difficulty in controlling
Tascosa, for there a large group of men were established before the XIT came and Jess Jenkins, the Mexicans, and the
little men that Jenkins influenced were still in power.

[5] *The Tascosa Pioneer*, December 8, 15, and 29, 1886.

The removal of the XIT warehouse and headquarters to the new town was a hard blow to Tascosa. Coupled with it was the policy of the ranch to fence out the herds and cut down traffic through what had once been an open country. The XIT fenced their entire property, and the Alamocitos Division fence ran on the caprock along where Adrian is now located. Here herds could have dropped down the Mujeros to the Alamocitos Creek, trailed down Skunk Arroyo and into Tascosa if the new fence and policy of the XIT and the LS had not cut them off. The LS fence closed in the section from Adrian to Wildorado. Any herd that came against this fence and the policy of the XIT found it much nearer and easier to move on to Amarillo for a shipping point. Thus Tascosa lost practically all of the business that had formerly come from trail herds which had been assembled from as far west as Phoenix, Arizona, Silver City, New Mexico, the Roswell and Pecos country, and the Davis Mountain region in Texas. In some instances the trail herds were allowed through the XIT; but Al Popham, boss of the LS, whose range surrounded the Tascosa shipping pens, was not co-operative with the visitors. The trail-herd business, which had been a big factor in Tascosa's early life, was gone by 1890. It had been killed by the fence, the railroad, and the hard-boiled business policies of the big ranches.

Drought has always been one of the most important factors in the life of the West, and in 1889, 1890, and 1891—in the dry cycle of the early nineties—Tascosa was severely hit. The country blistered from the intense heat of early June and gradually suffered the real tortures of the drought in July and August. A grasshopper plague, an ever-recurring blight in the plains area, added to the devastation. The grasshoppers would eat a large ring of vegetation to the ground, and then migrate to another spot to work again. These rings were soon joined, and hundreds of acres of grass were destroyed. Trees suffered the same fate.

The Pioneer, in its issue of September 21, 1889, gives an idea of the beginning phases of the drought:

"The Canadian River has reached the condition where it is not now running at all, and in this condition it has not previously been for a half dozen years—since April and May of '83, at which time it ceased to run for some six weeks, following a rainless and snowless winter. It is certainly a dry stream now—as dry as a Tascosa citizen would get if starting on a fifty mile journey with no more than a quart. It is dry, truly—as dry as we are at this very moment. Not a spoonful of water can be found in the neighborhood of the big bridge without digging, and even the sandy bed shows no particular degree of dampness, as indicating water at a shallow depth. It is rarely that it goes so completely dry, but we've written it up this time with perfect veracity—if we don't use the same again for a long, long time."

Rudolph's description of a two-day sandstorm reported in his issue of March 29, 1890, is a classic piece of writing about a common occurrence on the plains or any semiarid or desert country. The sandstorms followed the dry summer in the fall and winter of 1889.

"Wednesday was a windy enough day, but it was about midnight or a little after that things went to shaking and nodding in the breezes and getting a move on themselves about right. From that until daylight was the hardest windstorm the oldest inhabitant knows anything of. It just naturally blew and blew and blew, and blowed and blowed and blowed, and swept the country all up in one great big continuous sweep. In that latter half of the night it piled dust heaps everywhere, and sent it through and into the tightest buildings, and rattled the roofs and shook the fences and scattered the loose boards and boxes and barrels and bent the trees and roared and howled and shrieked and hissed till nothing else could be heard. It was frightful. It filled the river with sand till it went temporarily dry. It prevented the passengers who came in and were at the depot from getting over to town till morning broke and its fury had somewhat lessened. And then it kept up that lick all of Thursday. It made us tired and several others reported on the same line."

Great numbers of people who came West to farm or were running small herds were forced to leave in search of food and water. The big ranchers suffered great damage, and wherever possible they cut the number of men in their employ. The net result was a loss of population, drastic in most cases and fatal to the hopes of many new, booming towns.

The drying water holes and the terrific heat seemed also to make the great gray wolves more vicious and bolder than ever before. For some reason they were more numerous. Many nester farmers and ranchers discovered that if they put a long rope, a piece of wire, or a bell around the necks of their colts and calves, the wolves would leave the animals alone. Most of them took this precaution, but the loss was heavy over the entire range. Those animals which the drought did not get had to fight for their lives against the ravagers of the range—lean, hungry, vicious gray wolves.

Mel Armstrong said that one of the most pitiful scenes he remembered was the death of a beautiful white colt which belonged to H. B. Hayden's fine mare. Mel saw the mare acting strange in a part of the range in which she rarely fed, and he rode to her. She was standing over her colt, which had been torn to shreds by the wolves. The surrounding area gave mute evidence of a ferocious struggle for life on the range. It is no small wonder that many hardy souls left the withering plains country during those dry years.

The raw and tricky weather of the great plains thus was a factor in the gradual death of Tascosa and in the generally bad economic conditions throughout the West in the eighties. During the middle eighties there were several successive bad winters and the winter of 1886–87 seemed particularly severe. Thousands of cattle were frozen or starved on the plains or became the victims of the hungry bands of wolves. The terrific winters were followed by summer drought. The area affected covered many states and most of the range country from Young County, Texas, to Montana and Wyoming. The summer of 1886 brought a drought of great severity. The LS Ranch was forced to dig into the sand of the Canadian River and sink troughs to recover enough water for their cattle. Moreover, the drought did great damage to range grasses. Many large outfits were bankrupt as a result of losses sustained during these years. The period also saw the virtual end of buffalo hunting, mavericking, and mustanging, on the Western grasslands. Wild horse herds were caught or brought under control, and the barbed wire fence made hunting, mustanging, and mavericking far more difficult and less profitable. This reduced the number of people who bought supplies at range trading centers in the West. In a general way all these conditions affected Tascosa, but a more specific business element was dealing the little town effective body blows. Jess Jenkins and other persons who have been willing to tell their stories claim that many of the large cattle outfits conspired to be rid of Tascosa. They simply quit trading there and thus perceptibly slowed business.

The *Tascosa Pioneer* did not give up the ghost without a terrific and valiant struggle. Rudolph used every editorial art and license to kill despair, to bolster the hopes of the people, and to keep their faith strong. Some of his comments pay tribute to his fighting heart. Rudolph defended his position in the July 6, 1889, issue of *The Pioneer* with this pertinent paragraph:

"Occasionally someone laughs at us for anticipating or pretending to anticipate that we will get the Rock Island railroad. In this they do us great injustice. We have a right to look for it; we have a right to tell the country that we are looking for it, because if we don't claim it for ourselves nobody else will assign it to us; we even have a right to run a blind hog over the company and to bluff them into coming here if we can. And we have the exalted confidence and the sublimity of gall to believe that we can just naturally do this."

The next week, in his July 13, 1889, issue, he reported: "We can't point to any particular volume of real estate transfers in Tascosa, though occasionally some property changes hands; but you bet it will be a very different tale when the Rock Island comes."

In the same issue he told of the work that was being done to expand Tascosa's trade: "Tascosa is bending her energies in the direction of capturing New Mexico trade, and you needn't doubt but she will roll up a large quantity of it."

In the fall of 1889, trying to keep his chin up in the face of the drought, he reported: "The XIT ranch started two herds of beeves from the north end of their range to Liberal, last week, and shipped them over the Rock Island. By and by the Rock Island shipments will be made from Tascosa." In the same paper he reported the sale of the Cattle Exchange Saloon by A. L. Turner to J. H. East, who consolidated it with his Equity Bar. "Henceforth Tascosa will have but two saloons for a while," he commented.

One issue of the paper reported that Tascosa would have no school that fall, but the November 2, 1889, issue had this news: "Prof. B. Lawson opened school Monday, and will try it a round for the winter. He has the idea that he can make a success of it and so do we. The attendance for this first week was thirty-one."

On November 23, 1889, he published an editorial entitled "In the Spring of '90":

"Not long since The Pioneer got impatient waiting for news of the Rock Island, and decided to distinguish itself and to score a scoop over contemporaries by sending a representative north to the scene of operations and to learn definitely about the prospects of that road moving out. The young gentleman referred to, so long as he was going, made a point of accompanying a train of cattle through, but that was incidental while the other errand was special. We find that the representatives of that road at Liberal and its officials at Kansas City, and the surveyors and agents who throng along it, agree unanimously that it will surely commence building from Liberal in this direction in the early spring, and move out energetically. And Tascosa? The remark which they one and all made up there is that Tascosa is right square 'in the door,' and that they mean to follow the best and most direct route toward El Paso, and Tascosa is dead center on it. The item, dear friends, was treed and brought down with a whole lot of expense and assurance, and other qualities, and if it happens to be good news to any of you, we might suggest how you can reciprocate. For it's reliable. She's sure coming."

There were few favorable items in the spring of 1890, but the editor still had hope and breathed optimism. "Bridging the Tascosa" was the headline item on May 31, 1890. The story read:

"According to an order passed at the recent term of the Commissioners Court, and an agreement had with Road Overseer George Suddeth, work commenced this week and is being energetically pushed on a good substantial bridge for Tascosa Creek, at the west end of Main Street. It is to be twelve feet in width, seventy feet long, six feet over ordinary running water, a solid wooden structure, heavy floor, mudsill foundation. The cost of it will be some two hundred dollars.

"This bridge is an institution which we needed long ago, and the ordering of which now shows our commissioners to be alive to the needs of the times. Its construction too, just at this period in our history, ought to be enough to indicate to the man who was not previously 'on' that there is still a small band of us, a Thermopylean band, who have just gritted our teeth and spat on our hands and sworn that in spite of railroads or corporations or combinations and in spite of false friends and open foes and in spite of ——— and high water we'll hang and rattle with it till the Rock Island comes.

"After this enterprise, some other."

Titled "Volume Five," the annual anniversary editorial of Rudolph on June 14, 1890, was realistic but showed the spirit and sense of humor of the editor:

"This number of The Pioneer, dear reader, is the beginning of its fifth volume, its fifth year, and you'll hardly strike up with a snide country paper once in a hundred times that doesn't feel it's an inalienable right and a pressing duty to dip its pencil into a fresh fountain of gall on the occasion of the changing years, and spout grandiloquently of the things that have been and the things that probably are to be. This premise gives us the right to remark that just four years ago the tenth of this fair June this paper sprang into an existence that has been varying—a pioneer in the literal sense of having come a hundred miles farther out than other Texas papers, a Pioneer that may be—or may not be—four years more in the same field. We can all read the past, but even a newspaper man—candor forces the admission—cannot read with accuracy the future. So we say to you that the next thousand years are full of doubt and mist and smoke—who can tell what the impenetrable fog of time may hide? Not that The Pioneer is one whit dismayed; dismay and despair are articles which have been carefully eliminated from its diet, because they are poor food and bring bad dreams. But if we admit the future to hold things mysterious and unseen, we admit that anything may happen—and when we greet you at the end of the volume now commencing, this year five, as it were, it may be from a handsome brown stone of the Tascosa Daily Pioneer or it may be from its same old common quarters—it may bear the marks of prosperity or of poverty—it may tell of the materialization of its one great hope or it may still be breathing prophecies of the Rock Island.—it may record a town grown out of your knowledge or it may be figuring on a transfer of its affections and a new alliance—its next annual address may come indistinct and impossible to hear, but we will all refuse to think so unless matters grow much worse than now. Because the claim was boldly made in the opening number of the paper that this town was heir to a shining destiny: the claim has been unequivocally uttered and reuttered through succeeding numbers; and it is its high mission to brace up the weak and faltering, and to hang and rattle with Tascosa till these early prophecies come to their accomplishment, and everybody is compelled to acknowledge their timeliness and their inspiration. You may point to a slowly failing population, kind cynic, and ask what the finale will inevitably be; we may draw the old chestnut on you for an answer, and then ask you if Tascosa's well proven vitality doesn't give you patience. You may say that confidence like ours will have a deserved ending in some house of refuge for the very poor or the very demented; we may answer again that when the Rock Island comes you will see an editor, made by his strong bump of hope, and as affable toward you common short-sighted fellows as a bloated bondholder, or bank magnate, or maybe member of congress can afford to be.

"As we said, The Pioneer is now four years old, and now starts out for five. And when at the end of it we talk to you again thus frankly, we shall remember this moment and these sayings, and see what we shall see."

Editor Rudolph boosted his own stock and staying qualities in the June 21, 1890, issue, saying: "The Pioneer is pushing its little boat on out across the calm seas of the year five. The Pioneer has breasted all sorts of weather. It has stood the storms and sleet of adversity and they couldn't down it; it has seen days of prosperity and money getting, and they didn't make it proud. In all probability the Pioneer will be here still, doing mayhap better and mayhap worse when Gabriel blows his trumpet in the morning."

The struggle of the animals against raw nature and the fight of the people to hang on grimly until brighter days were accurately reflected in *The Tascosa Pioneer;* but finally in early 1891, after five years of brilliant reporting and valiant boosting, *The Pioneer* ceased publication. Business had simply reached the point where it was impossible for Rudolph to continue issuing the paper. He moved to Channing, where he published a paper for a short time before going on to more promising fields.

His last editorial was entitled "Here We Quit You" and was in the grand manner characteristic of the man:

"It is useless to make a long to-do about it, or to magnify a thing of no great moment, but this, kind friends, is the closing chapter in the history of The Tascosa Pioneer. For nearly five years it has gone forth proclaiming to the world that we had here a country and a town; has tooted his horn as faithfully as it knew how for the spot on which it hoped to grow up, has kept the best foot forward and a smiling face under every condition, has battled with difficulties and hoped against hope—but today we lay down the saber and give up the fight; and the Pioneer is an institution of the past, a back number, a remembrance, a reminiscence and a dream.

"It might have been different with The Pioneer—but it wasn't. Had Tascosa fared well at fortune's hands, that would have meant permanency for the paper; the citizens have been uniformly liberal in their support of it, and it acknowledges its deep debt of gratitude. But business has gone down to where profit is an unknown and undiscoverable quantity, and the near future holds no promise—and which one of you would do aught but give it up at that? Sentiment is creditable and the home feeling may be hard to stifle, but after all, duty points to go wherever labor hath a sure reward.

"So we quit to seek a new field—it would be childish to hesitate about it longer. We surrender the whole question— we feel that we have done all our duty—we go with a clear conscience, a heavy heart and a light pocketbook. Friends will be remembered for their friendship, and the years of pleasant association with place and people will never fade from memory. The warmest spot in our heart will long be for this little gem of a city on the turgid Canadian, sandy, sheltered, quaint Tascosa.

"No more will The Pioneer crack its ancient chestnuts in your tired ears—no more sing of the glories of Rockislandville—no more picture in wearisome detail the coming country—no more importune the young man to come west—no more chronicle the return of fly time—no more wage relentless war on the poor bachelors. We have had our say and now you can have yours—but as the pall of eternal silence settles down about us we are troubled with the thought: will they cuss us when we're gone?"

A town is not much of a place without a newspaper, and when a town lost its only paper, people in the West in the late nineties figured the town was through. The Quanah *Tribune-Chief* condensed the situation to this nutshell paragraph: "This leaves Tascosa without a paper, and judging from the contents of the last issue of The Pioneer, the town of Tascosa is almost a thing of the past."

In the plains country hard, dashing rains, often covering a full watershed, break a drought. This has happened time and time again over a long period of years. Therefore, when it started raining during the equinoctial storms of September, 1893, that the Canadian River might go on a considerable rampage was not entirely unexpected. As a matter of fact, Jess Jenkins, John Cone, and others interested in Hogtown, had for some time felt great concern about the danger of floods to this particular stretch of land. The Canadian River at that time made a great elbow bend that reached to within one hundred yards of the main street of Tascosa, and it drove straight toward Hogtown and the rich bottom acres that belonged to Casimero Romero. A previous flood had seen the

river out across country and eliminated at the height of
the flood the danger to Tascosa and to East Tascosa. The
river course did not follow this natural and straight basin,
and Jess Jenkins, John Cone, and others saw the possibility
of a channel eventually cutting out to straighten the river
and to remove the threat to their land and adobe buildings.
They conceived the plan of cutting a big ditch through the
river-bottom hay meadow and in this manner straighten the
course of the river at the next big flood. They assembled
teams and workmen and got in one full week's work on this
dry-land canal before McMasters of the LS swore out an injunction that prevented them from continuing their work.
The great scar had been made across the river bottom, however, and needed only a flood to change the course of the
river.

The awaited flood came in 1893. For three days the entire area was subjected to heavy, dashing rains. One old-timer
remarked that it rained cats and dogs with pitchforks thrown
in for good measure. The roof of one of the adobe buildings
at the Frying Pan collapsed, pinning a number of cowboys
underneath, but fortunately did not injure any of them, although it threw several large snakes into the room, much to
the disgust of W. H. Bush, manager of the ranch. Mel Armstrong and Charley Williams were at the Frying Pan the
night the rains started. The next day they made their way
toward Tascosa. Under the impact of the flood the Canadian
River went on one of the worst rampages of its early-day history. Charley and Mel rode their horses across the bridge
only a short time before the big stream took out one span and
headed across the meadowland bottoms, taking full advantage
of the canal which Jenkins, Cone, and Romero had cut.
Seventeen houses in Tascosa were washed away or collapsed
from the onslaught of the flood and torrential rain. Among
these were the old Cone and Edwards Hotel in Hogtown
and houses occupied there by an assorted group of gamblers

and women. Every depression, every buffalo wallow, and every stream in the entire watershed were filled to overflowing in the early stages of the three-day rain and from that time on spilled their contents into the ever increasing flow of flood waters.

When the flood abated and the bright sun shone again, the little town of Tascosa was in virtual ruins. Many buildings had been washed away, others had lost their dirt roofs, and walls had crumbled. The town presented a bedraggled and woebegone appearance. The river had changed its course as a result of the canal cut in the meadowland. The flood widened the stream to two or three times its former width and made a great sand bar out of land which formerly had carried knee-high grass and shrubs. The elbow curve, which had been the course of the river, was a lagoon of stale water. The land between it and the new course was wasteland. One span of the great Canadian River wagon bridge had been washed away and the entire bridge severely damaged. The danger of quicksand and bogging had been materially heightened by the erosion and cutting of the flood waters.

The question of repairing the bridge was immediately brought to the attention of county officials. The heavy taxpayers and big men who had fought its erection in the first place were now equally opposed to its repair. They made no pretense of hiding their objections. The general argument was that Tascosa was dead anyhow, that a bridge could not stand against the floods of the river, and that there was no use in throwing good money after bad. Petitions and protests were unavailing.

The population of Tascosa dwindled in the succeeding days and weeks as large numbers of persons moved to Channing, Hartley, and Amarillo. The big men, who were determined to be rid of the little men or reduce them to virtual peonage, now saw their hopes realized. After the flood the community took stock. Tascosa was simply the county seat with an empty rock courthouse, Joe Bowers' store, Bud Turner's saloon, two or three girls, and a few nester and Mexican families scattered about the immediate area.

An old dream faded for Tascosa when the Chicago, Rock Island and Gulf Railway built its line from Liberal, Kansas, across the north plains of Texas and into New Mexico some twenty miles north of the Canadian River. It missed the town by fifty miles. The line crossed the Canadian at Logan, proceeded on to Tucumcari, where its tracks joined those of the Southern Pacific. This route had the advantage of saving many miles on a transcontinental line and missed much rough country. The railroad boosters who had dreamed of its coming through Tascosa were crushed. The Rock Island line intersected the Fort Worth and Denver near the southwestern edge of Dallam County, and there immediately sprang into being a town which took its name from the letters of Dallam and Hartley counties and came to be known as Dalhart. It was designated as the division point and shop center for the Rock Island, a prospect Rudolph had long cherished for Tascosa. Almost from its birth in August, 1901, it was the metropolis of the north Panhandle, the spot Tascosa had hoped for in the railroad world. It was development such as this that Editor Rudolph had long boosted and strongly predicted. True to the spirit of the times, Dalhart got away to a great boom that embraced the enthusiasm and trade of the great country northwest of Tascosa. To the southeast, Amarillo, although having almost dried up and blown away in the early nineties, was staging a lusty comeback and could boast of being one of the largest cattle shipping points in the world. Both Dalhart and Amarillo were in the open plains country. Each had two railroads that crossed each other in the heart of a vast, undeveloped country. Tascosa was forgotten so far as railroad prospects were concerned. Three railroads had laid a solid network of lines to end the day of the big ranches and towns not favored by railroad promotion.

In the early nineteen hundreds a tremendous amount of land was put on the market in the Panhandle of Texas by the XIT Ranch, the state, and other owners. Companies organized for the purpose of colonizing the lands brought great trains of prospective land buyers to the country in 1904 and 1905. Soon ownership interest in the Panhandle was scattered over the nation, and large groups of people, especially from the Midwest, came to try their hands at farming and stock farming. This development brought about great growth for Channing, Hartley, Dalhart, Amarillo, and many other places throughout the plains country. Naturally this activity detracted from Tascosa, and many of her residents left for new communities where opportunities and business beckoned. Tascosa and the Canadian breaks, except for a few spring-fed and subirrigated valley spots, were entirely unsuitable for farming. That land which could be farmed was a long, long distance from a market.

Coincident with this development and settlement, the Rock Island Railroad in 1908 pushed a line from Amarillo west to Tucumcari, and in doing so saw such small towns as Wildorado, Adrian, and Vega come into being. Vega, the Spanish name for "meadow," soon developed into the most logical rival for Tascosa as the county seat of Oldham County. The farmers and stock farmers who now settled in the country found land on the plains near Vega ample for their use, and as a result the growth of that part of the country exceeded by far any possible growth around Tascosa. About this time the last of the counties attached to Tascosa for judicial purposes was organized, and Tascosa was left to fight it out with a vigorous, hard-hitting rival to retain even the county seat of Oldham County.

A county-seat election was held in 1911 with Adrian and Vega challenging Tascosa's right as county seat. The results favored Tascosa; but sharp controversy arose within the Commissioners' Court over the regularity of the election.

The controversy was settled, but the issue was not. Everyone knew that it was only a matter of time until the influx of nesters on the plains would enable the booming promoters behind some of the townsites on the Rock Island west of Amarillo to win.

As a town dies, picturesque and lovable old characters cling to it until with each death it seems that a definite part of the old town has been buried. This happened in the last years of Tascosa. In 1912 Uncle Billy Urion, who with Scotty Wilson and Jack Leonard had hunted the plains for buffalo and had fought in the first battle of Adobe Walls, died. He was being cared for by his old friend, Scotty Wilson, the *alcalde* of the dying town. Uncle Billy's body was prepared, or "laid out," by his men friends, and a crude wooden casket was made. The next afternoon the casket was placed in a wagon, Scotty Wilson was the driver, and seated in the wagon about the casket were the pallbearers and Judge H. H. Wallace, who was to read the burial service. Behind the wagon were a number of carriages and wagons filled with men, women, and children. As the burial procession pulled up Main Street to head toward the Casimero Romero Cemetery, it passed a saloon. Scotty, with his flowing white hair and beard tousled by the wind, pulled on the reins and stopped the team.

"Well, b'yes, I think Uncle Billy would like this. Let's all go in and have one last drink on Uncle Billy."

Out in the street the burial procession waited, with women fuming because of the delay. Mrs. Mel Armstrong, in describing the scene a few years later, said, "I thought they were going to stay in the saloon all afternoon."

The funeral of Uncle Billy might well have been prophetic, a symbol of the dying town, for three years later, on May 24, 1915, a second county-seat election made Vega the county seat. W. H. Fuqua and others interested in speculation, and the Vega Townsite Company, did what has often been done in the West. They gave 160 lots to cowboys, nesters, and others who would vote with them to move the county seat. Some of the land titles and tax records in Oldham County show the lack of interest of these newcomers after election day.

The day after the election, officials packed those county records which they did not burn and drove across the river and over the dim wagon trail that led southeast to the upland-meadow farming region of the county. The officials could see as they drove away from Tascosa a few small farms and shacks and they knew of other nester places on the pleasant little creeks near by, but their records could tell of the struggle these nesters were having to live and to pay taxes. Immediately after they crossed the river, they could see a few people who were located on some subirrigated land that included the site of the old Borregos Plaza; but it was evident that the people who lived there were finding it difficult to maintain themselves as the county became more isolated.

The officials continued on their journey toward Vega, taking with them the records of Oldham County. In those records were the legal authorization that in a former day had made Tascosa the capital of ten western counties and that now permitted those same records to be transferred to a punier and far less colorful rival. Among the records which Scotty Balfour and Allen Stagg had burned before starting on the trip were the old brand books, records of the symbols of a Western aristocracy and the little maverickers who challenged the right of the big men to the open range.

In 1915 Father Patrick J. Murphy, who served the crumbling adobe St. Barnabas Catholic Church as a missionary from St. Anthony's Church at Dalhart, reported: "On account of the dangerous condition of the building it was decided by the congregation to hold Mass in the future in the home of one of the two families." The following year his annual report had written in fine script across the top of the page: "Town gone. County seat transferred to Vega. All Catholics gone."

In 1917 as Americans engaged in their first World War, there came a demand for more wheat and more farm products. Level plains land was given to the plow. Great fields, some of them miles in length, were turned under and put into wheat and grain. The land around Tascosa was not fit for agriculture, and consequently the community's place in the sun was further darkened by the expansion of farming to the north and south on the plains and the increased attention of cattlemen to the Canadian River ranges. People were called away from the range country to the farming regions. This exodus gave those sections new impetus. The land more suitable for cattle was left for that purpose and to further isolation.

The XIT spent twenty years or more doing its best to colonize and dispose of its spread. Some employees and officials on the ground were a bit reluctant to carry out the sale order because it meant the end of their jobs. The cowboys who made a last stand on the vast acres were eager that it should remain the great open spaces. The organization, nevertheless, brought hundreds of farmers and stock farmers to the plains country.

Much of the XIT range, however, was not suitable for farming, especially the Alamocitos Division. This magnificent section, in itself a vast ranch of more than 200,000 acres, was sold to the Matador Land and Cattle Company, one of two big ranch outfits owned in Scotland and England that succeeded in the West. The sale offered Tascosa no new hope, because the Matadors merely enlarged and improved the XIT headquarters near Channing.

Tascosa was now scarcely remembered. Al Morris was growing fine apples on the Casimero Romero place and failing to find a market for them. Bud Turner had established himself in a good estate on the Rica. One by one the adobe buildings collapsed and crumbled as people moved away. The courthouse was sold to Julian Bivins, who began using it as a ranch headquarters. Scotty Balfour moved his family into a small house between old Tascosa and Al Morris's place. One day in the nineteen twenties Morris and his boys tore down the remaining old adobe houses in Hogtown and planted squash in a ground that had once been fertilized by the blood of real Western men.

EPILOGUE. Tascosa Today

CHARLES M. RUSSELL, great Western cowboy artist, once said, "The West is like a sweetheart. You may lose her but you will not forget her." Russell could have made the same statement about towns. It is the spirit of a town that lives.

In 1945 the spirit of Tascosa and its little men is alive. The open-range world passed long ago to make way for the big fenced cattle empires. These in turn were challenged and largely replaced by the man with the hoe; but the man with the hoe has been on the road in a broken-down jalopy hunting work and food these many years, while the big farmer with the tractor and power-farming methods has taken over. The Panhandle has grown into the era of the big stock farmer, just as Rudolph predicted in his *Pioneer*. The Canadian River Valley, because of its rough terrain, has been kept by the cattleman, and the famous brands of yesterday are seen on fine cattle and horses, and other brands are joining them in modern popularity. The cowboys ride the ranges, repairing fences and windmills, and go about the job of running a ranch, their horses many times giving way to trucks. The battle of Nature and of a raw economy has depopulated the Canadian River Valley in the Tascosa country, while less than a hundred miles downstream a great oil and gas field has brought tremendous industrial development and rich cities. Thousands of people live near the old Dixon Creek stage stand which was such a welcome sight to the men who carried the mail in 1878 and 1879. In contrast, less than fifty adults live in the vast range empire, the center of which is Old Tascosa.

Frenchy McCormick lived the fading years of a glorious romance. When she, the last of the girls of the Golden West, was buried beside her Mickey at Tascosa in 1941, the thin thread which linked the new with the old West was broken. Her loyalty to an ideal and to the love of a little Irish gambler inspired many writers and poets and just plain people of the city and the range. Tascosa bathed in the glory of this limelight.

Among those who sang "Home on the Range" at her funeral was a group of boys. They were from Boys' Ranch, created by Julian Bivins' gift of the old courthouse and the Tascosa townsite to an organization of ranchers and businessmen in Amarillo who, under the leadership of Cal Farley, were working in behalf of underprivileged boys. The little men were and are once again in the saddle at Tascosa. These big-hearted men have become big brothers. Plans are being carried out for vast improvements at Boys' Ranch because the fifty boys are crowding the place.

Time, which seemed to focus its events and its men there, is playing again with Tascosa. Boys' Ranch has attracted national publicity to the place and a major motion picture has been filmed about it by Metro-Goldwyn-Mayer. Thus once again Tascosa takes the center of the stage, as Editor Rudolph was wont to say, and doffs its hat to an audience larger than it ever dreamed of playing to before.

In the Panhandle, leaders, or sons or grandsons of lead-

ers, in busy, thriving cities speak with pride and affection
of Tascosa and Boys' Ranch. They recall their own experiences or background there. Tascosa was the mother of Amarillo, Queen City of the Panhandle, and of Channing, Hartley, Vega, Dalhart, and many more Panhandle communities.
Her citizenship made a great contribution to a fast-changing,
ever-developing empire. Everywhere there is a pride in her
crowded, turbulent history. Everywhere in this country
there is some cowboy who loves and remembers her when
he drinks to the old West.

BIBLIOGRAPHY

I. INTERVIEWS

Armstrong, Mel, with the author, 1941–45.

Arnot, John, with the author, 1941–45.

Baird, Ed, with the author, Canyon, Texas, 1923.

Baird, W. F., with the author, Canyon, Texas, August 10, 1941.

Baldwin, S. D., with Earl Vandale, Lordsburg, New Mexico, n.d.

Bugbee, Harold, with the author, 1941–45.

Bush, J. A., with the author, 1941–44.

Bush, W. H., with J. A. Bush, Amarillo, Texas, n. d.

Coots, Gus, with the author, Amarillo, Texas, March 7, 1943.

Dobbs, Kid, with the author, Farmington, New Mexico, September 12–14, 1942.

Fuqua, W. H., with the author, 1942–44.

Gough, Judge L., with the author, Amarillo, Texas, 1928.

Gurules, Ysabel, with Mel Armstrong, Tascosa, Texas, 1898–1912.

Hamlin, J. D., with the author, 1941–44.

Hooks, Bones, with the author, 1941–45.

Howard, Jules, with Mel Armstrong, Tascosa, Texas, n. d.

Ingerton, W. H., with the author, 1941–43.

Jenkins, Jess, with the author, 1937–45.

Lang, John, with the author, Amarillo, Texas, 1941.

McDonald, Mrs. E. M., with the author, Tascosa, Texas, August 5, 1928.

Martínez, Celso, with E. E. Miera, Buyeros, New Mexico, April 7, 1941.

May, Mrs. J. E., with the author and Earl Vandale, Vega, Texas, September 23, 1941.

Mooar, J. Wright, with the author, Amarillo, Texas, September 20, 1938.

Morris, Al, with the author, 1930–44.

Neff, Boss, with the author, Spearman, Texas, April 24, 1941.

Oliver, J. G., with the author, 1941–42.
Potter, Colonel Jack, with the author, 1941–44.
Queen, Beall, with the author, 1941–44.
Romero, José, with Roy Riddle, Amarillo, Texas, July 10, 1938.
Snider, John, with the author, 1941–45.
Stagg, Allen, with the author, 1942–44.
Sullivan, D. A., with the author, Amarillo, Texas, May 1, 1940.
Thompson, A. W., with the author, 1941–43.

2. LETTERS

Collinson, Frank, to the author. El Paso, Texas, May 7, 1941.
Dills, Lucius, to the author. Roswell, New Mexico, December 10, 1942.
Giles, Bascomb, commissioner of the General Land Office of Texas, to the author. Austin, Texas, May 12, 1941.
McCrea, Clayton, to the author. Pacific Grove, California, October 22, 1942.
O'Connell, Ambrose, first assistant postmaster general, to the author. Washington, May 10, 1941.

3. MANUSCRIPT MATERIALS AND GOVERNMENT RECORDS

Armstrong, Marion. "Memoirs." Bound vol. in library of John L. McCarty, Amarillo, Texas.
Commissioners' Court Records, Oldham County, Texas. Vega, Texas.
Hamner, Laura V. "Life Began in the Seventies." 2 bound vols. in library of John L. McCarty, Amarillo, Texas.

4. NEWSPAPERS

The Amarillo Sunday Globe-News, Amarillo, Texas, August 14, 1938, May 3, 1940, April 6, 1941, October 26, 1941, and November 2, 1941.
The Arkansas Gazette, Little Rock, Arkansas, March 23, 1941.
The Dallas Morning News, Magazine Section, 1922 (no further date).
The Tascosa Pioneer, 1886–91. Bound volume of editorial comment in Panhandle-Plains Historical Museum, Canyon, Texas.

5. BOOKS

Arnold, Oren. *Wild Life in the Southwest*. Banks Upshaw and Company, Dallas, 1935.

Babb, Dot. *In the Bosom of the Comanches*. Published by the author, Dallas, 1912 and 1923.

Bechdolt, Frederick R. *Tales of the Old Timers*. The Century Company, New York, 1924.

Bolton, Herbert Eugene. *Athanase de Mezières and the Louisiana-Texas Frontiers, 1768-1780.* The Arthur H. Clark Company, Cleveland, 1914.

——(ed.). *Spanish Exploration in the Southwest, 1746-1771.* Charles Scribner's Sons, New York, 1916.

Burns, Walter Noble. *The Saga of Billy the Kid*. Grosset and Dunlap, New York, 1926.

Carroll, H. Bailey, and J. Villasana Haggard (trans. and eds.). *Three New Mexico Chronicles; the Exposición of . . . Pino, 1812; the Ojeada of . . . Barreiro, 1832; and the Additions . . . by Escudero, 1849.* The Quivira Society, Albuquerque, New Mexico, 1942.

Culley, John H. (Jack). *Cattle, Horses and Men of the Western Range*. The Ward Ritchie Press, Los Angeles, 1940.

Dale, Edward Everett. *Cow Country*. University of Oklahoma Press, Norman, 1942.

Dobie, J. Frank. *The Longhorns*. Little, Brown and Company, Boston, 1941.

Dodge, Colonel Richard Irving. *Our Wild Indians: Thirty-three Years' Personal Experience Among the Red Men of the Great West . . . .* A. D. Worthington and Company, Hartford, Connecticut, 1884.

Foreman, Grant. *Pioneer Days in the Early Southwest*. The Arthur H. Clark Company, Cleveland, 1926.

Fulton, Maurice Garland (ed.). *The Authentic Life of Billy the Kid, the Noted Desperado,* by Pat F. Garrett. The MacMillan Company, New York, 1927.

Garretson, Martin S. *The American Bison*. New York Zoological Society, New York, 1938.

Goodwin, Cardinal. *The Trans-Mississippi West.* The Appleton Company, New York, 1927.

Gould, Charles M. *The Geology and Water Resources of the Western Portion of the Panhandle.* Government Printing Office, Washington, 1906.

Gregg, Josiah. *Commerce of the Prairies.* The Southwest Press, Dallas, 1933. (A reprint edition of *Commerce of the Prairies, the Journal of a Santa Fé Trader.)*

Guyer, James S. *Pioneer Life in West Texas.* Published by the author, Brownwood, Texas, 1938.

Haley, J. Evetts. *Charles Goodnight, Cowman and Plainsman.* Houghton Mifflin Company, Boston, 1936.

——. *George W. Littlefield, Texan.* University of Oklahoma Press, Norman, 1943.

——. *The XIT Ranch of Texas and the Early Days of the Llano Estacado.* The Lakeside Press, Chicago, 1929.

Hamner, Laura V. *Short Grass and Longhorns.* University of Oklahoma Press, Norman, 1942.

Harper, Minnie Timms, and George Dewey. *Old Ranches.* Dealey and Lowe, Dallas, 1936.

Hewett, Edgar L. *Ancient Life in the American Southwest.* Bobbs–Merrill Company, Indianapolis, 1930.

Holden, W. C. *Alkali Trails.* The Southwest Press, Dallas, 1930.

Hoyt, Henry F. *A Frontier Doctor.* Houghton Mifflin Company, Boston, 1929.

Kelly, Erick P. *On the Staked Plain, El Llano Estacado.* The Macmillan Company, New York, 1940.

Logue, Roscoe. *Tumbleweeds and Barb Wire Fences.* Russell Stationery Company, Amarillo, Texas, 1935.

McCarty, John (compiler and ed.). *Some Experiences of Boss Neff in the Texas and Oklahoma Panhandle.* The Globe-News Publishing Company, Amarillo, Texas, 1941.

MacDonald, A. B. (ed.). *Hands Up! True Stories of the Six-Gun Fighters of the Old Wild West as Told by Fred E. Sutton and Written Down by A. B. MacDonald.* A. L. Burt Company, Chicago, 1927.

Marshall, T. M. *A History of the Western Boundary of the*

Louisiana Purchase, 1819–1841. University of California Press, Berkeley, 1924.

Nye, Captain W. S. *Carbine and Lance.* University of Oklahoma Press, Norman, 1937.

Paxson, Frederick L. *History of the American Frontier, 1763–1793.* Houghton Mifflin Company, Boston, 1924.

Phillips, Philip Lee (ed.). *The Lowery Collection, A Descriptive List of Maps of the Spanish Possessions Within the Present Limits of the United States, 1502–1820,* by Woodbury Lowery. Government Printing Office, Washington, 1912. This volume lists these maps showing Quivira, not always in the same location: Agnese, Barrista, 1543–50; Lopez de Velasco, Juan, 1571–74; and a seventeenth century map of the world without name, date, or title.

Poe, Sophie A. *Buckboard Days.* The Caxton Printers, Ltd., Caldwell, Idaho, 1936.

Potter, Colonel Jack. *Cattle Trails of the Old West.* Laura R. Krehbiel, Clayton, New Mexico, 1935.

Raine, William MacLeod. *Famous Sheriffs and Western Outlaws.* Garden City Publishing Company, New York, 1928.

Rhodes, May D. *The Hired Man on Horseback.* Houghton Mifflin Company, Boston, 1938.

Russell, Charles M. *Good Medicine.* Garden City Publishing Company, Garden City, New York, 1930.

Siringo, Charles A. *A Cowboy Detective, an Autobiography.* W. B. Conkey Company, Chicago, 1912.

———. *A Lone Star Cowboy.* Published by the author, Santa Fé, New Mexico, 1919.

———. *Riata and Spurs, the Story of a Lifetime Spent in the Saddle as Cowboy and Ranger.* Houghton Mifflin Company, Boston, 1931.

Swan, Oliver G. *Covered Wagon Days.* Grosset and Dunlap, New York, 1928.

Toulouse, Joseph H., and James R. *Pioneer Posts of Texas.* The Naylor Company, San Antonio, Texas, 1936.

Webb, Walter Prescott. *The Great Plains.* Ginn and Company, Boston, 1931.

Wellman, Paul I. *The Trampling Herd, the Story of the Cattle Range in America.* Carrick and Evans, New York, 1939.

Wharton, Clarence R. *L'Archevêque.* The Anson Jones Press, Houston, Texas, 1941.

Winship, George Parker (trans. and ed.). *The Journey of Coronado, 1540-41, from the City of Mexico to . . . the Buffalo Plains . . . .* A. S. Barnes and Company, New York, 1904.

6. ARTICLES

Arnot, John. "My Recollections of Tascosa Before and After the Coming of the Law," *The Panhandle–Plains Historical Review,* Vol. VI (1933), 58–97.

Bugbee, Mrs. Helen. "A Sketch of the Life of Thomas Sherman Bugbee," *The Panhandle–Plains Historical Review,* Vol. V (1932), 8–22.

Donohue, David. "The Route of the Coronado Expedition in Texas," *Southwest Historical Quarterly,* Vol. XXXII, No. 3 (January, 1929), 181–92. (Reprint.)

Haley, J. Evetts. "Charles Goodnight, Pioneer," *The Panhandle–Plains Historical Review,* Vol. III (1928), 3–29.

———. "Jim East—Trail Hand and Cowboy," *The Panhandle–Plains Historical Review,* Vol. IV (1931), 39–61.

———. "Pastores del Palo Duro," *The Southwest Review,* Vol. XIX, No. 3 (April, 1934), 279–94. (Reprint.)

INDEX

Adams, President John: 7
Adkinson, Dave: 233
Adobe Walls: 14, 37, 65, 116, 238, 254
Adrian, Texas: 240, 253
Alamocitos Ranch: 102, 111, 168, 239-40, 256
Albuquerque, New Mexico: 210
Allen, Bill: 46
Allen, C. C.: 227
Amarillo, Texas: 159, 174, 183, 214, 223, 234-37, 240, 251-53, 259-60
Amarillo Creek, East: 70; see Amaryllis Creeks
Amaryllis Creeks, West and East: 159; see Amarillo Creek
Anderson, Bill: 130, 182
Antelope Springs: 188
Anton Chico, New Mexico: 18, 86
Anza, Don Juan Bautista de: 9
Archevêque: see l'Archevêque
Arkansas: 7
Arkansas River: 44-45
Armstrong, Mac: 154
Armstrong, Marion: 38, 54, 60-68, 70, 74, 97, 101, 150-51, 154, 167, 194, 237
Armstrong, Mel: 150, 154, 160, 182, 242, 250
Armstrong, Mrs. Mel: 254
Armstrong, Sam: 66
Armstrong, Tom: 154
Arnot, John: 55, 186
Arrington, Captain G. W.: 100, 175, 239
Atascosa, Texas: 56
Atascosa Plaza: 16
Austin, A. M.: 194
Austin, Mrs. A. M.: 201
Austin, Texas: 218

Babcock, Bud: 71

Baca: 21
Baca, Francisco: 29
Baca, Sacramento: 23, 25-27
Baird, W. F.: 166
Bajo del Sol: 11
Baldwin, Lieutenant: 14
Balfour, Scotty: 255, 257
Bar WA brand: 123-24
Barber shop: 172
Barnes, Dad: 64
Bassett, Bob: 137
Bates, W. H. (Deacon): 45-46
Beals, David T.: 45
Beaver Creek: 164
Beeman, Mr.: 44
Bell, Mr.: 29, 33
Bell brand: 126
Berry, Mr.: 29, 33-34
Big Grey (Kid Dobbs' horse): 72
Billy the Kid: 12, 20-21, 27, 36, 41-42, 48, 50, 77-81, 82-86, 88-93, 97, 109, 125, 128-29, 136
Bissell, F. E.: 218
Bivins, Julian: 45, 257, 259
Bivins, Lee: 45
Black Springs Draw: 81
Blanco Canyon: 14
Bloodworth, Rev. J. T.: 201
Blue Creek: 46, 238
Bogman, Mr.: 60
Boise City, Oklahoma: 214
Bonita Creek: 50, 64, 67-70, 75
Bonney, William: see Billy the Kid
Boothill: 96, 99, 101-106, 152, 153
Boothill Cemetery: 53, 96, 154
Borina, W. B.: 110
Borregos, Justo: 16
Borregos, Ventural: 16
Borregos Plaza: 15-17, 22-23, 29, 36, 40, 58, 217, 253
Bouldin, John: 182

267

Edwards, Idalene: 60
Edwards Hotel: 103
Elizabethtown, New Mexico: 53
El Llano Estacado (the Staked Plains): 4, 5, 8, 10–11, 22, 25, 29, 57, 58, 201
El Morro, Colorado: 163
El Paso, Texas: 7, 212, 226, 245
El Paso del Norte: *see* El Paso, Texas
Ely, George (Pidgeon): 173
Emory, Charley: 149
Emory, Sally: 134, 142–43, 145–46, 175
Emory, Tom: 85–86, 88–90, 146–47, 155, 176
Entrania Springs: 188
Equity Bar: 55, 145, 172, 199, 244
Escabadas, the: 237
Evans Canyon: 238
Ewing, Uncle Billy: 59
Exchange Hotel: 55, 60, 145, 148, 151, 173, 193

Farley, Cal: 259
Farwell-Taylor and Company: 204
Feliz River: 75
First Street: 193
Florentine: 27, 32
Fort Bascom, New Mexico: 12–14, 67–68, 70–71, 78, 80, 85
Fort Dodge, Kansas: 28, 186
Fort Elliott, Texas: 28, 33, 65–69
Fort Griffin, Texas: 14, 58
Fort Sill, Oklahoma: 65
Fort Smith, Arkansas: 7–8
Fort Stanton, New Mexico: 91
Fort Sumner, New Mexico: 91
Fort Sumner–Portales road: 87
Fort Union, New Mexico: 17, 21
Fort Worth, Texas: 218, 227
Fort Worth and Denver City Railroad: 169, 200, 210, 212–15, 217, 225–27, 252
Fort Worth Gazette: 232
Frio Creek: 110
Frio Draw: 15, 29
"Frisco": 234
Frog Lip Sadie: 100

Frosty Lane: 193
Frying Pan Ranch: 49, 126, 159–62, 166–67, 182, 250
Fulton, Pete: 105
Fuqua, W. H.: 254

García, Miguel: 21, 26, 39
García's store: 188
Garrett, Pat: 84–86, 88–89, 91–93, 129–32, 136–39, 178
Gate of the Moon: 86
Gatlin, Bill: 125–27, 132, 136–38
Gaton, W. A.: 110
Get Even Cattle Company: 123
Gibson, Bill: 103
Gizzard Lip: 100
Glidden, Joseph: 156, 158
Glidden and Sanborn: 49
Gober, Jim: 149
Goddard, C. F.: 110
Godwin-Austen, E.: 36–37, 48, 150
Godwin-Austen, Mrs. E.: 179
Gomez, Claudio: 151
Gomez, Juan A.: 110, 194
GMS herd: 52
Goodanuf: 23, 33–34
Goodnight, Charles: 12, 18, 20–22, 26, 28–29, 36–37, 46, 58, 82, 91, 205–206, 232
Goodnight, Mrs. Charles: 58
Goodrich, Bish: 44, 46
Gough, John: *see* Catfish Kid
Grace Street: 193
Graham, Texas: 83
Gran Quivira: 4
Granada, Colorado: 45
Grayson County, Texas: 52, 159
Great American Desert: 4
Greathouse, Jim: 14
Great Plains: 6–7
Greeley, Horace: 57
Green, Padre: 42
Greer County, Texas: 202, 209
Griffin, Button: 145–46, 172, 199
Griffin, Roy: 109–10
Griffin's Saloon: 144
Grisson, J. L.: 110
Groesbeck, Texas: 57
Guadalupe Mountain: 75

Index

Gunter, Jules: 112
Gunter and Munson: 52, 54, 107
Gurules, Agapito: 27, 39
Gurules, Felix: 26, 30–31
Gurules, Ysabel: 23, 32

Hackamore: 126
Haley, J. Evetts: 25, 29, 34
Hall, Lee: 83, 85, 88, 90
Hall, W. H.: 44
Hamilton, Miss Nellie: 182
Hamlin, Judge James D.: 205
Hansford Land and Cattle Company: 44
Hardesty, W. H.: 188
Hardin, John Wesley: 155
Harris, Tom: 109–13, 123–24, 126, 131, 135–37
Harris Syndicate: 124
Harrold, Texas: 200
Hartley, Texas: 234–36, 251, 253, 260
Hartley County, Texas: 63, 161, 195, 223, 235, 239, 252
Hassen, Frank: 183
Hayden, H. B.: 242
Hays, Jim: 111
Hays, President Rutherford: 77
Head, P. G.: 44
Henrietta, Texas: 33
Henry, Dutch: 28
Herara, Pablo: 62
Hereford, Texas: 110
Higgins, Colorado: 45
Hines Crossing: 188
Hogg, Governor James: 129
Hogtown: 56, 102–103, 135, 142, 144, 194, 249–50, 257
Hollicott, John: 36
Holliday, T. D.: 110
Homely Ann: 100
Home Rangers: 129, 138, 141
Homestead laws: 236
Hondo River: 75, 125
Hood, Mac: 182
Hooks, Bones: 109
Horsehead Crossing: 12
Hosack, J. A. H.: 227
Houston, General Sam: 79

Houston, Temple: 79, 102, 176–77
Houston and Texas Central Railroad: 51, 212
Houston County, Texas: 118
Howard, G. J.: 32, 53, 192
Howard, Julius: 56, 67, 94–95
Howard, J. L.: 110
Howard and McMasters: 54–55, 59, 67, 79, 98, 146, 192
Howard and Rinehart: 46
Howard's Fort: 32
Hoyt, Dr. Henry C.: 49, 78, 80, 185
Huerfano (Martínez' horse): 30
Hughes (employee of Colonel Goodnight): 28
Hughes, Colonel T. S.: 83
Hullett, C. M.: 110
Huney, New Mexico: 68
Hutch, Bill: 42
Hutson, H. H.: 192

India Creek: 144, 160, 214–16
Indian Territory: 44, 72, 81, 162
Ingalls, Senator: 8
Ingersoll, Robert: 73
Ingersoll's Infidel Ranch: 73
Ingerton, W. H.: 52, 110

James, General Thomas: 7
Jamerison family: 59–60
Jaritis Creek: 188
Jefferson, President Thomas: 6
Jenkins and Dunn Saloon: 144–45, 150, 172, 193, 199
Jenkins, Charles: 155
Jenkins, Jess: 110, 112, 123–24, 131, 134, 155, 173–74, 194, 205, 219, 223, 234–35, 237, 243, 249–50
Jenkins, Lon: 123, 176, 230
Jenny: 102
Jerry Springs: 142–43
Jicarillo Mountains: 75
Jinglebob Ranch: 49
Jinks, Captain: 103, 142
John, Uncle: 113
Johnson, Owl Head: 46
Johnson County (Wyoming) War: 153
Jones, George: 129

271

Index

Reynolds, P. G.: 68, 70
Reynolds brothers: 47–48
Rhodes, Eugene Manlove: 107
Rica Creek: 40, 99, 256
Rice, Jo: 175, 194
Rigan, Jack: 47
Riley, John: 76
Rinehart, Ira: 53–54, 59, 61, 67, 194
Rinehart, Irvin: 60
Rinehart, John: 97, 99
Rinehart, Lizzie: 94, 182
Rinehart Addition: 193
Rinehart's store: 193
Rio Colorado: 4
Rio Grande: 48
Rita Blanca Creek: 36–37, 39, 42, 126
Rivers, Texas: 239
Robbers' Roost band: 33
Roberts, Britt: 235
Robinson, Bob: 45, 85–86, 90, 111
Robinson, Tobe: 127, 151, 154, 178, 230, 235
Robinson Livery Stable: 193
Rocking Chair Emma: 142–43, 175
Rock Island Railroad: 212, 232, 234, 236, 243–44, 245–46, 253–54; see also Chicago, Rock Island, and Gulf Railway
Rockislandville: 214, 249
Romero, Casimero: 16, 32, 36–40, 53, 55, 143, 178, 184, 249, 256
Romero, Casimero, Cemetery: 135, 254
Romero, Francisco: 43
Romero, Frank: 194
Romero, José: 38
Romero, Martina: 59
Romero, Pedro: 79, 184
Rosencrans, H. C.: 45
Ross, Charley: 172, 199
Ross, E. G.: 200
Ross, John: 194
Ross (Charley) and Wife Millinery Shop: 193, 199
Roswell, New Mexico: 91, 230
Roswell country: 240
Rowdy Kate: 100
Rowland, Mrs.: 179, 201

Rudebaugh, Dave: 87–89
Rudolph, C. F.: 104, 171, 194–95, 197, 205–206, 212, 214, 218, 224, 225, 227, 229, 232, 235–36, 238, 243, 246–48, 252, 258–59
Ruidoso River: 75
Russell, Bob: 94–95
Russell, Charles M.: 157, 258
Russell, Fisherman: 194
Russell, H. A.: 54, 57, 61
Russell, Mrs. H. A.: 57
Russell, Molly (Mrs. J. E. May): 58
Ruth, Bill: 123–24
Ryan, Jack: 50, 55, 172, 177, 194, 199, 215, 219, 232
Ryan, Mrs. John: 232
Ryan's Saloon: 143
Ryland, I. P.: 194
Ryland, Mrs. I. P.: 179, 200
Ryland Avenue: 193

Sacramento Mountain: 26, 75
St. Anthony's Church at Dalhart: 178, 255
St. Barnabas Church: 178, 255
St. Louis, Missouri: 186
Salinas, Texas: 16, 102, 140
Salinas Plaza: 82
San Andreas Mountain: 75
Sanborn, Henry B.: 156, 159
Sandoval, Agapito: 16, 38–43
Sanger Brothers: 183
San Jacinto Heights: 159
San Hilario, New Mexico: 85
San Lorenzo, New Mexico: 85
Santa Fé, New Mexico: 6–7, 11, 19, 89–90
Santa Fé Mol: 175
Santa Fé Railroad: 188, 213–14, 234–35
Santa Fé Trail: 7–8
Scott, Lucien B.: 48
Second Street: 193
Seven Cities of Cibola: 5–6
Shackelford County, Texas: 212
Shannon, J. M.: 163
Sharps buffalo rifles: 33
Sheffy, L. F.: 195
Sherman County, Texas: 195

275

Sheets, Dave: 154
Sheets, Ella: 154
Sheets, Jesse: 144, 147–48, 150, 152, 155
Sheets, Mrs. Jesse: 148, 152, 194
Shelton, Dr. J. M. (*or* P. L.): 150, 185, 192, 196
Shelton Drug Store: 193
Sherman, Texas: 63
Shinebarger and Truscott: 151, 200
Sierna, Ysedero: 39, 194
Sierrata de la Cruz: 22, 216
Silver City, New Mexico: 29, 72–73, 240
Siringo, Charley: 46, 50, 81, 85–86, 90
Skillet brand: 49
Skunk Arroyo: 240
Slippery Sue: 100
Smith, Widow: 105
Snider, John: 192
Southern Pacific Railroad: 252
Southwestern Cattle Raisers' Association: 83
Spanish: 4
Spanish settlements in New Mexico: 8
Sperling brothers: 74
Sperling's store: 85
Spider brand: 71
Spider X brand: 126
Spotted Jack: 175
Spring Street: 98, 144–46, 172, 190
Springer, New Mexico: 16, 54, 57, 61, 133, 188–89, 226
Steeple Bar: 126
Stafford, Henry: 110
Stagg, Allen: 255
Staked Plains: *see* El Llano Estacado
Stambaugh, Vince: 182
Stewart, Frank: 83, 86, 88, 90
Sewall Jewelry Store: 193
Stock Grower (Las Vegas, New Mexico): 209
Strohm, George: 62
Suddeth, George: 227, 245
Summerfield, John: 52
Sweetwater Creek: 33
Swisher County, Texas: 63

T-48 brand: 126
Tabletop brand: 125, 132
Tabletop cattle: 133
T-Anchor Ranch: 52, 112, 115, 126
Tafolla, José: 14, 39
Tafolla, Miguel: 194
Tanner, Ruck: 235
Taos, New Mexico: 15, 34
Tascosa, Texas: 16, 35–43, 45, 47–51, 54, 56–57, 59–65, 67–68, 71, 73–74, 78–82, 90, 92–94, 96–107, 110, 113–14, 123, 126, 130–31, 133–36, 139–44, 149–57, 159, 162–63, 165–260
Tascosa, New, Texas: 217–20, 223
Tascosa Creek: 17, 193, 210, 214, 229, 245
Tascosa *Pioneer:* 104–105, 158, 164, 171–72, 178–79, 184–85, 187, 191–95, 195–228, 230, 234–36, 241, 243–44, 246–47, 258
Tascosa-Springer Trail: 188
Tascosa Valley: 53
"Tascosy": 35
Taylor, Dan: 42
Teats, Mr. (holder of mail contract): 80
Terry, Charles: 57
Tecolote Plaza: 16
Tesquesquite, New Mexico: 188
Texas, East: 43
Texas, South: 35, 117
Texas and Pacific Railroad: 163
Texas Panhandle: *see* Panhandle, of Texas
Texas Rangers: 129
Texas Supreme Court: 51
Texas tick fever: 237
Thompson, A. W.: 164–65
Thompson, C. B.: 110, 136, 138
Thurber, Jim: 104–105
Tierra Blanca Draw: 15, 29, 237
Tomb, Frosty: 194
Tonsorial parlor: 172
Torrey, Ellsworth: 40–41, 82, 85, 108
Torrey Peaks: 41
Tramperos Creek: 188

Maverick Town: THE STORY OF *Old Tascosa*

HAS BEEN SET ON THE LINOTYPE

IN THE JANSON TYPE FACE

AND PRINTED UPON

WOVE ANTIQUE

PAPER

UNIVERSITY OF OKLAHOMA PRESS

NORMAN